Conservation Communities

Creating Value with Nature, Open Space, and Agriculture

Edward T. McMahon

Copyright 2010 by the Urban Land Institute
1025 Thomas Jefferson Street, NW
Suite 500 West
Washington, DC 20007-5201

All rights reserved. No part of this book may be reproduced in any form or by any means, electronic or mechanical, including photocopying and recording, or by any information storage and retrieval system, without written permission of the publisher.

Library of Congress Cataloging-in-Publication Data

McMahon, Edward, 1947-
 Conservation communities : creating value with nature, open space, and agriculture / Edward T. McMahon.
    p. cm.
  ISBN 978-0-87420-132-1
 1. Planned communities—United States. 2. Open spaces—United States. 3. Housing development—United States. I. Urban Land Institute. II. Title.
  HT169.57.U6.M39 2010
  307.76'8—dc22
                                            2010015335

978-0-87420-333-2
Printed in the United States of America.

About the Urban Land Institute

The mission of the Urban Land Institute is to provide leadership in the responsible use of land and in creating and sustaining thriving communities worldwide. ULI is committed to
- Bringing together leaders from across the fields of real estate and land use policy to exchange best practices and serve community needs;
- Fostering collaboration within and beyond ULI's membership through mentoring, dialogue, and problem solving;
- Exploring issues of urbanization, conservation, regeneration, land use, capital formation, and sustainable development;
- Advancing land use policies and design practices that respect the uniqueness of both built and natural environments;
- Sharing knowledge through education, applied research, publishing, and electronic media; and
- Sustaining a diverse global network of local practice and advisory efforts that address current and future challenges.

Established in 1936, the Institute today has more than 29,000 members worldwide, representing the entire spectrum of the land use and development disciplines. ULI relies heavily on the experience of its members. It is through member involvement and information resources that ULI has been able to set standards of excellence in development practice. The Institute has long been recognized as one of the world's most respected and widely quoted sources of objective information on urban planning, growth, and development.

Project Staff

Dean Schwanke
Senior Vice President
Publications and Awards

Adrienne Schmitz
Project Director

Lydia Bjornlund
Researcher

Karrie Underwood
Project Assistant

James A. Mulligan
Managing Editor

Julie D. Stern
Manuscript Editor

Betsy VanBuskirk
Creative Director

Byron Holly
Senior Designer

Anne Morgan
Graphic Designer

About the Author

Edward T. McMahon, senior resident fellow at the Urban Land Institute, holds the ULI/Charles Fraser Chair for Sustainable Development and Environmental Policy. McMahon, whose work focuses on sustainable development, land conservation, and smart growth, is the author of numerous books and publications.

An attorney, community planner, and popular speaker, McMahon joined ULI after 14 years as vice president for land use planning at the Conservation Fund in Arlington, Virginia, where he helped protect over 5 million acres (2 million ha) of land with natural or historical importance. He is also the former president of Scenic America, a national nonprofit organization devoted to protecting America's scenic landscapes. Before that, he taught law and public policy at Georgetown University Law Center and served in the U.S. Army, both at home and overseas.

McMahon is an honorary member of the American Society of Landscape Architects and is the winner of the Chevron Conservation Award, the Maryland Vision Award, and the Stafford Award for Leadership in Scenic Conservation. McMahon has a juris doctor from Georgetown University, a master's degree from the University of Alabama at Birmingham, and a bachelor's degree from Spring Hill College.

 **Foundation**

Support for this book was provided by the ULI Foundation. The ULI Foundation is the philanthropic partner of the Urban Land Institute, providing an assured source of funding for ULI's core research, education, and public service activities. Through its various giving and support programs, the Foundation helps strengthen ULI's ability to provide leadership in the responsible use of land and in creating and sustaining thriving communities worldwide.

This book was developed in cooperation with the ULI Climate, Land Use, and Energy (CLUE) Initiative.

Acknowledgments

Many individuals contributed their time and talent to this book, and to each one I would like to extend my sincere appreciation. First, special gratitude goes to Lydia Bjornlund, who led ULI's research efforts on this book. Without her special assistance and untiring support, this book would not have been possible. Second, I would like to thank Randall Arendt, the "godfather" of the conservation development movement, for his inspiration, encouragement, and insightful review of a draft of this book and other contributions.

I would also like to thank all the developers, landowners, and designers who worked on the projects detailed in this book. I would especially like to thank Todd Mansfield, CEO of Crosland LLC and immediate past chair of ULI, for supporting this book project; Jim Chaffin, chairman of Chaffin/Light Associates and another former ULI chair, for his pioneering efforts in smart growth and for helping bring me to ULI; George and Vicky Ranney, the developers of Prairie Crossing, for inspiring my interest in conservation development; Bob Baldwin, managing principal of QROE Preservation Development, for sponsoring a very useful forum on conservation development; and Frank Martin, project manager of Hidden Springs, for all his advice and encouragement. Ted Harrison, the president of Commonweal Conservancy, joined Randall Arendt, Bob Baldwin, and Frank Martin in reviewing the book, improving upon every word and concept.

Countless others helped with the book by sharing their knowledge, insights, and experiences related to conservation development. Thank you to the many people who helped gather photos and other project-related materials. Special thanks go to the following people who helped provide information for the case studies:

- Bundoran Farm: Bob Baldwin and David Hamilton.
- Galisteo Basin Preserve: Ted Harrison and Lauren Whitehurst.
- Hidden Springs: Frank Martin.
- Homestead Preserve: Charles Adams, Don Killoren, and Deborah Huso.
- Santa Lucia Preserve: Tom Gray and Lisa Guthrie.
- Serenbe: Tucker Berta and Steve Nygren.
- Spring Island: Jim Chaffin and Glenny Ryan.
- Tryon Farm: Ed and Eve Noonan.
- Jackson Meadow: Carol and Harold Teasdale.
- Storm Mountain Ranch: Jeff Temple.

I would also like to thank Adrienne Schmitz for guiding the project through the production process and Julie Stern for editing the text and ensuring that the information was written and presented clearly to make it most useful to our audience. Thanks also to Dean Schwanke and Maureen McAvey for their direction and insights; ULI information specialist Joan Campbell for her research and information packets; and Karrie Underwood for helping whenever I asked. And, finally, thanks to Sherry McMahon, my wife and partner, who has always encouraged my love of nature and interest in travel to special places and good developments.

Edward T. McMahon

Contents

viii	**Foreword**
2	**Chapter 1: An Introduction to Conservation Development**
2	Why Conservation Development?
7	What Is Conservation Development?
11	The Roots of Conservation Development
14	Types of Conservation Developments
23	The Future of Conservation Development
24	**Chapter 2: Benefits and Limitations of Conservation Development**
26	Ecological Benefits
27	Health and Social Benefits
29	Economic Benefits
38	Limitations and Obstacles
48	**Chapter 3: Assessing the Feasibility of Conservation Development**
48	Landscape Suitability
52	The Regulatory Environment
58	Determining the Market
63	Refining the Project Concept and Setting Goals
68	**Chapter 4: Conservation Development Planning, Design, and Marketing**
68	Site Selection
76	Creating a Vision and Goals
81	Identifying Natural, Cultural, and Historic Features
83	The Design Process
90	Marketing
93	Measuring Success

94	**Chapter 5: Management and Stewardship of Open Lands**
94	Landownership
97	Land Protection Tools
104	Restoration and Enhancement
108	Land Management
111	Stewardship and Funding
113	The Environmental Team
118	**Chapter 6: Conservation Development Case Studies**
120	Bundoran Farm, Albemarle County, Virginia
134	Galisteo Basin Preserve, Santa Fe, New Mexico
148	Hidden Springs, Ada County, Idaho
160	Homestead Preserve, Bath County, Virginia
174	Jackson Meadow, Marine on St. Croix, Minnesota
184	Santa Lucia Preserve, Monterey County, California
198	Serenbe, Fulton County, Georgia
208	Spring Island, Beaufort County, South Carolina
220	Storm Mountain Ranch, Steamboat Springs, Colorado
232	Tryon Farm, Michigan City, Indiana
242	**Appendixes**
243	Examples of Conservation Development by Region
244	How to Evaluate a Conservation Development Ordinance
244	Conservation Subdivisions Fact Sheet
246	Resources

Foreword

Can development be good both for the land and for the pocketbook? I believe the answer is yes, particularly in the case of conservation development projects.

Conservation communities—sometimes described as golf course communities without the golf course—require the same careful attention to site layout and design as do developments centered on golf. Conservation communities and golf course communities also share certain economic dynamics: buyers pay a premium price for access to a shared amenity. In the case of a golf course community, buyers pay for proximity to a recreational amenity—the golf course. Homebuyers value views across the fairway and are willing to pay more to guarantee that the green space—the tees, greens, and fairways—will remain in place in perpetuity.

Similar factors drive the market in conservation communities: buyers pay for access to trails and protected open space. They value views of woodlands and meadows, and these community amenities contribute to increased home values, even if providing the amenities results in smaller lots or a more compact layout of houses, or both.

As early as 1956, Charles Fraser, the late founder of Sea Pines Plantation, South Carolina's first masterplanned resort, identified nature as the top attraction for Hilton Head Island. Fraser, who started the Heritage Golf Tournament in 1969, often told friends that more people came to walk the resort's trails and beaches than to play golf.

The same dynamic holds true in today's resorts and communities: far more consumers are drawn to green space than to greens. And it is becoming increasingly apparent that conservation development will drive growth in suburban and rural regions for decades to come. The potential for change is great. At least two-thirds of the development expected to exist in the United States by 2050 is not yet built, and the bulk of what is coming will be constructed outside city centers, on the outer edges of urban regions. In addition, many retirees, empty nesters, and buyers of second homes are seeking homes in high-amenity rural locations, near water, mountains, or public lands, such as national parks and forests.

Conservation development principles can help developers design communities that accommodate this growing market while sitting lightly on the land and preserving the natural amenities that are most attractive to people. What's more, conservation communities prove it is possible to reconcile density and compactness with America's expectation of wide open spaces. Successful projects such as Rancho Santa Margarita in California, Celebration in Florida, and Hidden Springs in Idaho illustrate the value of emphasizing public rather than private open space.

Conservation communities also can help developers find common ground with environmentalists and cash-strapped local governments. Conservation communities work with nature, not against it. They save open space, reduce infrastructure costs, increase property values, and help protect rural character. Sometimes people want parks and natural areas without any development, but when developers put homes and green space together, they create green and golden opportunities for collaboration and community.

This book showcases communities of widely different sizes, densities, and locations. Though they vary greatly, the projects share two defining features: they protect open space and promote community. They do so by recognizing the value of preserving nature and open space, the importance of views and vistas, and the growing interest in communities that link people with their neighbors and surroundings. Communities are places where people know their neighbors and can count on them, where people share both common interests and community pride. They also are places where people can walk from one place to another.

In the years ahead, while America no doubt will see much more infill development, brownfield redevelopment, and urban revitalization, it also will continue to experience substantial development in pristine greenfields outside cities. America needs both types of development—better cities and better models for suburban, exurban, and rural development. This book and the conservation developments it describes offer one path to that end.

Todd W. Mansfield
Chairman and Chief Executive Officer
Crosland LLC
Charlotte, North Carolina

Conservation Communities

An Introduction to Conservation Development

CHAPTER 1

Mike Sands and his wife Betsy love walking to the Station Square shops, the farmers market, and the horse stables near their home, even on chilly northern Illinois days. They also love the organic farm, the ten miles (16 km) of trails, the commuter railroad station, and the 400 acres (162 ha) of ponds, preserved prairies, and oak savannas at Prairie Crossing, a master-planned community outside Chicago.

Prairie Crossing is a critically acclaimed conservation community that was designed to combine responsible development, open-space preservation, environmental restoration, and easy commuting by train. This type of community is a relatively new approach to real estate development that is growing in popularity because it has shown that it is possible for developers to design and build communities that are good for the land, good for the residents, and good for the pocketbook.

Why Conservation Development?

New approaches to real estate development are needed now more than ever. New housing options are needed to support the growing U.S. population, which is expected to increase from 306 million in 2009 to more than 438 million in 2050.[1] Still, it is the inefficient use of land, not population growth, that is fueling the rapid conversion of open space and working land to houses and commercial areas. The average lot size for each residential unit is half an acre (0.2 ha), but more than 50 percent of the land developed since 1994 has been broken into housing lots of ten acres (4 ha) or larger.[2] Large-lot subdivisions are one of the major factors contributing to the accelerating consumption and fragmentation of land.

According to the most recent statistics available from the U.S. Department of Agriculture's (USDA's) National Resources Inventory, between 1982 and 2003 more than 35 million acres (14.2 million ha)—an area the size of Illinois—were converted for developed uses. About 6 million acres (2.4 million ha), 28 percent of this land, was prime farmland, defined by the USDA as "land that that has the best combination of physical and chemical characteristics for producing food, feed, forage, fiber, and oilseed crops and is also available for these uses."[3]

Statistics further suggest that the rate of land conversion is accelerating. A 2009 research report using data from the U.S. Census Bureau and the National Resources Inventory predicts that the developed area in the United States will increase by 54.4 million acres (22.0 million ha) during the next 25

Prairie Crossing—one of the nation's first conservation developments—has served as a model for developers who want to balance the need for housing with land preservation.

years.[4] "The impact of development on rural nonfederal land is a concern in the balancing of development needs with conservation of natural resources," concludes the USDA's Natural Resources Conservation Service. "This is an especially important consideration when the lands best suited to producing food and fiber come under development. Conversion of agricultural land to developed uses can also result in fragmentation of landscapes, leading to diminished values for wildlife, water management, open space, and aesthetic purposes, among others."[5]

Further enabling of the sprawling, haphazard pattern that has

Conservation development is a way to have both cows and condos.

characterized America's approach to development—and to conservation—will exacerbate many of the problems sprawl already has created, including less functional open spaces, degraded watersheds, fragmented wildlife corridors, deteriorated working lands, and increased air and water pollution. People living in sprawling neighborhoods also feel the impacts of increased traffic congestion, longer commutes, and little sense of community.

Many rural communities also are suffering devastating economic consequences. When farms are plowed under to make way for development, the businesses that once depended on these farms can no longer survive. A growing body of evidence shows that far-flung, large-lot residential development rarely generates enough revenue from property taxes to cover the services it requires. Building the roads, schools, sewer service, fire, police, and other infrastructure needed to support homes and neighborhoods that are dispersed helter-skelter across the landscape is inefficient and expensive. Cost of community services (COCS) studies undertaken by the American Farmland Trust show that, on average, for each dollar generated in revenue through taxes, it costs $1.15 to support residential subdivisions, compared to $0.28 for commercial and industrial uses and $0.36 for working and open land.[6] As the old saying goes, "you don't have to pay for cows to go to school."

Many smart growth advocates suggest that development needs should be met through infill development and the redevelopment of existing urban neighborhoods. This is a good idea. Unfortunately, the finite amount of land in urban areas is insufficient to support all of the nation's future housing and commercial development needs. In addition, the high cost of this land—as well as political and regulatory obstacles to its development—lead many developers to avoid compact, mixed-use, new urbanist–inspired approaches on infill sites. Moreover, many Americans who once found satisfaction in suburbia are choosing to retire in rural communities where nature and open space are easily accessible. While infill development will continue to be a critical goal for smart growth, experts suggest that most new development will continue to take form in greenfield locations, where virgin land has been undeveloped or used for agriculture or forestry. In *Greenfield Development without Sprawl*, Jim Heid writes that Portland, Oregon's metropolitan regional plan projects that 70 percent of near-term growth will be on greenfield land as opposed to built-up areas. Other U.S. jurisdictions predict numbers closer to 90 percent.[7]

Support for Land Conservation

While many Americans want to live in rural areas, they also want to protect the assets that draw them to the countryside. Nearly two-thirds of the respondents in a recent National Association of Realtors survey said that it is "very important" to preserve land being used for farming and/or agricultural purposes (64 percent) and natural areas such as forests, wetlands or deserts, and stream corridors (62 percent). A significant majority also responded that it is "very important" to create certain types of open spaces, including playgrounds for children (75 percent), playing fields for soccer and baseball (61 percent), and easily accessible neighborhood parks (60 percent).[8]

Another measure of Americans' interest in land protection is the number of ballot measures to fund land preservation that have been passed in recent years. In 2008, despite the nation's severe economic and fiscal crisis, voters approved 90 measures totaling $8.4 billion in new public funding for land conservation—a single-year record.[9] Minnesota passed the largest open-space state referendum in the nation's history, increasing the sales tax by three-eighths of a cent to generate $5.5 billion over the next 25 years for land preservation and environmental protection. A $500 million bond measure on the East Bay Regional Park District in California was approved by 71 percent of voters, while a $200 million bond measure in Hillsborough County, Florida, was passed by 79 percent. Voters supported open-space preservation measures even in areas where open space seems plentiful. Voters in Johnson County, Iowa, for instance, approved a $2 million bond for open space, while those in Blaine County, Idaho, established the first county land conservation program in Idaho with the passage of a two-year property tax measure.

Public financing and private charitable donations can protect only a small amount of land, however. In rapidly growing areas, where governments are struggling to pay for infrastructure and other needed public services, there may be no funds available to carry out citizens' desire for land preservation.

Americans' interest in land preservation does not always reflect antigrowth or antidevelopment sentiments. When new development is balanced with plans for the permanent protection of open space, Americans are more likely to accept responsible development initiatives as reasonable and appropriate. In the National Association of Realtors survey, for instance, 50 percent of respondents said that their position on growth depended on "the situation and circumstances."[10]

The first principle of better development is figuring out where *not* to develop. This principle applies at every scale, from the individual site, to the neighborhood, to the region. Every community needs a long-range conservation plan, just like it needs a long-range transportation plan. When citizens think all land is up for grabs, they are likely to oppose all new development everywhere.

Limitations of Land Use Regulations

Local governments have responded to citizens' calls to stem the tide of rural land development with new land use plans, laws, and regulations. Outside of major cities, county comprehensive plans typically call for the preservation of "rural character" and "rural lifestyles." But the well-intended growth plans and development codes that guide the decision making of elected officials and staff often subvert their stated objectives. Conventional zoning ordinances advance a seemingly logical, Euclidian model of development planning in which large-lot zoning is proffered as a "silver bullet" to protect open space. A bit of land is set aside as open space, and every other

The Carneros Inn, in Napa, California, is a 27-acre resort (11-ha) community surrounded by vineyards, with lush views of neighboring farmland and the Mayacamas Mountains.

acre of unpaved and buildable land is zoned for residential, commercial, or industrial development. Subdivisions are designed with cookie-cutter precision, because subdivision ordinances require rural and suburban land to be systemically divided into uniform house lots and streets. Development manuals and planning staff insist on it.

Local zoning laws often have unintended consequences. In an effort to protect small farms and ranches, many local governments dictate minimum lot sizes for development. Requiring large minimum lot sizes in rural areas, however, often fragments and degrades the landscape's scenic, wildlife, and watershed values. It also denies landowners an opportunity to advance their development goals while concurrently sustaining a viable working landscape for farming, ranching, or forest management. Instead, large-lot zoning forces many landowners to subdivide their land into five- or ten-acre (2- or 4-ha) lots, creating parcels that are "too big to mow, but too small to plow." Mandating large-lot development as a strategy for protecting rural character often fails; instead, it may transform the landscape in ways that are not productive for agriculture, aesthetically inspiring, or effective as new communities.

Decades of attempts to preserve rural areas—including purchase of development rights, conservation easements, zoning overlays, deed restrictions, and agricultural zoning—have achieved mixed results. Society has succeeded in protecting some extraordinary individual properties but has largely failed to protect the overall rural environment.

The Conservation Development Approach

Conservation development offers a valuable tool for accomplishing land preservation goals while providing communities with a sound development strategy that will meet their exurban housing needs. In conservation development, land protection measures are funded by market forces and private capital. Although conservation development tools once were used primarily by conservationists and wealthy landowners to help preserve land targeted for conservation, in recent years, increasing numbers of mainstream real estate developers have used conservation development techniques to plan housing subdivisions, resorts, and large-scale master-planned communities with ample green space.

Benefits of Conservation Development

The benefits of conservation development include:
- Reduced capital costs (primarily through a reduction in the amount of built infrastructure);
- Reduced risk of environmental hazards, including flooding and water pollution;
- Better health for residents and the broader community;
- Better land stewardship;
- Market differentiation;
- Positive press, free publicity, and editorial endorsements;
- Higher perceived value and quality; and
- The satisfaction of doing the right thing.

Conservation communities have grown in popularity because market forces are converging to create demand for authentic, livable communities in once-rural areas. Homebuyers have shown that they value natural open spaces, native plants, wildlife, and beautiful surroundings—and that they are willing to pay for these amenities. Developers are responding by incorporating large-scale open-space areas into their development plans.

From a developer's perspective, there are several reasons for conservation development. Some conservation developers have engaged in this practice to protect a cherished piece of land—a place they have grown to love. Others have used conservation development to overcome entitlement challenges and thwart anticipated public opposition to their projects. Perhaps the greatest benefit for developers, however, is that conservation communities help differentiate their product. Nationwide, houses that abut open space and/or are located in communities that feature open space as an amenity sell faster and at higher premiums than comparable homes elsewhere. Some studies have found as much as a 15 to 30 percent increase in the value of properties adjacent to parks and open space. (For additional information, see "Sales Advantages" in Chapter 2.)

What Is Conservation Development?

Conservation development defines the process of planning, designing, building, and managing communities that preserve landscapes or other community resources that are considered valuable for their aesthetic, environmental, cultural, agricultural, and/or historic values. The term also can refer to a community that results from this process.

Conservation development requires an integrative, systemic, and holistic approach to land use planning and development. It can help communities preserve open space and protect rural character. Most important, it can enhance property values, minimize infrastructure costs, and foster the development of graceful, environmentally responsible, and livable communities that appeal to today's increasingly sophisticated consumer.

Conservation developers undertake a deliberate, conscientious, and engaged approach to site planning, land preservation, infrastructure design, landscaping, architecture, and community governance. Conservation development typically is accomplished through the use of a layered, iterative planning process. Initially, scenic, environmental, cultural, and historic values are clearly delineated and set aside for permanent protection. In the land area that extends beyond these conservation areas, new development is often—but not always—tightly clustered. Clustering development both facilitates the protection of open space and enables communities to minimize the number and extent of roads. Reducing impervious surfaces, in turn, enables natural areas to function more effectively. As an alternative to clustering, some conservation developments distribute homesites across the parcel in a manner that is strategically designed to ensure that the development sits lightly on the land.

How Conservation Development Differs from Conventional Development

Conventional development is largely guided by the rules of geometry, the principles of physics, the protocols of engineering, and the values of efficiency and wealth maximization. Land is the raw material of the developer's craft—an imminently pliable and subservient surface from which plans take form. Perhaps more poetically, land sometimes is viewed as the canvas on which developers express their creative and/or wealth-creating vision. Notwithstanding the developer's utilitarian or romantic priorities, conventional development is largely a practice of imposing a land use program on a landscape, regardless of its unique physical, ecological, cultural, agricultural, or historical attributes. When open space is incorporated into a design, it often is done as an afterthought, with little consideration of the aesthetic, ecological, cultural, and community value of a particular property.

Conservation development differs from conventional development in its focus on *all* the uses of the site—on the open space as well as the built environment. The open space in a conservation community may be preserved and protected for natural, aesthetic, or cultural purposes, as well as for passive and active recreation. While many conventional development projects include open space for these purposes, conservation development focuses on the quality, quantity, and characteristics of the land to be preserved. Conservation development goes beyond simply setting aside open space to identify *which* land should be preserved and for what purposes.

Conservation development typically clusters houses to preserve natural features.

Principles and Goals

Conservation development is a practice of land use planning and community design that strives to maintain a respectful relationship with nature. Conservation development embraces a broad range of techniques and strategies to advance specific development objectives, while concurrently protecting a landscape's essential natural and environmental values. In many cases, conservation development initiatives seek to preserve and restore sensitive plant and animal habitat, protect cultural and historic resources, conserve scenic vistas and inspirational landscapes—including mountains, ridgelines, farms, ranches, or river corridors—and support and enhance the quality of a rural community's economic and social values.

Conservation development aspires to an unusually high standard of landscape protection. In most cases, conservation developers set aside 50 percent or more of a property for open space, agriculture, wildlife habitat, and/or cultural resource protection purposes. Protected land may include meadows, prairies, and other natural areas; endangered species habitat, wildlife movement corridors, and other environmentally sensitive land; riparian areas and other parts of the natural water system; farmland, ranchland, and other working lands; and culturally or historically significant land, such as stone walls, burial grounds, archaeological sites, and battlefields. Conservation development techniques also can be used to protect specific features on this land, such as large trees, rock formations, ponds or lakes, and historic buildings.

Conservation design begins with a careful analysis of the site to determine what lands should *not* be developed. Conservation developers also look at the natural features of the landscape to see how the natural environment can best support the built environment. One important goal of conservation development is to preserve valuable natural, cultural, and historic resources as part of an interconnected open-space system. Preserving working landscapes and rural heritage also are goals of many conservation development projects.

Conservation development projects capitalize on natural features for stormwater management, erosion control, and roadway design. Conservation corridors may be created to facilitate the protection and restoration of water flows or other ecological functions. In addition to preserving land of conservation value, some conservation development projects also may restore degraded land, remove nonnative exotic species, reuse already developed land and the structures on it, and/or carefully site house lots, roads, and other aspects of the built environment to blend in with the natural environment.

While all conservation development projects share a fundamental emphasis on preserving natural values, the unique characteristics of the land result in projects with widely different priorities and goals. In rural areas, conservation development can help the community protect its most ecologically valuable land while directing development toward areas best suited for human use and nature-based recreation. On smaller parcels in more suburban areas, conservation development may provide walking trails, a nature center, and a strong sense of community. Many conservation-minded developers take pride in helping restore the land, planting trees, improving water quality, and building trails.

Conservation development also considers the broader context in which a project takes place. This involves examining both the entire project site and the area surrounding it. In ecology, as in development, nothing exists in isolation. Conservation development demands a deep understanding of the interconnections among the various attributes of the landscape to ensure that the whole is more than a sum of its parts.

Notwithstanding its commendable intentions, conservation development is not without critics. One persistent criticism is that conservation development can encourage sprawl in rural areas. Some experts say that conservation development attracts high-income people to the countryside, increasing land values and undermining the ability of small farms to survive. Since homes in conservation developments often sell for a premium and appreciate at faster rates than those in conventional subdivisions, experts caution that conservation development projects can lead to the premature development of the resources they propose to conserve.

In communities with strong anti-growth sentiments, conservation development may be viewed as nothing more than the proverbial wolf in a less offensive style of sheep's clothing. While elected officials and other community members may appreciate the developer's conservation values, development imposes an unavoidable and fundamental change in land use conditions—a change that

What Conservation Development Is Not

Conservation development is *not*:

A Panacea. Like any planning effort, conservation development requires tradeoffs. It is not appropriate in every setting or on every site.

Inherently Altruistic. While land trusts and wealthy landowners may have altruistic motives, developers often can make more money implementing conservation development projects than they would by taking more conventional approaches to land development.

A Tool for Stopping Growth. Conservation development, like any other type of development, focuses on how to develop land. By deciding what land should be preserved at the outset of a project, conservation development provides developers with a tool to generate competitive risk-adjusted returns from highly scenic, environmentally sensitive, and/or recreation-serving properties.

Cluster Development. While the terms "cluster development" and "conservation development" often are used synonymously, cluster development is a means of *concentrating* land uses in a manner that minimizes infrastructure development and, in some cases, facilitates pedestrian access across neighborhoods and to commercial and civic facilities. Cluster development does not necessarily involve a conscientious investment in natural or cultural resource protection; conservation development does. Cluster development also lacks conservation development's focus on the preservation of land and the quality, quantity, and configuration of the resulting open space or on the linkages among open spaces within and outside a development's boundaries.

Green Building. Green building and conservation development are not mutually exclusive. They can go hand in hand, but whereas green building emphasizes the vertical dimension (the use of environmentally sensitive building materials, indoor air quality, water use, energy efficiency, construction waste management, and other elements of the built environment), conservation development emphasizes the horizontal dimension (good site planning and design, the preservation of ecological resources, the protection of open space, identification of view corridors, and other elements of land planning). Conservation development focuses on how land is used, setting the preservation of conservation land and its natural functions as a priority.

Elitist. Conservation subdivisions and master-planned green communities have a reputation for being affluent and homogeneous, but there is no reason that the same design principles cannot be applied to projects for residents with more moderate means. In fact, 30 percent of the housing in the Village at the Galisteo Basin Preserve, a conservation development near Santa Fe, New Mexico, is designed for lower- and moderate-income residents. Similarly, Myers Farm in Greenfield, Massachusetts, is a conservation development with condominium units designed for older retirees and families with modest incomes.

Low Density. People often assume that a conservation subdivision, by definition, will have fewer lots available for development than a conventional subdivision. Many conservation development projects are low density, but many others are density neutral—they have the same number of units as a conventional project, but are designed in a compact form with urban-scale lots. A few conservation development projects have even received waivers to increase density beyond what had been allowed.

Golf Course Communities. While some conservation developments incorporate golf courses into their design, golf courses should never be included in a development's natural open-space calculations and should only be considered *after* the property's ecologically valuable lands have been set aside for permanent protection.

some people may feel overrides any perceived conservation benefits.

The Roots of Conservation Development

Historically, conservation and development have been at odds with one another. As the saying goes, conservationists look at land as a community resource and a gift of nature that needs no improvement. In contrast, developers typically view land as an economic asset—something that yields its greatest value once it is transformed for human use. The lack of dialogue between seemingly antithetical forces has created an "either/or" approach to conservation and development: Land *either* is protected *or* it is developed.

Notwithstanding their inherent appreciation for wildlife habitat and open spaces, many conservationists become passionate about a parcel's protection only after a developer has proposed transforming it. The conservation community's reactive response to development proposals generates untold frustration for landowners and developers who have not previously considered their property appropriate for public protection—much less impassioned public protest. Late-in-the-game brinksmanship between developers and conservationists can inspire expensive buyouts from the public sector or philanthropic community and often leads to protracted and expensive entitlement battles. In some cases, projects that would have offered the community a number of benefits are aborted in the process.

Fortunately, the no-holds-barred conflict that traditionally has characterized the developer/conservationist relationship is evolving into a more cooperative and big-picture approach to land use problem solving. Over the past decade, a number of planning strategies have converged, creating a new awareness of the need for conservation and development to work in harmony. As sprawl creeps out from the suburbs into once-rural areas, communities are searching for efficient and productive tools to guide future development. The quest to reduce our carbon footprint and the emergence of a green building movement have further encouraged conservationists, developers, and community leaders to find new approaches to sustainable land use.

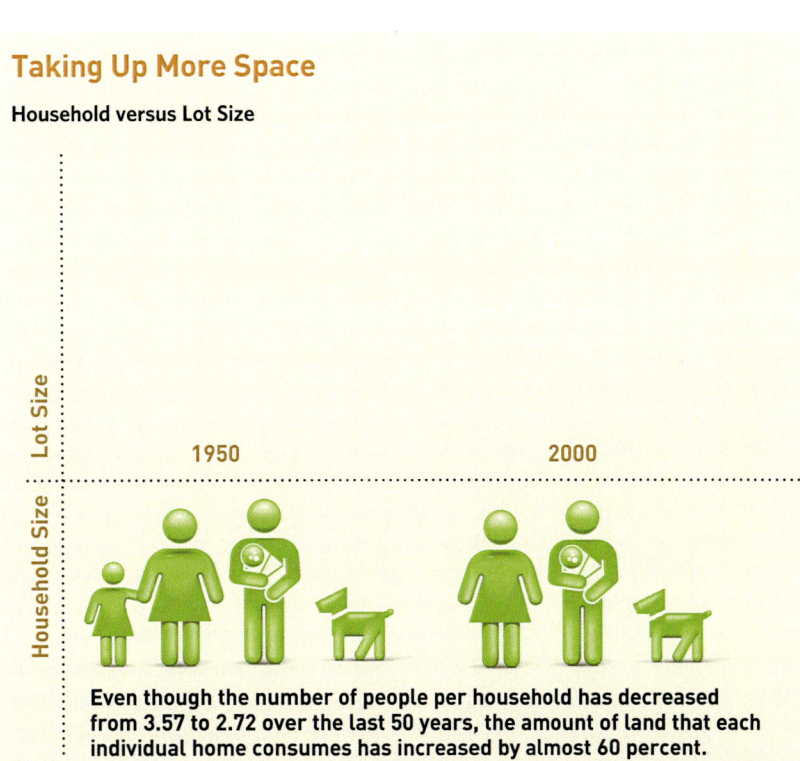

Taking Up More Space
Household versus Lot Size

Even though the number of people per household has decreased from 3.57 to 2.72 over the last 50 years, the amount of land that each individual home consumes has increased by almost 60 percent.

Local and state governments have initiated smart growth initiatives and green development strategies as part of a plan to provide a framework for development. Cluster development and other higher-density zoning strategies have given communities a valuable tool for preserving open space. In response to market demand, developers increasingly are incorporating the design values and planning principles of traditional neighborhood development to create more authentic, livable, and walkable communities. This planning strategy is being applied to exurban and rural areas in ways that some people are calling "new ruralism." To accommodate a growing demand from green consumers, developers are incorporating sustainable development and green building principles and practices into their projects. All of these strategies share many complementary values and purposes with conservation development, but each has a different approach and emphasis, as described below.

Smart Growth. In general, smart growth invests time, attention, and resources in restoring community and vitality to center cities and older suburbs. New smart growth is town-centered, with a mix of housing, commercial, and retail uses. Smart growth also focuses on designs that are transit and pedestrian oriented and on the preservation of open space and other environmental amenities. Conservation development can be an important tool for furthering smart growth efforts.

Green Infrastructure. Green infrastructure is a strategically planned and managed network of natural lands, working landscapes, and other open spaces designed to maximize ecological values and functions. Green infrastructure often mimics the form and function of natural ecosystems—with low-tech stormwater management systems, for example—to improve hydrological function, water quality, and so forth. Green infrastructure networks are informed by their unique and productive ecological attributes—woodlands, wetlands, rivers, streams, grasslands—that work together as a whole to sustain the health and functionality of human and natural systems. The goals of conservation development are aligned with green infrastructure. Conservation subdivisions of all sizes often link to and expand broader green infrastructure networks.

Cluster Development. Cluster development is a planning strategy that aggregates development into discrete zones of interdependent land uses so that the remaining land can be conserved as green space. When carefully designed and executed, cluster development can protect a significant percentage of a property's land area and provide an attractive and efficient living environment for residents and business owners. Although the terms "cluster development" and "conservation development" often are used interchangeably, there are important differences. Cluster development often places homes and commercial buildings on the most easily developed portion of the land, setting aside as open space the site's steep slopes, wetlands, and other hard-to-develop terrain. The primary goal of clustered development is to reduce infrastructure costs, not to preserve land with high conservation value. Conservation development, on the other hand, focuses on the quantity, quality, and configuration of the preserved land. Its top priority is the environmental, scenic, cultural, and recreational attributes of a property; it ensures that these values are permanently protected before development envelopes and infrastructure systems are identified. Conservation development focuses on the relationship between the development and the open space to maximize the value of both. It also strives to connect green spaces among adjacent subdivisions and existing parkland so that regional habitat corridors, riparian environments, and trail networks can be optimized.

Golf Course Development. Golf course communities are commonly viewed as the progenitor of contem-

Golf course developments have long been popular with homebuyers, even though most of the buyers do not play golf. A conservation development substitutes greenways for fairways and neighborhood greens for putting greens.

porary open-space developments. Developers incorporate golf courses into their subdivisions because homebuyers consistently pay a premium for homes in golf course communities. Within the community, homesites adjacent to fairways cost far more than those without easy access or clear views of the golf course's pastoral landscape. Ironically, countless studies by market research firms have revealed that the opportunity to play golf has not been the driving force for most buyers; rather, it is the opportunity to live near protected open space that motivates a majority of buying decisions. With this humbling revelation, a handful of developers began to ask whether people would be attracted to communities that offered a similar scale of open space, *without* the golf course. The success of a number of conservation development pioneers suggests that the answer is a resounding "yes!"

Traditional Neighborhood Development. Traditional neighborhood development (TND)—sometimes referred to as new urbanism—is a comprehensive planning system that may occur in infill or greenfield settings. Traditional neighborhood developments typically include a range of housing types, a network of well-connected streets and blocks, clearly delineated parks and public spaces, and a mix of uses—including stores, schools, and offices—all within walking distance of homes. TND projects usually have strict architectural guidelines, but they can accommodate many different architectural styles, from traditional to modern. TND often is used for relatively large parcels that incorporate several villages and hamlets into an overall community design.

Conservation developments often draw from the principles and practices of TND to create a unique sense of community character.

New Ruralism. Building on the principles and practices of new urbanism, new ruralism involves the conservation and enhancement of rural areas as places that are indispensable to the economic, environmental, and cultural vitality of metropolitan areas. New ruralism marries the development of livable communities with the preservation of a community's rural character, often through sustainable agricultural practices and clustered homesites. Conservation developments, particularly those in rural areas, often build on the design values and planning principles espoused by new ruralism.

Low-Impact Development. Low-impact development (LID) is a natural systems–based approach to site planning that focuses on stormwater management and landscape design and development. LID emphasizes the integration of site design and planning techniques that conserve a property's natural ecological and hydrologic functions. Like conservation development, LID takes its cue from the architecture and artistry of nature's forms and systems. It often incorporates wetlands and stream corridors as design elements; protects natural systems such as drainage, vegetation, and soils; and decentralizes and micromanages stormwater at its source. Conservation developments often include LID features such as porous pavement, reduced street widths, green roofs, and nonstructural approaches to stormwater management.

Green Building Design. Green building design strives to improve the quality of environmental responsiveness and resource efficiency. For many developers, green building design and conservation development go hand in hand. Green building emphasizes the vertical dimension of development (building materials, indoor air quality, water use, construction waste management, and so forth), whereas conservation development emphasizes the horizontal dimension of community design (site planning, street design, preservation of sensitive ecological resources, protection of open space, identification of view corridors, and so forth). Conservation development directs its attention to the preservation of wildlife habitat, scenic landscapes, and open spaces as well as to the sustained functionality of natural systems. By combining the values and sensibilities of environmentally healthy, long-lived, thermally efficient indoor environments with healthy and functional outdoor environments, green building and conservation development multiply conservation values and principles.

Sustainable Development. Sustainable development is a systemic and holistic approach to building and site planning. It integrates green principles and practices into every aspect of a community's planning, design, construction, marketing, and management. While the goals of sustainable development are closely aligned with conservation development, sustainable development principles and practices can apply to almost any type of development, regardless of the land use principles on which the development is based.

Types of Conservation Developments

Conservation communities vary tremendously in scope and size. Developers have experimented with a number of strategies for achieving conservation and development goals. The most common types of conservation developments are conservation buyer projects, limited development projects, conservation subdivisions,

Principles of Conservation Development

Not all conservation developments are the same. A residential project designed for a large, open tract of land in the western United States will be inherently different from one designed to protect a small working farm in New England. Regardless of the specifics, however, all conservation development projects share several basic principles. These include the following:

- A focus on preserving ecologically and culturally valuable lands;
- A layout that maximizes linkages among people and open space;
- Separation of lot size from density;
- Protection and preservation of land and natural resources, by clustering housing and infrastructure and/or designing development so that the built environment lays lightly on the land;
- Restoration and maintenance of open space and natural features;
- Protection of viewsheds, particularly as viewed from homes and from the public right-of-way;
- A flexible approach to development that follows the pattern of the land and capitalizes on its unique ecological and cultural values; and
- Beneficial use of open space for functional needs, including stormwater management, flood mitigation, passive and active recreation, minimization of curbs and gutters, and elimination of stormwater sewers, pipes, and other infrastructure.

Habersham, South Carolina, is a traditional neighborhood development that includes numerous green open spaces.

and master-planned conservation development communities.

Conservation Buyer Projects

A conservation buyer is an individual who wishes to purchase and protect a property that has natural, agricultural, scenic, or historic attributes while enjoying the benefits of private landownership. Conservation buyers typically donate a conservation easement to a land trust that will permanently protect the special features of their property. A conservation easement typically limits, but does not necessarily prohibit, future development. Many conservation development projects begin when an owner—often a rancher, farmer, conservation organization (such as the Nature Conservancy), or other large landowner—elects to sell his or her property while retaining interest in and authority over its future development. The landowner may want to limit the amount, the location, or the nature of the development that will take place on this land. Conservation buyer projects are designed to match site-protective owners with a buyer who shares the seller's aesthetic, recreational, cultural, and/or environmental sensibilities.

For most conservation buyers, the protection of wildlife habitat, cultural resources, scenic views, or other landscape features is the driving force in their purchase decision. Many conservation buyers have a passion for nature and the recreational opportunities it affords, such as hiking, horseback riding, bird watching, or fishing. As an affirmation of their public benefit purposes, land trusts and other environmental nonprofit organizations can serve as conservation buyers for "signature," one-of-a-kind properties.

To ensure that the properties they acquire are permanently protected, conservation buyers typically donate conservation easements to qualified nonprofit organizations and public agencies. Conservation easements are designed to limit or, in some cases, prohibit future development on properties of special concern. Land trusts can facilitate conservation buyer transactions, matching environmentally sensitive landowners with value-aligned conservation buyers. In addition to their marketing and brokerage functions, land trusts sometimes assume the role of conservation buyer, if only on an interim basis. In these cases, a land trust can purchase a high-priority tract, design a conservation easement to protect a targeted property's public values (such as its scenic, agricultural, or wildlife resources), and subsequently

Reasons to Become a Conservation Buyer

Real estate buyers can become conservation buyers for a number of reasons, including the following:
- Buying and preserving land benefits the community and creates an opportunity to offset a portion of the buyer's investment cost with potential tax incentives.
- Conservation easements are individually tailored to meet the buyer's goals while preserving the values of the land. These agreements allow the buyer to keep control of the land and maintain its historic uses.
- Conservation buyers who preserve land with an easement are in a unique position to take advantage of generous income tax savings. Donating an easement on land within a year of its purchase can result in increased federal income tax deductions compared to standard easement donations. Qualified easements also may generate state income tax credits and reductions in inheritance taxes.

resell the property to individuals or like-minded developers. The Nature Conservancy is a national organization that has a strong conservation buyer program. It purchases unique properties and then markets them with the goal of selling them directly to conservation buyers. Conservation easements ensure that the conservation buyer will protect in perpetuity a property's most fragile environmental features.

Many regional and local land trusts have strong conservation buyer programs. Given their limited staff resources, land trusts typically engage local real estate agents to identify and catalog high-value conservation properties for sale to qualified buyers. Such properties may include working farms or ranches, valuable old-growth forests, hunting preserves, and/or significant wildlife habitat. Land trusts can be a resource for landowners interested in selling their property to conservation buyers—in this case, by acting as an adviser to the landowner, in lieu of a real estate broker.

Conservation buyer transactions offer a wide range of benefits to participants. For the seller, conservation transactions can yield competitive returns relative to traditional development sales. For the buyer, a conservation easement can be donated to a qualified entity such as a land trust shortly after his or her purchase. Conservation easement donations create an opportunity for federal and state tax deductions, estate tax savings, and state tax credit certificates. In some cases, developers can benefit from the sale of designated conservation parcels, creating community goodwill that, in turn, can speed up entitlement approvals.

Notwithstanding their many attributes, the opportunity to successfully market conservation buyer programs is limited to properties of unique scenic, environmental, cultural, and recreational quality and significance. In order for conservation development to be productive, a property must be of sufficient size to allow a reasonable development program to be pursued without threatening the land's underlying conservation values. Ted Turner and Robert Redford are among the many wealthy individuals who have engaged in conservation buyer projects. For example, the Sundance Preserve, outside of Park City, Utah, is a well-known conservation buyer project dedicated to maintaining the balance of art, nature, and community, as well as the cultivation of independent, innovative thought among area residents.

Limited Development Projects

Limited development can yield effective conservation results with a voluntarily constrained development program. In most cases, limited development involves a lower-density development than may otherwise be allowed by local subdivision and zoning codes. In conservation limited development projects, a landowner may develop part of a property and leave the remainder as permanently protected open space.

For example, a green developer might choose to buy 100 acres in an area that is zoned for two-acre residential lots. Assuming that all of the land is buildable, the developer might be able to subdivide the property into 45 two-acre lots, setting aside ten acres for roads, stormwater retention, and other infrastructure. In a limited development context, rather than dividing the land into 45 two-acre lots, the developer might elect to subdivide half the property into five ten-acre lots and set aside the remaining 50 acres for conservation. To further limit development, the owner might sell the lots with a covenant that limits each parcel to one house.

In some limited development projects, the portion of property sold to a new landowner may have conservation easements or contract zoning that restricts the type and extent of development that will be allowed. Cluster development often is used to maximize the developed portion of land to reach the densities allowed by the current zoning, helping ensure that limited development can compete with conventional development projects.

Limited development allows a landowner to realize financial gain while protecting a significant portion of the property. In the example above, if the market for ten-acre properties is sufficiently strong, the net return to the developer may equal the profits that would have been earned by dividing the property into two-acre lots. In many cases, a landowner may be able to sell homesites for a far higher price than if the land had been developed at maximum density. In a growing area, people often are willing to pay far more for a lot in a protected rural setting than in a more typical "cookie-cutter" subdivision. In addition, effective large-lot development might result in an "enhancement premium" for adjoining properties, even if they are developed at a higher density.

Limited development projects often are facilitated by nonprofit land trusts that identify properties as high-priority conservation candidates but lack the financial capacity to effect a timely purchase. In such cases, a land trust can work with a private landowner or developer to buy the property in whole or in part, and then subdivide it into two sections. This approach can result in the part of a property that includes important conservation values being put under the stewardship of a land trust or public agency, while the lands with limited conservation value could be resold to a qualified buyer who appreciates the property's conservation values.

In the late 1990s, the Groton Land Foundation in western Massachusetts was alerted to the prospect of a large development on a nearby 70-acre (28-ha) parcel that served as a critical wildlife corridor and habitat for the threatened Blanding's turtle. The property's price tag put it out of reach for the foundation to purchase and conserve in its entirety, so the foundation laid out a 12-house subdivision on about one-fourth of the land to avoid infringing on the property's most sensitive habitat areas. After securing entitlements, the land trust sold the platted portion of the property to a sympathetic developer. By designing the development to take advantage of the adjoining open space and habitat areas, the foundation was able to sell 17 developable acres (7 ha) for more than it had paid for the entire property. Subsequently, revenues from this sale were used to purchase an adjacent 40-acre (16-ha) parcel that enabled the foundation to control more than 93 acres (38 ha) of environmentally sensitive habitat now known as the Duck Pond Conservation Area.

Conservation Subdivisions

Conservation subdivision may be the most commonly used conservation development strategy. In contrast to limited development, conservation

Serenbe, Georgia, is the first community to be built following the Chattahoochee Hills Land Use Plan, which calls for green space to be preserved by focusing development in historic villages and hamlets.

subdivision allows the maximum number of legally permitted units to be developed on a site, provided they are clustered in a tight planning envelope and platted with relatively small lots. Concentrating lots on a relatively small part of the property enables the developer to set aside the majority of the remaining land as permanently protected open space, natural areas, or working land. Conservation subdivision often is used to protect agricultural land and/or natural resource lands near already developed areas. To be effective, the local political jurisdiction—the county or municipality—must allow conservation subdivision as a development strategy within its zoning and/or development code.

Revisiting the example of the 100-acre parcel zoned for two-acre lots may offer a useful illustration of this practice. As noted previously, in a conventional development, the entire property could be subdivided into 45 two-acre homesites. In a conservation subdivision, 45 half-acre lots might be clustered into a 25-acre area, leaving 75 acres of protected open space. If the project is laid out creatively and effectively, the adjoining open space can add to the appeal of the subdivision and hence to the value and price of the smaller-than-average lots.

Conservation subdivision generally requires 40 percent or more of a property's developable area to be set aside as permanent open space. In rural areas, a conservation subdivision may need to dedicate land for agriculture or forestry. In urbanizing areas, publicly accessible parks, trails, sports fields, or stormwater storage facilities may be required. Conservation subdivision zoning also may dictate that the open space be contiguous and/or that it connect to conservation areas beyond the site's immediate boundaries. Some jurisdictions offer a density bonus to landowners to encourage conservation subdivision development. Baltimore County, Maryland, for example, has used a conservation subdivision option to successfully protect more than 2,000 acres (809 ha) of rural open space.

Master-Planned Conservation Development Communities

Master-planned conservation development communities are the most complex, economically ambitious, and technically demanding form of conservation development. Drawing from their historical antecedents, master-planned developments typically are large residential and mixed-use communities that include diverse residential product types and neigh-

Land Trusts and Limited Development

Local, regional, and national land trusts have used limited development to protect large and small parcels under imminent threat of development. In New York, for instance, the Peconic Land Trust has used limited development to protect thousands of acres of farmland on eastern Long Island. The trust works with each participating landowner to prepare a site plan that will meet the landowner's revenue goals while protecting important conservation values.

Colorado Open Lands also has used limited development as a tool for large-scale conservation initiatives. In 1982, with assistance from the Gates Family Foundation, Colorado Open Lands purchased a 3,200-acre (1,295-ha) parcel in Clear Creek County that was slated for the development of 1,100 residential lots. After a thorough site analysis, land management evaluation, and wildlife survey, the trust platted and sold five conservation-restricted ranches to ensure permanent protection of the property's agriculture and wildlife values. In 1996, Colorado Open Lands purchased an 830-acre (336-ha) ranch in a rapidly developing unincorporated portion of western Douglas County. In an effort to protect the property's high-priority agricultural and wildlife values, Colorado Open Lands designed and implemented what it calls a "protective development strategy" in which ten carefully sited lots were platted and sold to conservation buyers. Today, 96 percent of the Allis Ranch Preserve is protected with a conservation easement, 1.5 miles (2.4 km) of riparian corridor and critical wildlife habitat have been preserved, 638 acres (258 ha) of productive agricultural lands are available for continued farming, and ten residential landowners have been engaged as active stewards of the land.

Working with landowners typically requires land trusts to educate themselves about development and to educate owners about the potential benefits of conserving part of their land. In addition to a landowner's interest in what becomes of the land, benefits might include lower taxes, more flexibility for the landowner in the sales process, and access to funds from government open-space and/or farmland protection programs.

---

borhood demographics, parks, recreational areas, schools, community shopping centers, and other amenities. Master-planned communities (MPCs) often include golf courses, greenbelts, walking trails, and other informal green spaces that connect and shape neighborhoods.

Master-planned communities come in a wide variety of types and sizes. During the past two decades, large mixed-use, new urbanist neighborhoods have been developed on a wide range of infill parcels, including the sites of the former Stapleton Airport and Lowry Air Force Base in Denver, Colorado. In other cases, mixed-use MPCs have been developed in exurban locations such as Ladera Ranch in Orange County, California. Resort and second-home communities like Sea Pines Plantation on Hilton Head Island, South Carolina, are celebrated examples of master-planned development. Open space is an organizing principle in the design and development of all these MPCs. That said, an appreciation for and application of conservation principles to *actively* inform and direct open-space protection efforts in MPCs is something of a lost art.

Master-planned conservation development projects have been around for many years. England's garden city movement of the late 19th century grew from a belief in the importance of balancing development with people's need for nature. In a book written at the turn of the century, Ebenezer Howard described his plan for Victoria, England: a 1,000-acre (405-ha) town surrounded by a 9,000-acre (3,642-ha) agricultural greenbelt. The proposed town also featured 120-foot-wide (37-m)

> **Model Ordinance Provisions: Recommendations for Local Officials Considering Conservation Subdivisions**
>
> A conservation subdivision that combines both land conservation and residential development can be a useful tool, but it is not a panacea capable of meeting all of a community's conservation and housing needs. Local officials should keep the following recommendations in mind:
>
> - Limit conservation subdivisions to urban fringe areas as a transition between urban and rural landscapes. Consider how the marketability of conservation subdivisions may lead to the premature conversion of rural landscapes.
> - Consider using conservation easements, agricultural zoning, urban service boundaries, and compact design to protect productive farmland and distinctive rural landscapes.
> - In addition to requiring the protection of a minimum percentage of open space, ensure that conservation subdivision ordinances also identify a minimum percentage of developable land to be conserved.
> - Encourage creative conservation community design—for example, by providing design flexibility in minimum lot sizes, lot configurations, and building setbacks.
> - Have a good land management plan. The development and implementation of the land management plan is crucial to ensuring the stewardship of protected open space.
> - Offer appropriate incentives to encourage the development of conservation communities. Incentives could include a faster and more predictable approval process for conservation subdivisions, reduced development fees, and small density bonuses for dedicating open space and trails for public use or for providing affordable housing.
> - Encourage low-impact development techniques, such as bioretention areas, vegetated swales, permeable pavement materials, and flexible design standards for roads, parking lots, driveways, and sidewalks.
>
> **Source:** Adapted from Neil Fleckenstein, "Conservation Subdivisions Coming to the Panhandle," *Florida Planning* (June 2006), http://www.talltimbers.org/images/ttlc/conservationsubdivision.pdf.

radiating boulevards "planted on each side of the pathways with trees, and in many places with shrubs and evergreens." Howard's vision was for "a Garden City that, as it grows, the free gifts of Nature—air, sunlight, breathing room and playing room—shall be retained in all needed abundance."[11] Although this plan never came to fruition, several English cities built at the time—including Letchworth and Welwyn, both in Hertfordshire—incorporated some of Howard's ideas for a garden city.

During the 1930s, a number of pioneering greenbelt communities were established in the United States. These communities used large-scale protected open spaces and natural lands as a physical and psychological buffer against the congestion and dysfunction of nearby urban areas. Greenbelt, Maryland, was the first of three "green towns" built from scratch by the Resettlement Administration, an initiative of President Franklin D. Roosevelt's New Deal. From the beginning, Greenbelt was designed as a complete city, with businesses, schools, roads, and facilities for recreation and town government. In addition to the built or "gray" infrastructure, green infrastructure was included as an integral part of the community design. Modeled after the English garden cities, Greenbelt's plan included a system of interior walkways and corridors, a forest reserve on the town's perimeter, and heavily landscaped pathways and protected riparian corridors designed to separate neighborhoods while

The Agriburbia Concept

Agriburbia™, a term coined by Quint Redmond, chairman of the TSR Group in Golden, Colorado, is an innovative concept that incorporates sustainable practices—such as the use of alternative energy, natural stormwater management, and walkability—with the reintegration of food production directly within the living environment. Agriburbia includes characteristics of new ruralism, modernism, and historic preservation—as well as other environmentally sustainable principles of real estate development—in a new land use concept that features food production as an integral element in the community design, social network, and financial viability of the neighborhood.

Each Agriburbia mixed-use development is centered on an agrarian concept in which conventional suburban landscaping and open space are replaced by orchards, vineyards, and other high-yield crops, which are grown for the benefit of the neighborhood and surrounding communities. The organically farmed agricultural lands are owned and actively managed by the homeowners association or metropolitan district, which in turn awards farm contracts for professional cultivation of the land. In addition to this shared civic farm, each mixed-use campus is designed to have a significant number of homesites capable of useful agricultural production. On their private lots, homeowners may participate in the agricultural program at any level that suits their needs. Homeowners can have their backyards professionally farmed, farm them themselves, or choose not to farm them at all. The real requirement is that they provide stewardship of their homesites in a suitable, productive way.

One example of Agriburbia design is a 640-acre (259-ha) parcel in southern Weld County, Colorado, that includes 980 homes, ranging from multifamily dwellings to detached, single-family homes on two-acre (0.8-ha) lots. The homes are arranged around a series of drip-irrigated vineyards and fields of high-yield crops. This benefits both homeowners and developers. "Developers can grow market produce or specialty crops and earn revenue while waiting for people to buy houses," says Redmond.

Increasingly, master-planned and other large subdivision developments are treating organic farms as an amenity. In South Burlington, Vermont, for example, David Scheuer, a developer who specializes in pedestrian-friendly communities, is developing a 16-acre (6.5-ha) organic farm as part of a 220-acre (89-ha) project called South Village. Likewise, the Angwin Ecovillage in Napa County, California, a joint project of Triad Communities and Pacific Union College, includes a 50-acre (20-ha) sustainable farming operation as part of a 350-unit development.

Source: "The Agriburbia Concept," www.Agriburbia.com.

Village Homes, Davis, California

Since the early 1970s, Village Homes in Davis, California, has been respected by planners and designers as a solid example of an ecologically based planned community. Its 240 residential units—including single-family houses, townhouses, and apartments—and office and commercial space are interspersed with common green space. Village Homes also includes low-tech ecological features such as open drainage channels designed as creeks and play areas, solar roof panels, and shared vegetable gardens. Narrow streets reduce stormwater runoff and enable simple infiltration swales and on-site detention basins to handle stormwater. As a result, conventional storm sewers were not required, and the savings—nearly $200,000 (in 1980 dollars)—enabled developers Michael and Judith Corbett to fund public parks, walkways, gardens, and other community amenities. The narrow streets also left more room for trees, which keep ambient air temperatures down and reduce the need for air conditioning. Pedestrian paths and traffic-calming street designs have helped foster a strong sense of community with extremely low crime rates and higher property values.

The creation of Village Homes was not without obstacles. The Corbetts had to win countless variances from city codes and ordinances. Securing loans from a cautious real estate market also was difficult in the project's infancy, but persistence paid off. Since the community's completion in 1981, the market for homes there has exceeded that of the competition.

"You know you are on the right track when your solution for one problem accidentally solves others," observes Corbett. "You decide to minimize automobile use to conserve fossil fuels, for example, and realize that this will reduce noise, conserve land by minimizing streets and parking, multiply opportunities for social contact, beautify the neighborhood, and make it safer for children."[1]

Note
1. Rocky Mountain Institute, *Green Development: Integrating Ecology and Real Estate* (New York: John Wiley & Sons, 1998), 38.

---

concurrently allowing residents easy access to nature. Many more green towns were planned during the New Deal, but only two others were built: Greendale, Wisconsin, and Greenhills, Ohio.

Today's practitioners of master-planned conservation development draw important lessons and experience from the greenbelt and garden city planners of the past two centuries. Innovative conservation developers also aspire to broaden the impact of their predecessors' work to address increasingly complex and threatening environmental challenges. With the prospect of global climate change, species collapse, and energy crises looming, some progressive developers are trying to use development as a tool for far-reaching environmental protection.

The portfolio of master-planned conservation communities in the United States is relatively small, but their early success demonstrates how urban design, low-impact design engineering, green building, and comprehensive development regulations can advance a wide range of environmental purposes and preserve fragile and increasingly threatened natural lands. Today's master-planned conservation communities expand upon the goals of building authentic community to explore how development can be used as a tool for protecting valuable land and resources.

The Future of Conservation Development

Although conservation development projects vary greatly in terms of size, goals, and approaches, they share a number of defining principles. Each of the conservation development approaches described here is grounded in an overriding emphasis on looking at all potential land uses—including conservation as well as developed uses—when determining how land should be used. Whether a project involves designing a small conservation subdivision on the outskirts of a Midwestern city or building high-end housing on a huge ranch in rural Montana, the conservation of land becomes an integral element of the planning process.

Many skeptics remain firm in the belief that conservation development is too idealistic; that it is good in theory, but impractical in reality. A growing number of developers are proving them wrong. The success of conservation developments throughout the United States is demonstrating what many Americans already know: people cherish the land on which they live and are willing to pay to see it preserved. An increasing number of homeowners are demanding that conservation principles be incorporated into their homes and communities. In response, innovative developers are showing that developments that take into account people's desire to live in harmony with nature and nearby open space can be as profitable—if not more so—than more conventional types of development.

Early pioneers of conservation development have paved the way for generations to come. Over the next several decades, conservation development projects—in all possible variations—will become increasingly common. As elected officials, land use and planning professionals, lenders, appraisers, and real estate professionals become familiar with the concept of conservation development and its many advantages, it will become increasingly easy for developers and conservationists to find common ground in determining how to meet America's housing needs without destroying the land on which we live—and for developers to make a sizable profit in the process.

Notes

1. Jeffrey Passel and D'Vera Cohn, "Immigration to Play Lead Role in Future U.S. Growth," Pew Research Center, February 11, 2008, http://pewresearch.org/pubs/729/united-states-population-projections.
2. Smart Growth America, "Open Space and Farmland," http://smartgrowthamerica.org/openspace.html.
3. USDA Natural Resources Conservation Service, http://soils.usda.gov/technical/handbook/contents/part622.html.
4. E.M. White, A.T. Morzillo, and R.J. Alig, "Past and Projected Rural Land Conversion in the US at State, Regional, and National Levels," *Landscape and Urban Planning* (Vol. 89, 2009): 37–48, http://cfpub.epa.gov/si/si_public_record_Report.cfm?dirEntryID=191185.
5. National Resources Conservation Service, "Urbanization and Development of Rural Land," http://www.nrcs.usda.gov/technical/NRI/2001/nri01dev.html.
6. See American Farmland Trust, Farmland Information Center, "Fact Sheet: Cost of Community Services Studies" (August 2007), http://www.farmlandinfo.org/documents/27757/COCS_09-2007.pdf.
7. Jim Heid, *Greenfield Development without Sprawl: The Role of Planned Communities* (Washington, D.C.: ULI–the Urban Land Institute, 2004).
8. "Preserve, Create, Manage: The Public Voices Its Opinions and Priorities on Open Space," *On Common Ground* (Summer 2001).
9. The Trust for Public Land and Land Trust Alliance, LandVote 2008 (Boston: The Trust for Public Land, 2008), http://www.tpl.org/content_documents/landvote_2008.pdf.
10. "Preserve, Create, Manage."
11. Howard discussed this in his book, *Garden Cities of To-morrow*, initially published in 1898. Quoted from a 1902 edition, in "The Effect of Ebenezer Howard and the Garden City Movement on Twentieth-Century Town Planning" (Rickmansworth, Hertfordshire, United Kingdom: Norman Lucey, 1973), www.rickmansworthherts.freeserve.co.uk/howard1.htm.

Benefits and Limitations of Conservation Development

CHAPTER 2

America's suburban subdivisions frequently are characterized by look-alike houses on large lots set along wide streets. Many of these subdivisions have been designed with little concern or consideration for preserving open space or natural features; those that do preserve open space often do so as an afterthought, preserving land that is too steep or too wet to be built upon, or that is otherwise unsuited for development. In rural areas, forests often are clear-cut and hills are leveled to make way for development. Land clearing and mass grading increase soil erosion and release chemicals, sediments, and other substances that degrade water quality.

Land conservation and development traditionally have been undertaken in isolation from—or even in opposition to—one another. But when development is undertaken without consideration of the natural and ecological functions and processes on and under the land, it can have unexpected and unintended impacts on the developed property and the areas that surround it.

Conservation development provides a strategy for addressing these challenges. By definition, conservation development is about developing and managing land in harmony with nature, historic settlement patterns, and traditional land uses, particularly farming or forestry. This approach requires considering the environment on and around a proposed development site. It takes into account conservation needs and priorities at all scales, from the individual building lot to the streetscape, the neighborhood, and beyond, to the broader masterplanned community. At the individual lot scale, some conservation developments specify a building envelope within each lot, preserving large trees or other natural resources, protecting the more sensitive areas of the lot from development, and situating the home out of the viewshed and away from ridges where it would affect the site's natural beauty.

At the neighborhood or community scale, the first step usually involves identifying scenic or environmentally sensitive areas and designating them as unbuildable. During the subsequent planning process, care is taken to ensure that the areas of the highest ecological value are protected from development, so that home lots and infrastructure do not infringe on environmentally sensitive areas. Conservation developments also employ best practices in planning and constructing infrastructure and the built environment, reducing impervious surfaces and using natural stormwater drainage and wastewater treatment where possible.

By preserving natural open space, historic and cultural features, and beautiful views, conservation development helps forge connections between people and the natural and built environments. Conservation development respects

and promotes a sense of place by recognizing and protecting the unique characteristics of the land.

Designing in harmony with nature also focuses on the human context and the needs of the people who will live in and around the conservation community. This involves protecting resources and scenic views not only for the community's residents, but also for those who live in the surrounding area. By considering the needs of nature *and* humans, planners and developers can leverage specific cause-and-effect interconnections between natural and built systems to increase benefits and reduce costs. When undertaken in

Conservation communities are an attractive and ecologically sustainable alternative to the cookie-cutter subdivisions so common throughout America.

Benefits of Conservation Development

Conservation development offers many benefits for developers, local governments and communities, and homeowners.

For developers, conservation development can result in:
o Higher price premiums;
o Faster absorption rates;
o Cost savings from reduced infrastructure, as a result of clustering development on the site and taking advantage of natural stormwater and other systems;
o Cost savings from reduced grading and other land preparation costs; and
o Free positive publicity.

For local governments and communities, conservation development can result in:
o Decreased stormwater runoff, due to less impervious surface area;
o Decreased stormwater treatment costs;
o Reduced risk of flooding and other environmental hazards;
o Improved water quality, due to protection of riparian buffers, wetlands, and groundwater recharge zones, as well as to clustering development away from water resources;
o Protection of rural character, forests and fields, and tourism/agricultural economies;
o Land preservation at no cost to the community;
o Reduced demand for public land;
o Lower municipal service costs due to clustered development; and
o Protection of critical habitat for a variety of species.

For homeowners and residents of a conservation community, conservation development can offer:
o Protection from inappropriate development;
o Higher home appreciation rates;
o Access to natural areas and open space;
o Increased opportunities for healthy lifestyles;
o A greater sense of community and belonging; and
o A serene and aesthetically pleasing environment.

conjunction with the local government's comprehensive plan, conservation development can help a community achieve its land preservation goals while avoiding the conflicts that too often characterize land use decision making.

Ecological Benefits

Land preservation and conservation-based projects offer a variety of ecological benefits. Protecting forested areas, riparian corridors, and wetlands reduces stormwater runoff, which in turn lessens downstream pollution and the risk of flooding. Conserving woodlands, natural areas, and other open lands also can lower ambient air temperatures and improve air and water quality.

Reduced Stormwater Runoff

The roads, buildings, parking lots, and other impervious surfaces in many conventional development projects profoundly affect how water moves—both above and below ground—during and following rainstorms. The amount of paved surfaces also has an impact on the quality of stormwater and the ultimate condition of nearby rivers, lakes, and streams. Conservation development reduces impervious cover and protects natural areas, allowing them to perform valuable ecological functions.

Forests and wetlands store water, reducing stormwater runoff and providing invaluable flood mitigation services. In forests, some rainwater stays on the leaves of trees, giving it more time to evaporate directly into the air rather than adding to the amount of water flowing over the ground. Leaves also reduce raindrop impact, which in turn reduces soil erosion. Tree roots absorb water from the soil, keeping it drier and able to store more rainwater. In addition, tree roots hold the soil in place, reducing the movement of sediment that can shrink river channels downstream. Ground that is covered by vegetation also absorbs more water than ground that is paved or has structures on it. The U.S. Environmental Protection Agency (EPA) estimates that one acre (0.4 ha) of asphalt will generate 16 times the runoff of one acre of meadow.

The mass grading used in conventional subdivision development compacts soil, further adding to runoff, even in areas where there is no construction. Conservation development generally requires less grading than conventional development, further reducing the amount and speed of water running over the surface.

Reducing surface water runoff has several advantages. When more water is absorbed into the ground, less runoff empties into rivers and streams. As water leaves the ground it picks up sediment, depositing it in downstream rivers and waterways, reducing their capacity to hold water. This increases the risk that a river or stream will overflow, flooding the land and settlements around it. Water flowing over impervious surfaces also travels faster than over natural areas, increasing the risk of flash floods.

Another issue associated with stormwater runoff is water quality. As the runoff picks up sediment, it also carries away pesticides and other chemicals that have been used to treat the soil, affecting water quality and causing potential harm to aquatic life.

Improved Air Quality

In addition to reducing stormwater runoff, trees help purify the air. Some experts suggest that a built environment devoid of trees and other air purifiers is contributing to a rise in childhood asthma and other respiratory diseases. The EPA cautions that more than 50 percent of Americans live in areas where the air is unhealthy to breathe.[1]

Trees also offer a host of other benefits. Large shade trees absorb carbon and cool surface temperatures. According to the USDA, "the net cooling effect of a young, healthy tree is equivalent to ten room-size air conditioners operating 20 hours a day."[2] Lower temperatures can be an important factor in stemming the production of hazardous air pollutants like ozone. In 1985, the American Forestry Association estimated the yearly value of a tree at $73 for air conditioning, $75 for soil erosion and stormwater control, $75 for wildlife shelter, and $50 for air pollution control. Compounded over a 50-year lifetime, this totaled $57,152.[3]

Health and Social Benefits

A growing body of research shows that how we design our communities and buildings has profound impacts on our health. A 2003 study by Smart

Chicago Wilderness's Sustainable Development Principles for Protecting Nature

The Chicago Wilderness consortium sponsored a collaborative effort by representatives of local governments, developers, engineers, planners, site designers, and conservationists to provide guidance to local governments and developers on planning and designing new development and redevelopment projects as part of a broader effort to protect and enhance nature as an integral part of the development process. This effort resulted in the following principles:
1. Promote infill development;
2. Protect natural resources and habitats;
3. Enhance potential recreational and aesthetic amenities;
4. Preserve permanent linked open spaces;
5. Recognize water as a resource;
6. Minimize changes to topography, soils, and vegetation;
7. Establish ongoing management procedures; and
8. Design developments to achieve the broader sustainability of human and natural communities.

Source: The Nature Conservancy and Chicago Wilderness, "Conservation Development in Practice," http://www.nipc.org/environment/sustainable/conservation design/Conservation%20Development%20 in%20Practice/CD_Presentation.pdf.

> ### Stormwater Treatment at Prairie Crossing
>
> Prairie Crossing—one of the nation's first conservation developments—demonstrates how ecologically sensitive development can be used as a tool for the conservation of land that is threatened by inappropriate uses. The 678-acre (274-ha) site, located in Grayslake, Illinois, some 40 miles (64 km) north of downtown Chicago, has become a model for aspiring conservation developers.
>
> Although many recent residential developments incorporate environmental features, Prairie Crossing made ecological concerns its starting point, building a community around principles of enhancing and caring for the land. A prime example is the natural stormwater treatment system that was used instead of conventional storm sewers. The "water treatment train"—the first of its kind in the country—channels rainwater and snowmelt through open swales and wetlands into lakes, ponds, and streams.
>
> Each step in the treatment train reduces the volume of runoff, allowing greater water filtration and evaporation as well as the removal of pollutants. Water that reaches the wetlands has been significantly cleansed by the time it flows into Lake Aldo Leopold, an artificial water feature, and three other ponds, which act as detention basins. This treatment train decreases the amount of stormwater conveyed off site by approximately 50 percent compared to the predevelopment agricultural landscape, thus helping to prevent flooding downstream. The developer saved more than $200,000 in reduced stormwater management costs by taking a natural systems approach to stormwater management.
>
> **Source:** Adapted from Jo Allen Gause (editor), *Developing Sustainable Planned Communities* (Washington, DC: ULI–the Urban Land Institute, 2007).

Growth America that used census data from 448 U.S. counties identified a clear correlation between sprawl and health problems such as obesity and hypertension.[4] According to federal transportation studies, approximately half of all schoolchildren walked or rode a bicycle to or from school in 1969. Today, fewer than 15 percent walk to or from school,[5] a statistic that many health experts warn is a factor in the growing number of overweight, out-of-shape children and teens at risk of developing serious health problems.

A related impact of current development patterns is what author Richard Louv—in his book *Last Child in the Woods*—calls "nature-deficit disorder." Louv argues that children need to have a stronger connection to the natural world if they are to flourish as healthy citizens of the planet. He points out that although our schools may teach students about threats to the Amazon rainforest, conventional development patterns do little to encourage people's personal relationships with the natural terrain outside their own homes. When neighborhood green space is lost to development, children lose a place to play and adults lose a place to socialize.[6]

Many studies have demonstrated that nature can have a positive influence on mental and physical health. A 2003 study of children in public housing units concluded that girls who lived in units near nature have better concentration and more self-discipline than those in housing that lacked access to green space.[7] Similarly, employees whose workplaces offer them views of nature consistently report greater job satisfaction and productivity; research suggests that this also results in reduced absenteeism. Studies of hospitalized patients have shown that patients who can see greenery from their hospital windows recover faster than patients who cannot. It stands to reason that providing people with a view of nature on a daily basis may have major health benefits.[8]

Sociologist Robert Putnam, in his 2000 landmark study *Bowling Alone*, traced the decline of community since the mid-20th century. His research

> ### Benefits of Trees
>
> Research by the USDA Forest Service and others has shown that healthy trees:
> - Create cleaner, healthier, and more breathable air. An acre (0.4 ha) of mature trees can absorb as much carbon dioxide as that generated by a car driving 26,000 miles (41,842 km).
> - Shade homes and buildings, reducing air conditioning bills by as much as 30 percent.
> - Reduce stormwater runoff and soil erosion by slowing the impact of rainfall and allowing it to soak into the soil.
> - Mitigate the impacts of urban heat islands by lowering surface temperatures.
> - Block winter winds and reduce noise levels.
> - Provide neighborhoods with a sense of place.
> - Increase real estate values by as much as 20 percent.

shows that Americans sign fewer petitions, belong to fewer organizations, know fewer of their neighbors, and meet with friends less frequently than they did in the past. In addition to various time pressures and changes in the family structure, Putnam blames suburban growth patterns. He concludes that "suburbanization, commuting, and sprawl" are responsible for an additional 10 percent of the problem.[9]

Putnam warns that we are experiencing the loss of social capital—valuable social networks—in critical ways. Communities with less social capital have lower educational performance and higher rates of teen pregnancy, suicide, low birth weight, and prenatal mortality. Perhaps not surprisingly, Putnam's research also demonstrates a link between the loss of community bonds and high crime rates.

There is no doubt that conservation development can result in healthier, more livable, sustainable communities. Forests, lakes, parks, and other open-space elements are havens of tranquility, recreation, and inspiration for many people. The open space in conservation developments offers people peace of mind. The sound of running water, the smell of a garden, or a view of a grove of trees all can have a calming effect upon one's mental state. The sheer beauty of an uninterrupted ridgeline or a green valley adds to the quality of life of those who live in and around a conservation development. In conservation communities—developments where homes abut open space—homeowners have visual access to nature by simply looking out their windows.

The compact development in conservation communities also increases interaction among neighbors, fostering a stronger sense of community. Many conservation communities have nature centers, cultural programs, and/or community events that further encourage a sense of community. For developers, these become amenities that can increase a project's profitability.

Residents of conservation communities benefit from passive and active recreational opportunities afforded by conservation lands. Conservation design typically includes walking and hiking trails; many conservation lands also offer biking, fishing, horseback riding, swimming, gardening, and other forms of outdoor recreation. Where conservation lands are accessible to the general public, the benefits extend well beyond the conservation community. In addition to enhancing the quality of life of those in the surrounding area, the open space may even prove to be a draw for tourists, supporting and enhancing the local economy.

Economic Benefits

The benefits of conservation development extend beyond meeting broad community preservation or conservation goals. Conservation development also offers distinct economic advantages to all parties, including local governments, landowners, developers, and homebuyers. Conservation development enables communities to preserve land without a significant expenditure of public funds. Livingston County, Michigan, for example, has

The surrounding environment is the single most important factor affecting the market value of a home. A mountain vista or proximity to a park, water, or green space affects the value more than the size of the house, the number of rooms, the types of appliances, or even the presence of a swimming pool. Shown: Centerra, in Loveland, Colorado.

preserved more than 2,000 acres (4,942 ha) through this approach; Hanover County, Virginia, has preserved 5,000 acres (2,024 ha); and Monterey County, California, has preserved more than 20,000 acres (8,094 ha).

Conservation development provides a means for land to be preserved voluntarily, while owners and developers can still realize the fair market value of their property. In addition, many conservation developments in agricultural areas protect productive farmland by providing a way for owners to earn a profit by selling off a portion of the land. Allowing farming, vineyards, orchards, ranching, or selected timber harvests to continue protects the local economy in rural areas, as well as the rural character of agricultural communities. Part of the appeal of some conservation communities is the opportunity for people to buy property on or near a working farm, where they can live amid horses, cattle grazing in open pasturelands, vineyards, or fields of corn or wheat. Some of these communities contain organic farms that

Conservation development offers financial advantages to local governments. Clustering homes allows less infrastructure, shorter and narrower roads, fewer curbs and gutters, and other savings.

offer fresh produce to residents, while others offer opportunities for traditional family activities such as apple or strawberry picking.

Conservation development offers other financial advantages to local governments. Clustering homes and other elements of the built environment requires less infrastructure, shorter and narrower roads, fewer sidewalks, fewer curbs and gutters, and less underground piping for water and sewers. This amounts to significant savings for local governments in repair and maintenance. In addition, well-planned conservation developments limit future costs by reducing the government's need to control flooding, treat polluted water, and implement other environmental mitigation projects.

A development with fewer infrastructure needs offers obvious cost benefits to developers as well. Shorter infrastructure runs can reduce the cost of utilities. Clustering development can lower construction costs for roads, as well as for curbs, gutters, and sidewalks. Clustered development usually requires fewer streetlights and fire hydrants. All of these savings also can be achieved with limited development that does not use clustering. Projects with narrower, more rural roads and/or having no water or sewer services required have lower infrastructure development costs. In addition to these lower construction costs, conservation developers typically achieve additional savings in site preparation because a smaller portion of the property is cleared and graded. The use of natural stormwater systems rather than conventional curb-and-gutter systems may afford additional cost savings.

In a 2005 study comparing the economic costs of designing and building conservation versus conventional developments, the Conservation Research Institute found that cost savings for conservation developments ranged from $2,500 to $3,700 per lot. Similarly, a 2007 study undertaken by Applied Ecological Services (AES) that compared the costs of conservation development with those of conventional development on ten parcels of land found that stormwater management costs in a conservation development were an average of 39 percent less than those in a conventional development, roadways cost an average of

> ### Prairie Crossing's Infrastructure Savings
>
> The developers of Prairie Crossing in Grayslake, Illinois, saved almost $1.4 million—$2,000 per acre ($4,942 per ha)—in infrastructure costs, compared with conventional development, as a result of differences in the stormwater management system, curbs and gutters, paving, sidewalks, and landscaping. These savings were put back into the project budget and used for amenities and enhanced open space, to create a more aesthetically appealing community.
>
> | | |
> |---|---|
> | Decreased road width (8–12 feet [2.4–3.7 m] narrower than traditional subdivision streets) | $178,000 |
> | Elimination of paved sidewalk (except for Village area) | $648,000 |
> | Elimination of curbs and gutters (except for Village area) | $339,000 |
> | Decreased storm sewers (replaced by natural stormwater management) | $210,000 |
> | **Total savings** | **$1,375,000** |
>
> **Source:** Rocky Mountain Institute, *Green Development: Integrating Ecology and Real Estate*, (New York: John Wiley & Sons, 1998).

18 percent less, and reduced grading needs resulted in a 39 percent reduction of costs. Not all costs were lower, however. On all ten sites in the AES study, landscaping costs were higher for conservation development, because of the additional cost of landscape restoration. Although such costs may be higher in a conservation project that seeks to protect and preserve natural features, it is important to recognize that not all conservation development projects require extensive landscape restoration. Overall, the study found that conservation development cost on average 22 percent less than a conventional approach.[10]

Although site-to-site comparisons can be difficult to make in the real world, conservation developers suggest that AES's findings hold true for most conservation development projects.[11] Land planner Randall Arendt, one of the nation's foremost experts in conservation subdivision design, tells of his experience: "One developer in Texas who hired me to redesign his 60-acre [24-ha] subdivision told me that his site grading costs plummeted from $300,000 to $50,000 as a result of my redesign.... In Tennessee, my redesign saved one developer approximately $212,000 in street construction costs, while at the same time introducing significantly more quality open space into the layout. Another design is credited by an Indiana developer as having added $20,000 to $25,000 of value to each of his lots."[12]

Market Differentiation

An increasing number of Americans are searching for more variety and choices in both housing and neighborhoods. They are looking for communities that offer them places to walk, to socialize, and to commune with nature. Providing open space—and guaranteeing that the open space will remain in perpetuity—can be a valuable marketing tool.

Many people do not like the one-size-fits-all developments that so many Americans call home. One reason for shifting buyer preferences is the fact that there are so many different buyer profiles. Visual preference surveys that ask people to pick out pictures of the sort of place where they would like to live reveal an almost universally negative reaction to the visual appearance of sprawl and a positive reaction to communities with lots of common open space. At the same time, surveys indicate that Americans want to live in homes located near parks and natural areas, regardless of whether those homes are in infill or greenfield locations. As interest in green consumerism and protecting the environment grows, the pool of buyers for conservation communities will expand even more.

Sales Advantages

Market surveys have shown that a surprising number of potential homebuyers are willing to pay a premium for green space. In a 2008 study undertaken by the National Association of Realtors, more than 90 percent of first-time homebuyers said that environmentally friendly features were an important criterion in selecting a home.[13] According to the National Association of Realtors, trails for hiking and biking—*not* golf courses—are the top choice for open-space amenities in a development. Only 1 to 2 percent of respondents in a survey of who uses public recreational facilities said they use golf courses; 5 to 6 percent use public swimming pools, and 50 to 60 percent—more than half—use pathway systems. In another recent poll, more than three-quarters of respondents rated natural open space as "essential" or "very important"; walking and bicycling ranked third in the list of attributes homebuyers wanted. More than half of respondents—57 percent—said they would be more likely to purchase a home close to green space, and 50 percent said they would be willing to pay 10 percent more for a home located near a park or other protected area.[14]

Numerous market studies seem to confirm these findings. For example, a market study of Prairie Crossing suggests that attention to environmental features has resulted in both price premiums and increased property values. According to a market analysis by Robert Charles Lesser and Co., houses at Prairie Crossing were selling for $139 per square foot ($1,496 per m²), 33 percent higher than comparable houses in the market area.[15] At Hidden Springs, a 1,844-acre (746-ha) conservation community near Boise, Idaho, homesites adjacent to protected open space usually sold first, regardless of price. In addition, sites adjacent to protected open space generally sold at price premiums ranging from 10 to 20 percent over other sites in the conservation community. Sales at Hidden Springs also suggest the overall value of conservation development: most of the Hidden Springs sites achieved price premiums ranging from 15 to 30 percent over comparable sites in the market area.

Other studies support these findings. According to a 2005 report by the Alliance for the Chesapeake Bay, wooded properties increase home values by as much as 20 percent, and lots with mature trees or those that back up to forested land have sold more than 50 percent faster than others.[16] A comparative study of developments in Amherst and Concord, Massachusetts, found that clustered housing with open space appreciated at a higher rate than homes in more conventional subdivisions without open space. This translated into a difference in average selling price of $17,100 more for the subdivisions with common open space.[17] In Salem, Oregon, land adjacent to a greenbelt was found to be worth about $1,200 an acre ($2,965 per ha) more than land only 1,000 feet (305 m) away. In Oakland, California, a three-mile (5-km) greenbelt around Lake Merritt was found to add $41 million to surrounding property values. And a developer who donated a 40-foot-wide (12-m), seven-mile-long (11-km) easement along a popular trail in Front Royal, Virginia, sold all 50 parcels bordering the trail in just four months.[18] A 2006 study titled "The Economics of Conservation Subdivisions" concluded that "conservation subdivisions can provide higher profits to developers. Lots in conservation subdivisions carry a price premium, are less expensive to build, and sell more quickly than lots in conventional subdivisions."[19]

In Prince William County, Virginia, homes in the Forest Brook subdivision, a 62-acre (25-ha) conservation development in which 60 percent of the site remained untouched, sold 30 to 50 percent faster than those in a conventional subdivision located less than a mile (1.6 km) away. In northern

Studies show that developed lots with trees sell for 10 to 20 percent more than similarly sized lots without trees. Shade trees can also reduce air-conditioning bills by as much as 30 percent.

Florida, developer Jon Kohler could not keep up with demand for homes in the Centerville Conservation Community, a new 975-acre (395-ha) conservation development in which more than 70 percent of the land is permanently protected. During the initial release to "friends and family," all 86 homesites sold in just seven hours. "Our lot absorption rate was off the charts compared with traditional developments," Kohler says. "Given apples to apples, I think conservation lots sell for 20–30 percent more than traditional lots. The demand has been incredible. We haven't even finished our paving yet and, out of 200, we have 122 lots under contract."[20]

Sales at Dewees Island, a conservation development on a coastal barrier island near Charleston, South Carolina, have similarly surpassed expectations. Property values are far higher than on other sea islands, primarily because of the value of the project's hundreds of acres of protected land. Developer John Knott says that buyers appreciate the beauty and tranquility of the place, and feel they have a personal stake in its preservation.

In addition to the initial price premiums, research suggests that lots in conservation communities increase in value more quickly than comparable lots in conventional developments. In its annual study of real estate trends, PriceWaterhouseCoopers, for instance, found that communities with sensible land use policies that include the protection of a "meaningful" amount of open space consistently hold their value better in economic downturns and appreciate more in upturns of the market.[21] "Conservation subdivisions are vastly more appealing to consumers, have a much faster resale rate and higher resale value, and that is a fact," says Joe Flaherty, the developer of Jarvis Farm, a conservation community in Westford, Massachusetts.

Centerville Conservation Community, Leon County, Florida

Conservation easements, public acquisition, and deeds of covenant currently protect more than 135,000 (54,635 ha) of the 300,000 acres (121,410 ha) in northern Florida's Red Hill region. Located on the southern periphery of this region, the Centerville Conservation Community falls under Leon County's "urban fringe" zoning category, which typically requires three-acre (1.2-ha) lots. Developer Jon Kohler believed he had a better idea, however, and set about designing a community where clustered housing would allow roughly 65 percent of the 975-acre (395-ha) site to be preserved.

The land under conservation easement includes significant upland acreage set aside to provide habitat for the gopher tortoise, a species of special concern in Florida. The conservation land also provides amenities for homeowners, who have access to more than seven miles (11 km) of nature trails, two miles (3 km) of scenic pedestrian walkways, stocked fishing ponds, and horse stables.

The development team began by designating conservation areas, and then sited the houses in relationship to the protected land. The 200 homesites are strategically located on hilltops, lakefront, and in scenic areas with the purpose of protecting views and pristine habitats. Pervious pavements were used for the pedestrian walkway, which weaves around the trees that were in its way. Centerville's wildlife management plan calls for stocking and feeding bass for fishing and installing duck boxes that provide important habitat for the once-endangered wood duck. Prescribed burns replicate the natural processes of the land and minimize the risk of larger fires. Trails are marked with bluebird houses, fox squirrel boxes, and footbridges over the water crossings.

Centerville's path from concept to approval was long and at times cumbersome. Because it was the first conservation community in Leon County, the learning curve was steep for all involved. The county lacked a conservation subdivision ordinance to guide the development's review. The project also required the county to create a new land use map and make zoning changes before site planning and permitting could begin.

The developer's persistence has paid off, however. The public's response to the Centerville Conservation Community has been overwhelmingly positive. More than half the lots sold within days of the initial public offering. Residents of nearby neighborhoods, initially skeptical about traffic and smaller lot sizes, have become supporters of Centerville, citing the developer's willingness to address their concerns and to protect the integrity of the landscape. "Centerville is an excellent example of what can happen when you work together in respecting the environment and creating a development," says former Leon County Commissioner Tony Grippa. "[It] will be the model for conservation communities to come."[1]

For more information, see the project website, www.centerville-florida.com.

The Centerville Conservation Community in Leon County, Florida, preserves more than 65 percent of a 975-acre site.

Note

1. Quoted in Jason Dehart, "Big Plans for the Centerville Corridor," *Tallahassee* (Nov.–Dec. 2005), http://www.jonkohler.com/press-releases/Jon%20Kohler_TM%20Reprint.pdf.

Lenah Run, Loudoun County, Virginia

In Loudoun County, Virginia, one of the fastest-growing counties in the United States, Lenah Run features six separate housing clusters with a total of 256 lots on 460 acres (186 ha). More than 70 percent of the project—over 340 acres (138 ha)—has been preserved as open space. The homes blend into the natural features of the land. There are no sidewalks, curbs, or gutters; driveways are short to lessen the amount of impervious surfaces. Trees were transplanted from woodlands on the property to enhance common areas and to supplement the 800-foot (244-m) minimum buffer between hamlets.

The open space was designed as a permanent greenbelt around the community, providing a wildlife and vegetative corridor, as well as opportunities for passive recreation.

The Virginia Department of Forestry supervised the voluntary reforestation of 30 acres (12 ha) of perimeter and open-space areas with native plants. In addition, 1,659 feet (506 m) of Lenah Run, a local stream, was enhanced, restored, and protected by a conservation easement in a partnership between the landowner and the Virginia Department of Forestry.

All of the lots at Lenah Run back up to open space, which added an estimated $10,000 in value to each lot. The developer estimates that the project's homes have sold 30 percent faster than those in more conventional developments.

Source: Adapted from *Forest Friendly Development: Chesapeake Bay Watershed Case Studies* (Camp Hill, Pennsylvania: Alliance for the Chesapeake Bay, 2005).

"Consumers prefer the open space. Homes in conservation subdivisions sell as soon as they go on the market, within one week, even in a down real estate market. It is all about value."[22]

As land is developed and green space disappears, open space will become an even higher priority for homebuyers. Because land in conservation communities appreciates faster and holds its value in down markets, it is easier to obtain construction loans, speeding up the process from planning to buildout and absorption. Calvert County, Maryland, for example, has fast-tracked approval of conservation developments in rural areas as compared to conventional developments.

The Power of Positive Press

Conservation developments often derive enormous marketing benefits. Many people do not like the cookie-cutter developments that are so common throughout America. When a developer provides a positive alternative to the typical suburban subdivision, it gets attention from both the press and the public. Many of the projects showcased in this book have generated extensive national and regional press coverage. This is, in effect, free publicity for the development's lots and homes, which translates to increased visibility and demand. When—through visual preference surveys—people are asked to pick out pictures of the sort of place where they would like to live, almost all react negatively to the visual appearance of sprawl, selecting instead scenes of compact, human-scaled neighborhoods like those created through conservation design. As interest in green building and sustainability grows, conservation communities will have a growing pool of buyers.

Conservation developers also often benefit from the public goodwill derived from doing something that is perceived as good for the community. Conservation-based projects are far more likely than conventional development to generate positive press, which can significantly reduce the amount of marketing the developer needs to do and shorten the sales cycle. Prairie Crossing, Serenbe, Hidden Springs, and other conservation developments, for example, have generated positive news stories in dozens of major news outlets, including the *Wall Street Journal*, *New York Times*, *Atlanta Journal-Constitution*, and *Chicago Tribune*. Developers of communities in

Conservation-based projects, like Northwest Crossing, in Bend, Oregon, are more likely than conventional projects to generate positive press, which can provide free marketing and help to accelerate sales.

which land protection is a goal also generally meet with less resistance from the surrounding community. In fact, developers often are amazed at the level of community support for a plan that balances development with conservation. Gaining the support of the community may speed up the approval process for a development project and, as all developers know, "time is money." Again and again, the developers interviewed for this book said that little or no opposition was voiced at public meetings when the community understood that the proposed development would preserve valuable open space.[23]

Some local governments have created a streamlined permitting process for conservation-based projects. In Sarasota County, Florida, for example, administrators recently passed an

> **Conservation Subdivisions: Advantages to Communities**
>
> Conservation subdivisions offer many advantages. Communities should be aware that conservation development is *not* "clustering." Conservation subdivisions preserve 50 to 70 percent or more of the *buildable* land in unsewered rural areas in place of conventional "all lawn" lot sizes of two to five acres (0.8 to 2.0 ha). This is a much higher quality and percentage of preserved land than "clustering." Conservation communities are fair to developers and landowners, since they have been proven to be more profitable and sell more quickly while reducing some costs. They also are fair to homeowners, since they result in higher home appreciation rates.
>
> Conservation subdivisions also:
> - **Protect clean water** in lakes, rivers, and streams and reduce stormwater runoff and treatment costs;
> - **Conserve groundwater** as natural areas infiltrate water and reduce flooding;
> - **Clean the air**, because most trees and vegetation are left intact, helping combat climate change;
> - **Preserve a town's rural character**, forests and fields, wildlife, and tourism/agricultural economies;
> - **Save money**, by preserving land at no cost to the community;
> - **Reduce demand for public land** acquisition;
> - **Create the same number of homesites** as conventional subdivision development;
> - **Reduce costs**, because municipal service costs are cheaper when homes are not widely scattered; and
> - **Create trails through natural lands**, enabling children and adults to exercise and improve their health while enjoying nature.
>
> Source: Adapted from Land Choices, Conservation Subdivisions Fact Sheet, 2007.

ordinance that expedites building permits for green developments, reducing the waiting period from six weeks to six days for those who are committed to building a greener future. As local governments become more familiar with conservation development and recognize it as a tool for land preservation, an expedited permitting process for conservation development may become the norm.

Seasoned developers know that mutual trust and respect can eventually translate into financial advantages. Many pioneering developers have found that focusing on the land's environmental qualities has afforded them new, often unexpected opportunities. Conservation communities are gaining credibility, not just as a tool for protecting land, but also as a means of meeting market demand and making profits.

One additional benefit of conservation development is the sense of pride that developers feel when they do something good for residents and the community. "I feel good developing land this way," says Joe Flaherty, the developer of Jarvis Farm. "The farmer, Mr. Jarvis . . . used to walk around the open space at the subdivision I developed, proud that his land was kept intact after he sold for development. I was proud that I did not destroy his farm."[24]

Similiarly, Kurt Andrae—the developer of Sugar Creek Preserve, a conservation development in Elkorn, Wisconsin—says, "when I became a developer, I knew that there had to be a more respectful way to treat the land while also creating unique living spaces. "Conservation subdivision design is the perfect solution to accomplish both of these goals and is the only way I approach development. More often than not, this approach saves on project costs and accelerates approval timelines."[25]

Limitations and Obstacles

Conservation development is not a panacea. It will not work everywhere, nor will it appease staunch no-growth advocates. Residents may be particularly wary of projects containing high-density neighborhoods. Some rural

communities resist projects that include clustered housing because local residents think they look "too urban"; they may feel that clustering houses undermines the rural appeal of the community. Many rural areas attempt to maintain their rural feel by requiring minimum lot sizes that preclude clustered development approaches. Residents similarly may fail to appreciate lower-density projects with dispersed homesites, even when these projects are conscientiously designed to sit lightly on the land.

Change is inherently difficult. When a change involves the permanent alteration of the land one calls home, it can create a fierce, emotional reaction. The Santa Lucia Preserve, a 20,000-acre (8,094-ha) conservation development project near Carmel, California, met with significant opposition

Conservation development is designed to sit lightly on the land. Many designers experienced with this approach say it requires walking the land to handpick the appropriate sites for homes, buildings, and infrastructure.

from a small group of conservationists who fought to the end to preserve the entire parcel. For them, says developer Tom Gray, who planned to use limited development of a portion of the parcel to fund the preservation effort, "the perfect became the enemy of the good."[26]

Success in conservation development often requires a partnership among the original landowner, the developer, local government, and a local land trust that will hold a conservation easement on the protected property. Whereas the "rules" for conventional development are clear to all players involved, conservation developers may have to break down barriers to do things differently. If they are dealing with a unique or prized piece of land, this may happen amid intense scrutiny from the surrounding community. In fact, a major cause of the historic tension between conservation developers and land conservationists is that both sides are naturally attracted to the same parcels of land.

The most successful conservation developments take place in a context in which the community is engaged in determining the criteria that will be used in land use decision making. As with any project, involving more people in the decision-making process lengthens, but usually improves, the planning process. Pennterra, a master-planned community on 503 acres (204 ha) in Carlisle, Pennsylvania, used an innovative bioretention and stormwater treatment train technique that had never before been used in the township. Obtaining the approvals needed to implement this system set the project start date back a year. The fire department's concerns over minimal street setbacks and 20-foot-wide (6-m) streets further delayed approvals.

The Perception of Risk

A lack of experience with conservation development is often the biggest obstacle to developing a conservation community. This can make lenders, public officials, and the general public hesitant to embrace what they perceive to be an unusual and perhaps risky approach. In general, real estate investors tend to steer away from innovative, "unproven" approaches. Some conservation development projects do not fit the formula that banks use for financing. Following the housing credit crisis, this hurdle may become more difficult than ever to overcome. Homebuyers, too, often are confused about and suspicious of the covenants and restrictions that are part of a conservation development. Initial sales may be slower than they would be at more conventional projects, since it may take time for potential homebuyers to become familiar with the concept and how it affects their purchasing decisions.

Developers also may find it difficult to compile data for a comprehensive market analysis. Outdated assumptions often inform current market analyses, which may prevent developers from building projects for the narrowly defined market to which conservation subdivisions are thought to appeal. The lack of comparable developments can make it difficult to locate detailed and reliable cost information. Many early conservation developers say they often had to "go with their gut," because clear marketing and financial data were hard to find. Others relied on psychographic analysis, as well as traditional market analysis, to support their concept.

Zoning and Subdivision Regulations

Zoning and subdivision regulations can create further obstacles. In many localities, creative designs are subject to a "conditional use" process, whereas more conventional designs can proceed unimpeded. "Not many developers, and none of the big homebuilders, will apply for a special permit to build a conservation subdivision," says Joe Flaherty, who developed Jarvis Farm. "It is too risky and causes delays that can last six months or more. These businesses have a responsibility to shareholders."[27] It took the developer of South Village—a South Burlington, Vermont, conservation community in which 340 homes are clustered around a 40-acre (16-ha) farm—six

Overcoming Obstacles to Conservation Development

Developers must recognize—and take steps to overcome—the many obstacles to conservation development. These include the following:
- Conservation development is a relatively new concept. Educating elected officials, community residents, real estate professionals, and potential homebuyers may take significant time and attention.
- Change is inherently difficult, particularly when it involves land one calls home. Developers may need to be prepared to meet with resistance on the part of long-time residents.
- Approvals may take longer when a project uses innovative approaches. Developers should be careful to incorporate additional time into the development schedule.
- Lenders and investors may be reluctant to invest in an innovative, "unproven" approach. Conservation developers may need to explore creative financing approaches.
- A lack of comparable developments makes it difficult to compile data for market analysis. Developers may need to "go with their gut" and incorporate other types of data into their feasibility studies and market analyses.
- Conducting in-depth analyses of land features and values takes expertise, time, and money. Conservation developers must recognize, plan, and budget for this.
- Addressing the environmental features on the conservation land adds complexity to all phases of the project. Developers must take care to ensure that land is permanently protected and appropriately maintained.
- Projects with clustered housing may look too "urban" for some rural communities. Effective layout and architectural design can be important tools in making sure that higher-density projects blend into the rural countryside.
- Developers may need to educate the community to overcome minimum lot sizes, setback regulations, and other regulations intended to preserve the community's rural character. Variances to codes and zoning regulations may be required.
- Conservation developments often have a narrower target market than more traditional projects. Conservation developers need to clearly identify their target market and design marketing strategies that will reach this market.
- Initial sales of homes in nontraditional communities are often slow, as the market adjusts to new offerings. Developers must be prepared for a longer initial sales phase—although later phases may sell more quickly than those in conventional developments.

years to get approval, in part because of neighbors' objections to density.

Time is money, and many developers default to conventional development when regulations make conservation too difficult. "That is why conservation subdivisions should be the 'by right, permitted use' in ordinances, to make it easy for developers and their lawyers," adds Flaherty. "A lot of developers want to do the right thing but conventional subdivision ordinances and stubborn, inexperienced planning officials who lack vision force them to build the conventional subdivision that destroys the land."[28] Good conservation responds in specific ways to each piece of land, making it very difficult for any metrics-based zoning ordinance to accommodate it well.

Developers of conservation communities may have to spend considerable time educating policy makers and neighbors about their intentions and the benefits that this nontraditional approach will bring. Developers can more effectively educate policy makers by teaming up with local land trusts, watershed protection groups, or other environmental nonprofit organizations. The Natural Lands Trust in Media,

Pennsylvania, for example, has been particularly effective at educating local governments in Pennsylvania about the advantages of conservation development. When George Desmond wanted to pioneer environmentally friendly techniques at Millcreek, a 90-acre (36-ha) residential subdivision in West Lamenter Township, Pennsylvania, he spent two years working with the township to design a new ordinance option to "encourage development that complements rather than eliminates the distinctive resources of the site."[29] Millcreek was designed to preserve woodland and trees while achieving higher density than normally permitted. The developer sold more than 40 of the 230 homes per year, twice the rate of sales at neighboring developments.

Site Design and Development Challenges

Even when the zoning allows for conservation development and the community is open to it, conservation design sometimes can take more time upfront. Rather than looking at the land as a two-dimensional plot, conservation developers have to analyze various parts of the land to assess their relative conservation values. This typically is done through geographic information system (GIS) mapping—with overlays used to identify various values—which can be a time-consuming and sometimes costly proposition.

During the subsequent site planning phases, laying out lots and then setting building envelopes within these lots also may take extra work to ensure that they are consistent with the environmental, social, and ecological goals for the community.

Conservation development is designed to lay lightly on the land. Many designers and developers experienced with this approach insist that it requires walking the land to hand-pick the appropriate sites for homes, buildings, and infrastructure. The process of selecting sites and then figuring out how to get to them—planning roads and other infrastructure paths—is more labor intensive and time consuming, and thus can be more costly.

Transplanting suburban housing forms to a rural community contrasts with the basic premise of conservation development's focus on fitting the development into the existing landscape. To protect the rural character of the community, many conservation communities have strict design standards to which builders must adhere. Some design standards, for example, require local vernacular architecture for new houses. Other conservation communities extend the environmental benefits of the community through green building standards. Where residents are building their own homes, it can be a time-consuming process to develop

standards, educate homeowners and builders about what can and cannot be done, and enforce the standards.

Addressing environmental features on the conservation land further adds to the complexity of any project. Developers must be careful to ensure that the land is permanently protected and appropriately maintained. This may require finding an existing land trust to take on an easement or establishing a new trust. To ensure adequate funding for the restoration of ecologically valuable lands and the ongoing maintenance of open space, conservation communities sometimes include an assessment on the sale of property and/or the resale of homes, typically 1 to 3 percent of the lot or home price.

Sometimes the protected land is turned over to a land trust, the local municipality, or another entity. The developers of Homestead Preserve—a conservation community adjacent to the world-class Homestead Resort in Bath County, Virginia—for example, sold 9,250 acres (3,744 ha) of their 12,000-acre (4,856-ha) parcel in a bargain sale to the Nature Conservancy. The developer of the Santa Lucia Preserve, a 20,000-acre (8,094-ha) conservation development project in Monterey County, California, created a new nonprofit land conservancy to assume management of the preserved open land. The developer of Jackson Meadow, a conservation

community near Marine on St. Croix, Minnesota, contributed 53 acres (21 ha) of its site to the city, put another 120 acres (49 ha) under conservation easement, and constructed a clustered housing development on the remaining 40 acres (16 ha).

Other conservation developments retain full ownership of the open space. These communities often create a homeowners association to oversee the management of preserved land. When the open space includes working land—such as at Bundoran Farm, a high-end residential conservation community in Albemarle County, Virginia, or at Storm Mountain Ranch, a gated luxury ranch community, near Steamboat Springs, Colorado—it may be leased to one or more farmers, ranchers, or foresters to keep it in production. Putting in place the appropriate covenants on the property to address how it is to

Conservation communities emphasize commonly owned features—like the 350 acres (142 ha) of open space at Prairie Crossing—rather than focus on individual lot characteristics.

Real estate agents selling conservation communities must sell the community first and the specific lot second.

be managed and used adds another layer of complexity to conservation development decision making.

Educating the Market

In some cases, conservation developments may face marketing obstacles as well. The typical homebuyer is unfamiliar with conservation development and lacks a vocabulary to talk or think about it. People often assume that more money should buy them a larger lot. A buyer who is thinking in terms of a dollar-per-square-foot basis may find a smaller lot unappealing.

Success depends on marketing the environment, the shared open space, and the community rather than a specific lot. In other words, conservation developers should refocus prospective buyers' attention on the acreage they will gain as open space. For example, the sales director for a conservation community might emphasize the fact that the community features ten acres (4 ha) of open space per home. "Realtors selling conservation subdivision homesites must sell the community first, and the specific lot second," says a real estate agent at Sugar Creek Preserve, a conservation subdivision in southeastern Wisconsin in which the homes are clustered on 52 acres (21 ha) of the 176-acre (71-ha) site. "It is important to frame the lot purchase differently than a regular lot and block subdivision. At Sugar Creek Preserve we tell buyers that they aren't buying one acre lots, they are buying a 176-acre lot, of which they have one acre to build on."[30]

Not all real estate agents will readily understand or appreciate this approach. Agents may avoid showing a community that has higher-than-average home prices, particularly if smaller lots make it look as though homeowners are getting little for their money. Clearly, success in markets that are unfamiliar with conservation development principles will require ongoing education of the real estate community, including appraisers, lenders, real estate agents, and public officials.

Educating prospective buyers also can be challenging. Even after people are sold on the idea, it may take considerable time to explain how the concept translates to reality—what can and cannot be done with one's property. And not everyone is likely to agree with all of the rules. Bob Baldwin, Jr., the managing principal of Qroe Preservation Development LLC, tells of one wealthy client who decided not to purchase a lot at Bundoran Farm after failing to convince the development team to allow him to bypass some of the rules.

Experts warn that early sales of lots in a conservation development sometimes may be slower than in conventional development projects, as the market catches on to the idea. "Conservation subdivisions can be difficult to sell in the early stages," says Rob Keefe of Keefe Real Estate in Geneva, Wisconsin. "Prairie restorations look terrible for the first two years while the grasses are being established. The construction traffic and the excavation work take away from the peaceful natural setting."[31]

A Lack of Experience

A final obstacle to conservation development is the relative inexperience of the development profession in land conservation—and vice versa. Developers who want to build conservation-based projects must learn how to use easements, covenants, and other conservation tools. These projects also require significant knowledge and expertise to understand the biology, hydrology, and chemistry of the land in order to determine its relative ecological values. Conservation development requires looking not only at the land in its present state but also at its restoration potential. Adding a thorough investigation process extends the development time frame, as does working with the government to transfer densities and/or with a land trust to put easements on the property.

The developers who have successfully planned and created conservation communities have taken extra time to research existing projects, adapting what has worked to accommodate the unique characteristics of their own situations. As new conservation development projects are added to the litany of examples, land use professionals will have a growing body of knowledge on which to draw. Successful conservation development projects that offer a better quality of life for residents, a handsome profit for developers, and an opportunity for communities to protect and preserve land for future generations will serve as models for new conservation communities.

Notes

1. "EPA Issues Designations on Ozone Health Standards," U.S. Environmental Protection Agency news release, April 15, 2004.
2. "Urban Shade Trees," www.CoolCommunities.org, http://www.coolcommunities.org/urban_shade_trees.htm.
3. Gary A. Moll and Sara Ebenreck, *Shading Our Cities: A Resource Guide for Urban and Community Forests* (Washington, D.C.: American Forestry Association, 1989).
4. Jim Heid, *Greenfield Development without Sprawl: The Role of Planned Communities* (Washington, D.C.: ULI–the Urban Land Institute, 2004).
5. Centers for Disease Control and Prevention, "Kids Walk to School: Then and Now—Barriers and Solutions," http://www.cdc.gov/nccdphp/dnpa/kidswalk/then_and_now.htm.
6. Richard Louv, *Last Child in the Woods: Saving Our Children from Nature-Deficit Disorder* (Chapel Hill, N.C.: Algonquin Books of Chapel Hill, 2006).
7. F.A. Taylor, F.E. Kuo, and W.C. Sullivan, "Views of Nature and Self-Discipline: Evidence from Inner City Children," *Journal of Environmental Psychology*, Vol. 22 (2002): 49–63.
8. See M.D. Velarde, G. Fry, and M. Tveit, "Health Effects of Viewing Landscapes: Landscape Types in Environmental Psychology," *Urban Forestry & Urban Greening*, Vol. 6, Issue 4 (November 15, 2007): 199–212; Health Council of the Netherlands and Dutch Advisory Council for Research on Spatial Planning, *Nature and the Environment, Nature and Health. The Influence of Nature on Social, Psychological and Physical Well-being* (The Hague: Health Council of the Netherlands and RMNO, 2004); and R.S. Ulrich, "View through a Window May Influence Recovery from Surgery," *Science*, Vol. 224, Issue 27 (1984): 420–421.
9. Robert D. Putnam, *Bowling Alone: The Collapse and Revival of American Community* (New York: Simon and Schuster, 2000): 283.
10. Craig Q. Tuttle, Jill C. Enz, and Steven I. Apfelbaum, *Cost Savings in Ecologically Designed Conservation Developments* (Brodhead, Wisconsin: Applied Ecological Services, Inc., 2007).
11. Conservation Research Institute, *Changing Cost Perceptions: An Analysis of Conservation Development*, February 2005, http://www.nipc.org/environment/sustainable/conservationdesign/cost%5Fanalysis/Cost%20Analysis%20Report.pdf.
12. Quoted in Steve Wright, "Conservation Subdivisions; Good for the Land, Good for the Pocketbook," *On Common Ground* (Winter 2006): 15.
13. "NAR Home Buyer and Seller Survey Shows Rise in First-Time Buyers, Long-Term Plans," National Association of Realtors press release, November 8, 2008, http://www.realtor.org/press_room/news_releases/2008/11/home_buyer_and_seller_survey_shows.
14. Statistics in this paragraph are from the National Association of Realtors, "Realtors and Smart Growth," *On Common Ground* (Summer 2001), conducted by Public Opinion Strategies for the National Association of Realtors; Stanly Hamilton and Moura Quayle, "Corridors of Green and Gold: Impact of Riparian Suburban Greenways on Property Values," *Journal of Business Administration and Policy Analysis* (January 1, 1999).
15. David J. O'Neill, *The Smart Growth Tool Kit* (Washington, D.C.: ULI–the Urban Land Institute, 2000).
16. *Forest Friendly Development: Chesapeake Bay Watershed Case Studies* (Camp Hill, Pennsylvania: Alliance for the Chesapeake Bay, 2005).
17. Jeff Lacy, "An Examination of Market Appreciation for Clustered Housing with Permanent Open Space," Center for Rural Massachusetts Monograph Series (Amherst, Massachusetts: August 1990).
18. Steve Lerner and William Poole, *The Economic Benefits of Parks and Open Space: How Land Conservation Helps Communities Grow Smart and Protect the Bottom Line* (Washington, D.C.: Trust for Public Land, 1999): 13.
19. Rayman Mohamed, "The Economics of Conservation Subdivisions," *Urban Affairs Review* (January 2006).
20. Quoted in Jason Amundsen, "Subverting the Subdivision: Conservation Development in the United States," *Ecosystem Marketplace* (June 13, 2006).
21. *Emerging Trends in Real Estate 2008* (Washington, D.C.: ULI–the Urban Land Institute, 2008).
22. Quoted in LandChoices, "Download the Ordinance.org," http://www.downloadtheordinance.org/planners2.htm.
23. Unless otherwise noted, quotations and comments in this book are taken from direct conversations with the person named.
24. Quoted in LandChoices, "Download the Ordinance.org."
25. Ibid.

26. Edward T. McMahon and Michael Pawlukiewicz, *The Practice of Conservation Development: Lessons in Success,* ULI Land Use Policy Forum Report, Chicago, Dec. 3–4, 2002 (Washington, D.C.: ULI–the Urban Land Institute, 2002): 4.
27. Quoted in LandChoices, "Download the Ordinance.org."
28. Ibid.
29. Quoted in *Forest Friendly Development: Chesapeake Bay Watershed Case Studies* (Camp Hill, Pennsylvania: Alliance for the Chesapeake Bay, 2005): 8.
30. Quoted in Steve Wright, "Conservation Subdivisions": 16.
31. Ibid.

Assessing the Feasibility of Conservation Development

CHAPTER 3

Conservation development has evolved dramatically in recent years. Developers have proven that they can plan, design, and build communities that preserve the best of the land in perpetuity—and that they do not have to sacrifice profits in the process. In fact, conservation communities are becoming more marketable than conventional housing options. As people continue to look for green housing options and alternatives to the endless sprawl that characterizes so many of America's suburbs, the market for homes in conservation communities is sure to grow.

The types of conservation communities and the approaches used to create them vary considerably. Conservation development is applicable to many zoning environments, land uses, and landscape types. While most conservation developments are led by experienced developers who see a marketable advantage in preserving the landscape's natural, cultural, and/or aesthetic resources, others have emerged organically from the conservation movement, led by an individual, a family, or a nonprofit organization dedicated to preserving the environment for more traditional reasons.

Regardless of who spearheads the effort, the process should begin with a realistic assessment of whether the site and the surrounding environment are suited for conservation development. In addition to determining whether there is sufficient land available and what resources on that land are to be preserved or restored, this involves assessing the regulatory environment and determining what types of cost issues will affect the project. As with other types of development, these steps should be taken long before site planning begins.

Landscape Suitability

The basic premise behind a landscape suitability analysis is that each aspect of the landscape has intrinsic characteristics that make it more or less suitable for different uses. The landscape is the best scale at which to begin thinking about the conservation of land resources, particularly ecosystems and species. A landscape suitability analysis uses a detailed evaluation of the landscape's different characteristics and conditions to identify the types of activities that are most appropriate for a particular landscape condition, such as woodlands, farmland, floodplains, wetlands, and so forth. This analysis enables a local government or individual developer to determine whether the landscape is appropriate for the desired use, in this case conservation development.

A landscape suitability analysis considers a range of human and natural factors. Human factors include community needs, economics, community organization, demographics, zoning, and the current and historical use of the land under consideration as well as the surrounding area. Features such roads, utilities, and civic, educational, and commercial facilities also should be included in the analysis. Natural factors include wildlife and vegetation, as well as hydrology, topography, geology, soils, and climate. An independent analysis of these factors can determine whether each is favorable for the proposed development as well as for preservation and

A landscape suitability analysis considers a range of human and natural factors, such as roads, utilities, and civic, educational, and commercial facilities, as well as hydrology, topography, geology, soils, climate, wildlife habitat, and vegetation.

Chimney Rock Estates, Flower Mound, Texas

In the midst of the rapid development taking place in the Dallas/Fort Worth metroplex, the town of Flower Mound has proactively sought to protect the things that make it special. According to Flower Mound's open-space plan, the town wanted "to preserve the country atmosphere and natural environment that make Flower Mound a unique and desirable community." The town sought to preserve its character by protecting open space, wildlife habitat, and the environment. To achieve this goal, however, the town recognized that it would need to engage partners.

Flower Mound offers developers a variety of incentives to engage in conservation development. It is the only municipality in north central Texas to specifically encourage the use of conservation easements and partnerships with local land trusts in its land use plan. "In our land development code, Flower Mound provides several incentives to encourage developers to preserve open space with a conservation easement," says Town Manager Van James. "These incentives include expedited development review, permit fee waivers, and even a rebate of agricultural valuation rollback taxes."

Chimney Rock Estates began when the town invited national land conservation experts to speak at a symposium on smart growth and conservation development. Following this symposium, developer Willard Baker and his partners contacted Randall Arendt to

help them apply conservation planning principles on the 104-acre (42-ha) Chimney Rock property, located in Flower Mound's Cross Timbers Conservation Development District.

The resulting site plan consists of 48 one-acre (0.4-ha) lots for single-family homes arrayed along a single-loaded road that provides every house with views of open space. The remaining 56 acres (23 ha) of land, including one ten-acre (4-ha) "single-family conservancy lot," are under a perpetual conservation easement. The entire Chimney Rock Estates development is focused on providing a serene, country-style environment.

In addition, special care was taken in aligning streets and siting houses to protect the large live oak trees found throughout the property. The protected area includes scenic views, water features, native grasses and wildflowers, woodlands, and wildlife habitat. The purpose of the conservation easement is to protect a scenic vista designated by the town of Flower Mound along highway FM 1171, with the forested shoreline of Grapevine Lake visible in the distance. The easement prohibits obstruction of a view corridor that also overlooks the property's grassland, which is dotted with clusters of native oak trees referred to as oak mottes. In addition, the property includes a restored stock tank that serves as a water feature.

Chimney Rock also benefits from linkages to open space beyond the community. A segment along the western boundary adjoins property owned by the U.S. Army Corps of Engineers. A planned hiking and equestrian trail will connect to the town's extensive trail system.

Preserving scenic vistas and natural areas has proven to be financially as well as ecologically rewarding. "There are emotional and market demands for this type of residential development," says Willard Baker. Cliff Baker, a partner in his father's development company, adds, "A homeowner will be able to enjoy the scenic and recreational benefits of the preserved open space without having the maintenance responsibilities or property tax liabilities associated with owning it." Guaranteeing that the land will be protected in perpetuity has translated into higher sale and resale values. The first homes were constructed in 2003. The homes have a median price of $740,000 and range in size from 4,000 to 5,100 square feet (372 to 474 m^2). The Connemara Conservancy, a local land trust, will monitor and enforce the easement area.

For more information, see the project website, www.thepressleygroup.com.

restoration activities. The result may provide an assessment that a parcel of land is of high, moderate, or low suitability for development.

Ultimately, all of the suitability maps may be synthesized into a composite map to provide an overall picture of the landscape as a whole for the different land uses being considered. Data on different land characteristics are overlaid to identify the best locations for housing, conservation, outdoor recreation, agriculture, commercial development, and other land uses. This information often is compiled in a regional landscape conservation and development plan that shows the proposed location of core habitats, secondary habitats, intensive production areas (agriculture and forestry), and development areas.

If a landscape suitability plan has been completed, a developer or other person interested in developing a conservation community can determine whether the proposed plan is viable and, if it is, where development might best be located. In contrast to typical development proposals, a conservation development project might be well suited for a property that has significant conservation value. Many conservation developments site houses on secondary habitat or agricultural areas. They do this to preserve the most important natural habitat and/or prime agricultural areas from devel-

opment. In general, conservation communities are well suited for growing areas on the urban fringe, as part of the transition between urban and rural landscapes. In these areas, homes can be clustered and the open space can buffer developed areas from working rural lands.

Still, it is important to note that conservation development may not be appropriate for all parcels or in all locations. Within a geographic region, the viability of conservation development may vary considerably from one parcel to another. Limited or clustered development may have no impact in situations where conservation resources are located in a small geographical area, but conservation development may not be a viable means for protecting geographically large conservation targets or animals that are sensitive to habitat fragmentation. For example, even a few houses on a 100-acre (40-ha) forested site might displace birds that require large, undisturbed patches of interior forest to breed. As development is considered, it is important to take into account the scale and intensity of the development and its anticipated impact on habitat and species to determine whether limited development will be compatible and, if it is, how it should be designed. If the conservation land is intended to provide habitat for a rare or endangered species, for instance, the design should take into account not just existing wildlife habitat, but also wildlife migration corridors between the site and adjacent parcels.

Once a site has been selected for conservation development, the suitability analysis also can be used to identify discrete development envelopes within the site. The process is similar to a landscape suitability analysis; the result will help to identify the areas best suited for conservation versus those that are most appropriate for development. Then the development team can develop an overall plan to optimize the site design to accommodate these findings.

The Regulatory Environment

Regardless of the appeal of a conservation community, greenfield development of any kind often faces some opposition from the community. It is important to assess the political viability of each project and to lay the groundwork for approval early on in the planning process.

Almost all communities have concerns about growth. In some areas, residents and other stakeholders may want to limit growth; in others they may want to encourage it. In both situations, residents often are most concerned about the pattern or nature of growth. Environmentalists, quality of life advocates, slow growth proponents, and NIMBY residents all influence public attitudes toward community design and development. Growth often is blamed for congested highways, overcrowded schools, the loss of farmland and open space, and other negative impacts on community character and quality of life.

In almost every local jurisdiction, developers encounter county or municipal comprehensive or land use plans, zoning and subdivision requirements, environmental regulations, and other policies that have an impact on their development plans. Many state governments also have policies that affect the land development process and make additional demands on local governments and land use professionals. In some communities, residents see developers as the enemy and seek to put a stop to almost any major development proposal. This often translates into calls for restrictions on growth and higher standards of development. Governments respond by imposing limits on development to slow—or even stop—growth. Some communities seek to restrict growth by putting quotas on the number of building permits that may be issued during a specified timeframe or within a specified area.

Conservation developers often cite the regulatory environment as being one of the biggest obstacles to this concept. Implementing a plan for a conservation community may require changes to local ordinances and/or subdivision regulations. Conventional codes may need to be replaced with new design standards that address the goals of conservation development. "We've found that road waivers are often the biggest regulatory hurdle," says Bob Baldwin, Jr., managing principal of Qroe Preservation Development LLC. "We like private roads that are narrower and occasionally steeper to avoid massive cut and fill operations or running the roads through the open lands and the viewshed." Road frontages, lot sizes, setbacks, roadway dimensions and standards, and other conventional regulations may have to be relaxed to allow clustered development or smaller lot sizes, thereby enabling environmentally sensitive areas, historical sites, and other unique characteristics of the parcel to be preserved.

Zoning and other regulatory approaches often are combined with compensatory approaches, such as purchase or transfer of development rights, installment purchase agreements, or tax credits. Some communities use expedited permit review and approval processes as an incentive for projects that they expect to result in desirable outcomes. It is in the developer's best interest to fully understand all of the zoning and regulatory tools in play.

Assessing the Regulatory Environment

Most land use decisions are made at the local level. Local governments can use many different tools and techniques to encourage the protection and management of conservation lands. Such opportunities exist within zoning and subdivision ordinances, purchase or transfer of development rights, performance standards, property tax breaks, and impact fee structures.

Many federal and state agencies also have regulatory or incentive-based programs that can be used to protect land. These programs cover a wide spectrum, from wetland and forest protection to habitat restoration, to the installation of water quality best management practices, to the acquisition of easements or purchase of land in fee simple.

Land Use Plans

Many communities have responded to pressures to develop land at an increasing rate and density by developing new programs and using new strategies, such as smart growth regulations. In 1997, for instance, the state of Maryland launched a smart growth initiative to redirect the state's financial resources to communities and areas approved for growth while taking a more aggressive and strategic approach to preserving remaining

These drawings by land planner Randall Arendt illustrate how a conventional subdivision can be redesigned as a density-neutral conservation development that increases value by preserving open space, views, and special landscape features.

Numerous studies indicate that Americans are willing to pay extra for parks, natural areas, and other open-space amenities.

open space. The state's GreenPrint program, which emerged from this initiative, works to identify and protect Maryland's most ecologically sensitive lands through a comprehensive, statewide green infrastructure assessment and the expenditure of dedicated funds to preserve key sites. These types of efforts can help support a developer who intends to include land preservation as a design principle.

In addition to any statewide policies or open-space protection plans, developers should be knowledgeable about any and all existing regional, county, and municipal government comprehensive plans. A government's comprehensive plan describes the ways in which it wants the community to develop over a ten- or 20-year period. The plan usually consists of written development goals and policies, supplemented by maps that provide guidelines for local officials as they make decisions about the type, location, and amount of development to be permitted. Depending on state law, comprehensive plans may be either advisory in nature or legally binding on public decisions. They sometimes include detailed plans for specific development elements or for particular areas of importance.

Comprehensive plans and other land use policies can help guide development—and the built infrastructure needed to support it—into areas best suited for it. By directing development away from environmentally sensitive areas, comprehensive plans make it easier to protect sensitive lands through other means. This often helps speed up the approval process for development. A plan specifying that wetlands must be protected or that old-growth forests cannot be infringed upon, for example, can help a developer design a plan that will be approved. If developers can show from the beginning that their development plans fit into the local government's comprehensive plan and land use initiatives, fewer time-consuming delays will occur.

Zoning

In many communities, zoning is the only tool available to direct development and/or protect land. Local zoning laws may limit nonagricultural uses or emphasize planned unit development that preserves open space, floodplains, or other natural areas. Zoning also may be designed to protect a special feature of the land or a historic or cultural resource.

Zoning typically designates permitted uses of land based on mapped zones that separate one set of land uses from another. Zoning regulations may designate specific uses that are

> ### Urban Growth Boundaries
>
> Some states, including Oregon and Washington, as well as some localities in other states, have attempted to curb sprawl with urban growth boundaries. These are legal boundaries that separate urban land from rural land. An urban growth boundary circumscribes an entire urbanized area and is used by local governments as a guide to zoning and other land use decisions. The area inside the boundary is designated for high-density development, while the area outside it typically is designated for low-density rural development. Proposals for urban growth boundaries often are politically unpopular and can create disparity between the land values on opposite sides of the boundary. Depending on its scope and approach, conservation development might be appropriate within or beyond urban growth boundaries.

allowed and/or ban other uses. Zoning laws sometimes also regulate building height and/or size, lot size, lot coverage, or other land use characteristics.

When properly implemented, zoning can be a useful tool for protecting and maintaining a community's green space. Topeka, Kansas's open-space ordinance, for example, requires developers to set aside open space at a standard of five acres (2 ha) per 1,000 residents. The ordinance further requires that the area consist of at least three contiguous acres (1.2 ha) unless it is an addition to an existing park. The goal of this ordinance is to ensure that Topeka has enough open space to meet the needs of its growing population and to maintain its quality of life and neighborhood values. The ordinance also helps protect open space for park systems and trail connections, as well as for storing urban stormwater.

There are many different types of zoning. Planned unit development (PUD) zoning can be used to achieve a plan that satisfies zoning requirements while allowing density transfers or other variations. PUDs typically allow more flexible site design and housing types on relatively large sites. Open-space or cluster zoning requires new construction to be located on only a portion of the parcel, with the remaining open space permanently protected through a conservation easement. Cluster zoning usually allows the same number of units that could be built under conventional zoning. The cluster concept sometimes is restricted to detached, single-family homes, each set on its own downsized lot. Conservation development zoning takes these approaches a step further by encouraging people to consider the conservation value of the land that is set aside.

Some local governments also use agricultural zoning—sometimes called downzoning—as part of an attempt to manage growth by protecting farms from development. Agricultural zones usually are put in place to minimize competition for agricultural land and thus keep its cost down. Agricultural zoning limits the density of development, typically through a large minimum lot size, and restricts nonfarm uses of the land. One problem with agricultural zoning is that it makes it difficult for farming families to retire. Farmland typically is a small farmer's largest asset, and critics say that agricultural zoning unfairly restricts farmers' ability to cash in on this asset. Conservation development addresses this challenge by allowing limited growth and meaningful land conservation on the same parcels.

Some zoning ordinances provide density bonuses for developers who agree to protect desired features of the land. While cluster zoning is typically density neutral—it allows the same number of homes that would be allowed under conventional zoning—some communities have incentive-based ordinances that allow more homesites in exchange for protecting a certain percentage of open space or providing other public benefits not required by law. In communities where cluster zoning would meet with significant opposition, a bonus or incentive can accomplish the same purpose, by allowing a developer to apply for higher density or other variances in exchange for providing open space or other community amenities.

The open-space zoning provision in West Manchester, Pennsylvania, which applies to developments of 15 acres (6 ha) or greater, is just one example. The law requires developers to prepare a sketch plan showing the number of units that could be built under a conventional development pattern. This determines the allowable density that can be used when the project is redesigned in a clustered manner. According to Jan Dell, the assistant township administrator, allowing the same density was important to allay the concerns of landowners who worried that the open-space provision would diminish the value of their property. The zoning provision has had the opposite effect on home values, however: preserving green space and views has increased property values and made the area more attractive to homebuyers.

Other zoning options include performance zoning. Also known as "effects-based zoning," performance zoning uses goal-oriented criteria to establish review parameters for proposed development projects. For example, performance zoning might base development approval on the amount of sewage capacity available, the acceptable volume of surface water runoff, road capacity, or other factors. In addition, some localities have enacted buffer ordinances that prescribe a minimum width of vegetated land to be maintained on either side of a stream or drainageway, or adjacent to a public right-of-way. Larger streams require wider vegetated buffers to moderate peak flows and neutralize excess nutrients and contaminants.

Sometimes a conservation development project—like any innovative project—will require a change to zoning and/or subdivision regulations. Such changes can be hard to come by, particularly in areas where people are worried about the impacts of rural land development. Reworking codes and regulations often is a very time-consuming process that can delay the start of a project.

Purchase/Transfer of Development Rights

Purchase of development rights (PDR) and transfer of development rights (TDR) programs reward landowners for placing deed restrictions on their land that limit its future development. Because these programs are voluntary, they are an attractive option for landowners who want to keep their land and have access to new capital. They also allow local governments to protect land at a relatively low cost, because the landowner maintains the primary management responsibility.

While PDR and TDR programs typically are associated with conservation initiatives, they can help conservation-minded developers by identifying parcels that are appropriate for development. Understanding the PDR and TDR programs in place also may help a developer assess whether a local government will be amenable to a new conservation development approach that helps preserve high-priority lands.

PDR programs can help communities redirect development away from important natural or cultural resources. Madera, California, is among the many towns that have used PDRs as a conservation and growth management tool. Madera is using PDRs to create a four-mile-wide (6-km) "farmland security perimeter" intended to protect eight square miles (2,048 ha) of grape, alfalfa, and dairy farms from development.

TDRs are similar to PDRs. TDRs permit owners in development-restricted areas to sell their development rights to property owners in designated receiving areas. This requires a community to have designated "sending" areas (resource or rural areas) and "receiving" areas (developed or urban areas). A conservation easement is placed on the "sent" property to ensure that its resource values are protected in perpetuity.

Developers of successful conservation developments say one of the keys to success is meeting with community leaders and other key stakeholders early in the process.

TDRs allow landowners in sending areas to realize the market value of their land without developing it. Developers who purchase these rights can increase their profit margins by increasing the density of development in receiving areas.

Just 30 minutes southwest of Atlanta, the Chattahoochee Hill Country Alliance was created to protect rural land from sprawling development. The group is using TDRs to implement a plan that will concentrate homes and businesses in three compact, high-density development zones and several smaller areas, thereby preserving two-thirds of the rural land in the 40,000-acre (16,188-ha) area. Fulton County, which includes most of the hill country, has amended its zoning laws to approve the plan.

Navigating the Political Process

A careful review of existing zoning regulations can help developers determine whether a community is ready for conservation development. Innovative approaches to zoning may suggest that a locality is open to new ideas and willing to be flexible to accommodate a project that is out of the ordinary. Conventional zoning

laws, which mandate a strict separation of uses and uniform lot sizes, on the other hand, may suggest that local officials are resistant to change, or that there is no support for change among the citizenry. The attitudes of local officials and citizens are not always readily apparent, however.

Developers new to an area should try to learn as much as possible about any innovative development projects that already exist or that have been proposed. Developers also should research conservation initiatives and programs. For example, does the area have a local land trust or a PDR program? Have any local citizens advocated for alternatives to conventional subdivision design? Does the comprehensive plan advocate the protection of open space or the preservation of rural character? Has the community ever held a "visioning" exercise?

Leaders of successful conservation development projects say that one of the keys to success is building community support by meeting with key stakeholders and community leaders early in the process. By getting out in front of the required public approval process, developers are able to test the waters and assess support for or potential opposition to their

The town center at Serenbe, Georgia, was made possible, in part, by a new land use plan and TDR program. The new plan concentrates development in three compact zones (that is, rural villages), while preserving two-thirds of the rural land in the 40,000-acre (16,200-ha) area.

One of the most effective ways to encourage change is to offer technical assistance and education for local planning officials. Landowners and developers may need to be proactive in encouraging government leaders to learn about successful conservation development projects elsewhere and the benefits they provide to the community. Buildout maps showing the future of the area, if it is built in accordance with conventional zoning ordinances and land use plans, can be used to illustrate the downsides of the status quo. Alternative land use proposals can help people see that cluster zoning and other innovative approaches to land use can do far more than traditional zoning to protect rural character and other community assets.

project. It is important to allow neighbors to express their concerns—and for members of the development team to demonstrate that they are willing to work with neighbors and other stakeholders to address these concerns. The Bundoran Farm project in Albermarle County, Virginia, for example, was approved without a single dissenting voice, largely because the original landowner met with neighbors to explain the conservation development approach proposed for the land and answer questions before selling the property to a developer.

Determining the Market

A number of trends point to the feasibility and desirability of conservation developments. Numerous studies suggest that people want to live in authentic communities with ample open space—and that they are willing to pay extra for parks, natural areas, and other open-space amenities. For a growing number of Americans, "going green" is a lifestyle choice. Green consumers may look for communities in which they are less dependent on their automobiles or that grow their own food. As the baby boom genera-

Community Amenities Sought by Homebuyers

Feature	Percentage of Respondents
Walking trails/bike paths	36
Parks/natural areas	26
Playgrounds	21
Daycare	14
Soccer fields	9
Golf courses	6
Club houses	6
Security guard at gate	5

Source: National Association of Realtors, National Association of Homebuilders, April 2004.

tion retires, a growing market also may emerge for homes away from urban employment centers, in rural communities where retirees can relax and enjoy the natural world around them. Market analysts should not lose sight of these national trends when assessing the feasibility of a particular conservation development.

It is equally important to consider the regional and local demographic trends that may affect the marketability of a proposed project. Obstacles to preparing a comprehensive analysis of the market for conservation development do exist, however. Many developers are accustomed to relying on insights gleaned from comparable projects. This can be difficult when one is exploring the potential of conservation development in a new market because of the limited number of comparable projects.

It is almost impossible for a development concept that works on one site to be readily transferred to another. While this is true of conventional development, it is doubly true of conservation-based projects, where the natural features of the land dictate land design and development approaches. Developers need to learn from what has been done elsewhere. By traveling to other conservation communities and talking to those who have been successful in building these communities, developers can learn about the approaches used in different types of conservation communities. Then they can incorporate into their own development plan the elements that best fit their vision and their particular land parcel.

In addition, certain practices and features may work well in some parts of the country but not in others. A conservation development that incorporates a working farm may work well in areas where scarce farmland is threatened by development, for instance, but not in areas where the development of farmland is not imminent. Similarly, this concept works best in communities that want to preserve a traditional way of life. New residents in areas undergoing rapid suburbanization may lack the ties to the land that make this type of development attractive. Developers planning a conservation-based project therefore must take adequate time to consider consumer preferences at the outset of the planning phase.

Market Research

A market study conducted to assess the feasibility of a conservation development project may use traditional market research methodology, but conventional market analyses typically fail to accurately assess the market potential of innovative projects. For example, a conventional market analysis never would have foreseen a market for the 585 housing units in West Palm Beach, Florida's City Place development, because no new downtown housing had been built in the city in 40 years. Yet, all the units sold or leased in a short period and commanded higher prices than expected. Developers of innovative projects repeatedly talk of the need

At Daniel Island, South Carolina, the golf course was designed so as to be visually accessible to the entire community. Public roads and trails allow this open space to be enjoyed by everyone—not just those whose homes face the course—thus increasing the value of properties throughout the community.

to "go with their gut," testing out new ideas on would-be homebuyers.

Still, even the gutsiest developers recognize the critical importance of engaging in a sound analysis of the market. Like any project, a conservation development will compete against other new-home communities in the local market. Developers must take due diligence in researching past and present sales to gain a complete understanding of the housing market. Conventional market

Dewees Island, South Carolina

Can profitable development be not only harmonious with the environment but actually enhance it? John L. Knott, Jr., managing director and CEO of Dewees Island, thinks so. Claiming that "the environment and development are natural allies," in the early 1990s he set about developing an island protected by conservation law. Combining local climatic responses with new materials, Dewees Island contains a growing population while protecting its sensitive ecosystems.

When Knott and his colleagues set out to develop the coastal barrier island, located ten minutes by ferry from the mainland and 12 miles (19 km) northeast of Charleston, it was a natural area with just three existing homes. About 65 percent of the 1,206-acre (488-ha) scenic barrier island is set aside for permanent conservation by law. The development project began in 1995 with an inventory of the island's natural resources—wind, vegetative covering, topography, orientation, and views. The developers, Island Preservation Partnership, believed that harmonizing with these natural resources would reduce construction and maintenance costs.

Since the island contained several geological zones, the developers decided to place all houses in the sturdiest zone, which would buffer them from storm surges while preserving the more sensitive areas. Erecting dune fences (like snow

At Dewees Island, environmental guidelines strictly limit construction impact on each building lot, regardless of size, to 7,500 square feet (700 m^2) of disturbed space, thereby minimizing the development's impact on the island's environmental assets.

fences), planting sea grasses to stabilize the dune system, and providing beach access paths deter the erosion common to many beachfront properties. The dispersed homesites also were determined to be less disruptive to the wildlife zones than clustered development. The developers assert that this measure, together with creating additional ponds, triples the island's waterfowl habitat. By limiting development to 150 homesites at two acres (0.8 ha) each, the development effectively conserves 92 percent of the island, far more than the 65 percent required by the state's conservation law. This leaves more vegetation to absorb massive rains, protecting the island against flooding.

The developers saved money by using a variety of environmentally benign practices, enriching an already profitable venture. For example, the decision to cut back on the amount of paving reduced other costs, including those for stormwater drains and detention ponds. Mounting outdoor lighting on existing trees eliminated the need to clear them and install massive lampposts.

To ensure future preservation and resource efficiency, Dewees Island has its own architectural and environmental guidelines. Low-flow plumbing fixtures are required in all buildings, for example, and any watering of vegetation must be drip irrigation via cistern. Kitchen wastes are composted; garbage disposals are prohibited. Individual homes are limited to 5,000 square feet (465 m^2). There is an absolute limit of 150 homes on the island.

Dewees Island's developers attribute its success to an exclusive but wide-ranging marketing campaign. The approach is described as more personal and one-on-one, directed at a buyer with an environmental ethic. Ads are placed in specialized publications, and a substantial response has come through the company website. Additional interest is channeled through local real estate agents and friends of current Dewees Island homeowners. A certain amount of publicity is generated through the enthusiasm of John Knott, who travels extensively to give talks about the project and related sustainable development issues. In 2001, Dewees Island received a ULI Award for Excellence.

For more information, see the project website, www.deweesisland.com.

Source: Adapted from "TechPractices: Island Presentation Partnership, Dewees Island, SC," Toolbase Services, http://www.toolbase.org/Home-Building-Topics/Energy-Efficiency/Island-Presentation-Partnership.

research typically looks at new home sales, housing starts, closings, and/or lot supply over the past decade to determine what is selling well and what has sold in the past. Most developers also seek to obtain information about custom home sales and resales in desirable neighborhoods, which typically are sold at a price premium.

Of particular importance, of course, is whether a similar project has been tried in the community and, if so, with what result. Any information about innovative projects can help a developer determine whether the community is prepared to embrace new approaches to housing, particularly at a higher price point. It can be difficult to compare specific projects, as they may vary considerably in their product offerings and price points. One tool often used is an analysis in which the features of the project are adjusted up or down relative to a subject site. The study assigns values to conventional home and community attributes, such as lot size, shared amenities, and amount of open space.

The market study also should include an analysis of the density of new development projects and compare density to the amount of open space in a subdivision or master-planned community. This can help a developer better understand the potential market for a community with conservation land and the willingness of the market to pay a premium for this asset.

Surveys and focus groups are other typical market research tools. Visual preference surveys, for instance, can help a survey group or community narrow down its preferences and set priorities. These surveys ask people to choose between photographs or other visual images of different options by choosing one of two alternatives at a time. Visual preference surveys can be used to assess community preferences for all aspects of a development, from site layout—for example, cluster development versus a conventional layout—to street width and architectural features. Focus groups can be used to assess the reaction to a specific development proposal or specific design elements.

Demographics and Psychographics

Market research should include both demographic and psychographic information. Demographics refers to selected population characteristics such as age, race, income, education, household size, employment status, homeownership, and so forth. Psychographics, on the other hand, refers to a person's lifestyle, attitudes, beliefs, and values. It is important to distinguish between demographics and psychographics, because analyzing one without understanding the other can lead to misunderstandings about the market. George W. Bush and Bill Clinton, for example, have very similar demographic profiles. Both were born in 1946, and each attended Yale University. Both men held the same job (president of the United States) and they have similar incomes. However, their psychographic profiles—that is, their attitudes, lifestyles, and beliefs—are quite different.

It is important to consider both the demographic and the psychographic characteristics of potential buyers in the market research undertaken for a conservation development. Demographics can be used to determine the size of the retirement-age population or of a particular wealth cohort in a specific market. It is also important to know whether target buyers value nature, ecology, and healthy living, or whether they have more conventional interests such as golf or tennis.

Understanding psychographics has become increasingly important for real estate professionals and may be particularly relevant for conservation-based projects. Some conservation development communities seek to appeal to a wealthy segment of the population, people with ample time on their hands to enjoy the natural amenities that these communities provide—namely, retirees or empty nesters. Such projects obviously will

> **Assessing the Market for Conservation Development**
>
> The following questions can be used to help determine the feasibility of a conservation development project:
> - Will the project cost less than a conventional project? If not, can the additional costs be neutralized?
> - Are tax credits available for donated land?
> - Is the government offering incentives, such as streamlined approvals or review processes, for conservation-based approaches?
> - Will the project appeal to a target market currently not being served?
> - Will the market perceive the project to be of high value?
> - Will buyers understand and accept the covenants and rules that make conservation development a reality?
> - Will the green space and other natural amenities help differentiate the product?
> - Will the open space and other natural amenities help get the product on the prospective homebuyer's shortlist?
> - Are buyers willing to pay more for the project's open space and other natural amenities?
> - Is conservation development the right thing to do?

not succeed unless there are sufficient numbers of the target population looking for housing who also value nature and open space.

Refining the Project Concept and Setting Goals

Translating market analysis information and data about the land into a framework that relates potential risks and rewards to the developer's intended goals and objectives is an ongoing function during the refinement of any development concept. Many developers of conservation development projects feel strongly about preserving the natural features of the land. Others want to maintain a rural heritage and working land. Still others want to make sure that their project meets the needs of a diverse population of various ages and income levels. Success in achieving these goals depends on identifying one's priorities.

Cost Factors

Determining all of the costs involved—including the purchase price of the land parcel, as well as planning, marketing, and construction expenses—and the options for financing until a project is complete are key elements of any development project. Developers of conservation projects also must consider the cost of conducting the various environmental and landscape analyses of the land that are required to determine conservation targets and development opportunities.

Construction costs for conservation developments may differ from those for conventional development. While costs associated with infrastructure and grading typically are lower in conservation-based projects with clustered housing than in conventional projects, other costs may be higher, particularly if the project requires the restoration of wetlands or other degraded lands, reforestation, or other significant changes to the land. Projects that seek to minimize damage to trees and other natural features of the land also may incur higher excavation costs than those in which the parcel is clear-cut for development. For example, to preserve trees and accommodate elevation changes at Millcreek, a 90-acre (36-ha) residential subdivision in Lancaster, Pennsylvania, developers built massive stone retaining walls. While this added $150,000 to the project costs, the development team is quick to point out that the preserved trees added to Millcreek's property values and, subsequently, home sales prices.

Many developers—particularly those who are new to the concept—

Land cost is a key factor in the success or failure of conservation communities. The St. Joe Company, which developed WindMark Beach near Port St. Joe, Florida, had large land holdings because it started out as a timber company.

find it difficult to accurately assess the costs of a conservation development. The first-costs approach used in conventional development pro formas can be misleading, because it does not accurately evaluate the environmental costs and benefits of a conservation-based project. Developers of conservation projects also must consider the ongoing costs involved in maintaining the common open space. Some experts suggest that life-cycle costing is better suited to conservation development projects, particularly if the developer plans to retain ownership for a long time. In this approach, the analysis includes not only the first cost of certain features, but also the cost over their life span. Life-cycle costing aggregates costs and savings and calculates a net present value. Life-cycle analysis might not be useful for small-scale residential developers who intend to move price-sensitive products quickly. Even in these projects, however, it can help demonstrate to investors and buyers the long-term savings of green features and/or the ongoing benefits of using conservation development as a land preservation tool.

Cost considerations should be informed by sound market research. It is important to work with an appraiser who has experience appraising special, one-of-a-kind properties with unique natural, scenic, or historic attributes. Appraisals of homes in conservation developments must go beyond a simple comparison of square footage, acreage, and the other metrics used for conventional projects.

The sales projections of conservation developments may differ from those for more conventional projects. Although homes in conservation communities often reap higher prices than comparable homes in conventional developments, the target market for them may be smaller—at least at first. It also may take longer to educate the market, resulting in less predictable absorption rates.

Financing

Banks and other financial institutions tend to be conservative, which may make it difficult for a development team to obtain financing for an innovative project. Until comparable projects exist, conservative investors often are reluctant to provide financing for an innovative type of development project. When developers Jim Chaffin and Jim Light sought financing for Spring Island—a master-planned conservation community on the Atlantic coast near Beaufort, South Carolina—they met with skepticism from lenders. Although their firm, Chaffin/Light Associates, had worked with NationsBank for several years prior to the Spring Island project, bankers questioned the developers' market assumptions and were wary of Spring Island's unusually strong site protection covenants. The bankers also had reservations about the wisdom of reducing the number of homes on the island to one-tenth of the number allowed under the existing zoning provisions and wondered whether buyers would be willing to pay $300,000 for two-acre (0.8-ha) lots without beach frontage.

Unable to sell the financial establishment on the merits of the project, Chaffin purchased a one-year option on the island and set about figuring out how to make his concept for a conservation community work on Spring Island. Once the master plan was approved, Chaffin brought people to the island to experience its unique character and beauty, selling them on his concept over lobster bakes and walks around the island. He then presold lots to 35 buyers for $300,000 a lot. This "founders program" brought in $10 million, which Chaffin and Light used to finance construction of a bridge to the mainland and other infrastructure. Perhaps just as important, the developers' success proved their claim that this innovative idea was marketable, which convinced NationsBank to provide a $17 million loan for the project. About six months later, a Japanese firm provided an additional $20 million in venture capital as an equity partner.

Since completing Spring Island in 2000, Chaffin and Light have developed many other successful conservation communities and learned a lot in the process. Chaffin points out that financing likely will be an obstacle for any innovative project. He emphasizes the importance of having enough equity and being conservative in pro forma estimates. Having an established relationship with NationsBank—and his firm's track record in always paying off its loans—were critical to its success in getting a loan, he adds. Chaffin also argues that the best way to obtain financing for a conservation development is either to get an option on a property and prove through presales that a market exists or to locate sufficient equity investment in which investors own a percentage of the project above what is financed by debt. Equity financing allows more time for planning as well as greater flexibility, since it keeps more control in the developer's hands.

The fact that homes in conservation communities often are more

Partnerships between landowners and conservation organizations are becoming more common. A partnership between the Foothills Conservancy of North Carolina and Creston Development LLC established a conservation easement to preserve important hardwood forests, mountain views, waterfalls, and a system of hiking trails.

expensive than those in more conventional projects in the same market area presents another challenge. Even if the market is willing to pay a price premium for homes in conservation developments, lenders might be hesitant to finance a project in which home prices are higher than average. In the late 1980s, lenders were unwilling to provide financing for the Prairie Crossing project near Chicago, largely because they were skeptical that the homes would sell at the prices predicted by the pro forma—prices that were roughly $100,000 higher than those for a typical new home in the county. The developers succeeded in financing the project by using publicly held stock, rather than real estate, as collateral—a strategy that Frank Martin, Prairie Crossing's development manager, said also offered more flexibility. As it turned out, Prairie Crossing's homes did sell at a significant premium over the local market and the competition. In fact, the premium has increased steadily over the life of the project.

As at Spring Island and Prairie Crossing, developers may find it difficult to obtain the requisite financing for a conservation development project at the outset. In some cases, a phased acquisition approach might be required. Commonweal Conservancy secured an agreement with the owner of a 12,800-acre (5,180-ha) ranch in the Galisteo Basin near Santa Fe, New Mexico, to purchase the land in five phases over an eight-year period. Driven by its deep conservation values and public benefit mission, Commonweal Conservancy will protect the vast majority of the land—roughly 12,000 acres (4,856 ha)—by constructing a "stewardship community," the Galisteo Basin Preserve, that will contain 965 homesites and 150,000 square feet (13,935 m^2) of commercial and civic facilities. To help finance its initial land acquisition phases and the village predevelopment planning and entitlement expenses, the conservancy presold more than 30 conservation homestead parcels to conservation buyers and investors. The homesteads were sited so as to protect the larger property's escarpment viewsheds, open spaces, wildlife, and cultural resource values. Sales from the homestead offering gave Commonweal's lenders and investors confidence that the project would be well received by the Santa Fe market.

It is important to note that it is not *always* harder to find funding for conservation development projects. Many financiers and investors are sold on the idea that attention to environmental and community issues can make a project more marketable. As with any innovative idea, it will become easier to find financing as more and more conservation projects prove to be profitable investments.

Partnerships

In their attempts to protect environmentally sensitive lands while also generating capital to foster their mission, a number of large environmental organizations have begun pursuing partnerships with developers. The Conservation Fund, the Nature Conservancy, and the Trust for Public Land all have played major roles in creatively engineering agreements that allow limited development while also preserving open space and sensitive habitat. The Nature Conservancy, for instance, often uses a joint venture strategy or acts as a broker, purchasing critical land and holding it until another organization can come up with the capital needed to purchase it. Through its Conservation Buyer Program, the Nature Conservancy identifies properties with high ecological value and then matches them with conservation-minded buyers who agree to protect the land by entering into a permanent conservation easement that limits development and specifies compatible uses of the property.

The Nature Conservancy played an instrumental role in the development of Homestead Preserve, a conservation development project underway in rural Bath County, Virginia. The group analyzed the site that developers Charles Adams and Don Killoren had identified for their project to determine which land was most suitable for conservation. On the day Adams and Killoren acquired the 12,000-acre (4,856-ha) site, they sold 9,250 acres (3,744 ha) to the Nature Conservancy for the below-market price of $6 million. The developers now use this large nature preserve owned by the Nature Conservancy as a key marketing asset for their development project.

The Trust for Public Land also works to protect ecologically important lands from haphazard development. Among its projects is the Santa Lucia Preserve, a 20,000-acre (8,094-ha) conservation development in Monterey County, California, where 90 percent of the land has been donated to the nonprofit Santa Lucia Conservancy.

In addition to these large national organizations, countless local and regional land trusts have programs to identify and preserve land with high conservation value. Increasing numbers of community land trusts also focus on housing and community development needs. In rural areas, community land trusts have been established to ensure access to land and housing for low-income people and to preserve family farms.

Land trusts often have resources and expertise that can be tapped to further conservation development goals. For instance, a land trust may have mapping capabilities or ecological expertise. Local land trusts usually know most of the local landowners and can advise developers about which owners might be candidates for a conservation development. Some large land trusts also have real estate development divisions experienced in all phases of development. All of these resources and expertise can help developers to assess the feasibility of a particular conservation project.

Conservation Development Planning, Design, and Marketing

CHAPTER 4

A property's location, form, and quality play a fundamental role in determining its economic value and land use potential for any type of real estate development project. Successful developers of conventional projects take their cues from the site and its setting. But conservation design takes that evaluative process a step further. It requires developers to think seriously about the land—about the opportunities the land affords and the constraints it may present—at the outset of the planning and design process. Success, for a conservation development, depends on viewing the land holistically and carefully undertaking planning, design, and construction efforts to ensure that its most fragile and treasured resources are protected.

In many ways, the site evaluation process for conservation development mirrors the process employed for successful golf course communities. No golf course developer would lay out the golf course as an afterthought. On the contrary, the streets, lot lines, and houses are laid out *after* the golf course has been designed. So, too, with conservation development: the land dictates where the open space is located, which in turn is used to determine the layout of the project's built features.

This approach is not new. In his 1969 book, *Design with Nature*,[1] landscape architect Ian McHarg advocates a careful analysis of the development site to foster a greater sense of harmony between natural systems and the built environment. Raised in an industrialized suburb of Glasgow, Scotland, McHarg incorporated some of the principles used to design garden estates in England—particularly the inclusion of the natural world in the developed landscape—into the American housing developments he designed. McHarg also pioneered the use of map overlays as a way to display spatial data. Each of his maps included a different field of data, such as soil types, wildlife habitat, riparian areas, the built environment, and so forth. McHarg's system became the basis for the geographic information systems (GIS) that have become widely used planning tools today.

Site Selection

Many developers avoid sites that have natural lands of high ecological value because of concerns about the difficulty of permitting, entitlement procedures, environmental impact studies, and community opposition. Conservation development provides an opportunity to overcome these obstacles. In fact, conservation development often requires seeking out lands with high conservation value and

Creation of a conservation community often begins when a landowner or developer falls in love with a site's natural beauty, then is determined to find a way to protect it. Shown: Centerville, Florida.

then leveraging the development of one part of the land in order to protect the rest. This strategy is proving to be one of the most effective means of conserving natural resources throughout the country, from suburban subdivisions in the eastern United States to the farms of the Midwest and the large ranches and open spaces of the West.

As with any other type of development, the site selection process requires finding a location with sufficient acreage for the proposed project. The optimum size of a development site depends on the type of development to be undertaken and the size of the market. Large-scale master-planned communities typically tie up the land with long-term options, with individual projects constructed in phases. Many conservation communities are much smaller, ranging in size from a half-dozen to a few hundred lots. Determining the right site for a project also may require finding the appropriate topography, as well as desirable natural and cultural features that can be preserved and used as amenities as well as marketable features.

In a typical conventional development scenario, a developer identifies a property that may be available for purchase and analyzes the feasibility of a project's success, based on the price of the land, the permitted uses and densities, the specific attributes of the tract and the ease or difficulty of development. The planning process begins with a vision of what the developer hopes to achieve and aims to accommodate of the site's unique context and characteristics, as well as the demands of the market. While some conservation development projects have followed a conventional approach to acquisition and development, the site selection process often is more complex and time consuming when the developer's vision includes the preservation, protection, and restoration of land with high ecological, cultural, scenic and/or historic value.

Some conservation developments begin when a landowner, developer, or would-be developer falls in love with a site's natural beauty and vows to find a way to protect it. This is essentially what occurred when Jim Chaffin happened upon Spring Island, a 3,000-acre (1,214-ha) island off the coast of South Carolina. Similarly, Ted Harrison came across the Thornton Ranch property in southwestern Santa Fe County, New Mexico, when he was working for the Trust for Public Land, a national land conservation organization. John Jenkins loved the 850-acre (344-ha) Wyoming ranch that he had purchased from his siblings after his mother died. It was too expensive to conserve the entire ranch, but he did not want to see it cut up into homesites either, so he, like Chaffin and Harrison, decided to develop a small part of the land in order to preserve the rest. Each of these men—seasoned developer, conservationist, and landowner—asked himself the same question: How can I use development to help protect this land?

Not all conservation projects begin with a parcel to be preserved. Some developers look for sites with particular characteristics that are best suited for the project they envision. Qroe Preservation Development LLC, for instance, has developed several conservation communities throughout New England and the Mid-Atlantic region. Bob Baldwin, Jr., managing principal of Qroe, says the principles and processes his firm has developed require a landscape with rolling hills so that the homesites can be tucked out of view from the public right-of-way.

In many cases, the site selection process for conservation development requires finding an owner who wants to sell his or her property but is concerned about what will happen to the land after the sale. Finding these landowners may require significant detective work, since many owners of highly scenic, wildlife-rich, culturally significant properties do not present their properties to the market in conventional ways, such as through a brokerage firm. Many significant properties find their way to market only after the owner has died. In many cases, the executor of the estate offers the property for sale through a back-door offering.

Location and Context

As with any type of development, the conservation developer needs to consider a range of factors to decide whether the land parcel being considered for a project will attract the desired market and meet the desired goals. These factors include location, accessibility, surrounding land uses, potential for active and passive recreation, and proximity to employment, shopping, and schools. Site selection goes beyond an examination of the parcel under consideration for development; it must include surrounding parcels as well. Existing, proposed, and historical patterns of land use on and adjacent to a potential conservation development site should be studied carefully to determine whether any potential conflicts exist. If the uses on adjoining lands are compatible, they can enhance the desirability

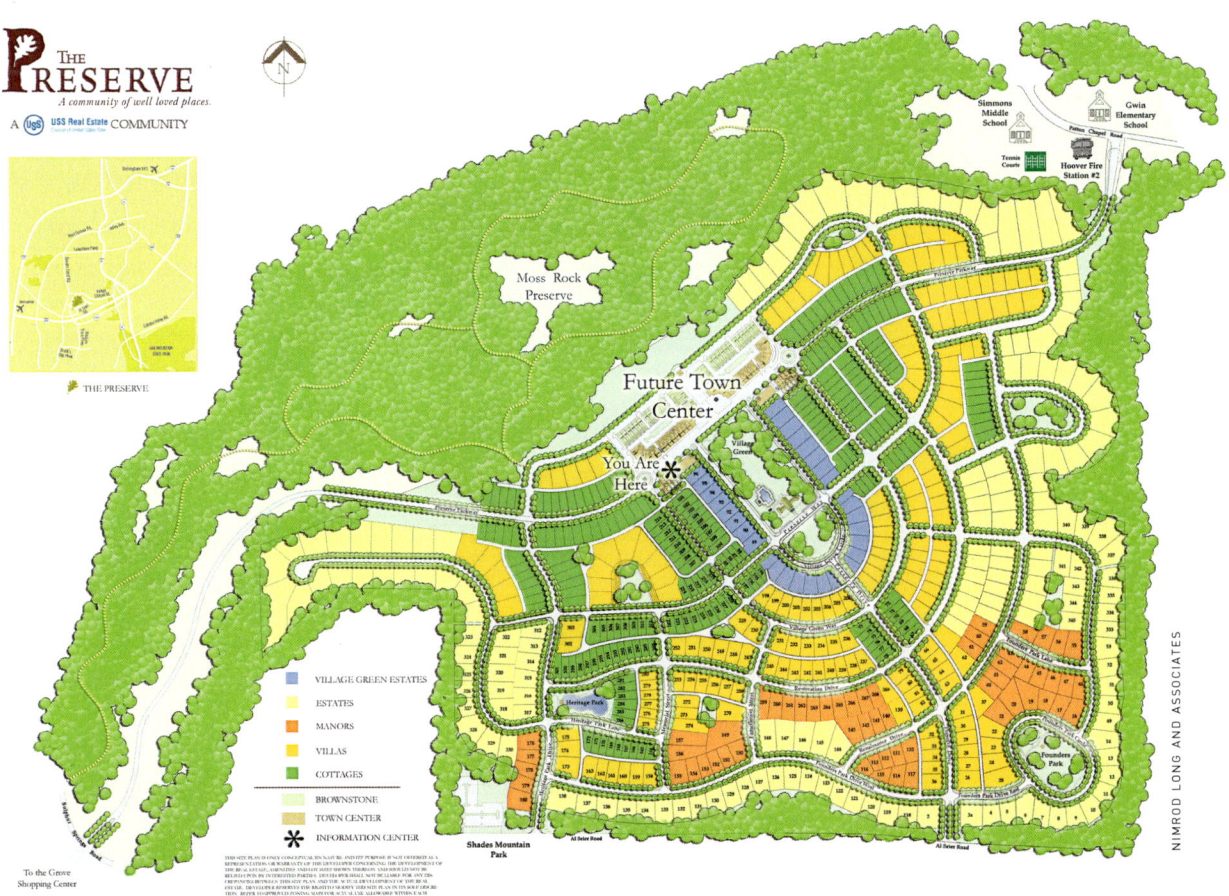

and marketability of a development project. Many successful conservation developments leverage the value of protected lands nearby, linking to adjacent national or state forests, to other public lands, or to privately owned land under conservation easement on adjoining parcels. Others may take advantage of smaller parks or other natural attractions. In 1991, U.S. Steel sold a portion of a 700-acre (283-ha) parcel it owned to the city of Hoover, Alabama, for use as a public nature preserve. Since then, the Moss Creek Preserve has become a well-regarded hiking and rock-climbing venue. Concurrently, a neotraditional development built by U.S. Steel Realty on an adjacent parcel has substantially benefited from having a large

U.S. Steel Realty sold a portion of a 700-acre (285-ha) property to the city of Hoover, Alabama, for use as a nature preserve, then built on the adjacent parcel a neotraditional community that substantially benefited from having the large natural area next door.

As is the case with any kind of development, for a conservation community the developer must carefully consider the site's location, accessibility, surrounding land uses, and proximity to jobs, shopping, and schools, as well as other factors.

natural area nearby. Another example is Homestead Preserve in Hot Springs, Virginia, where developer Celebration Associates has capitalized on the reputation and amenities of the Homestead Resort, a nationally renowned 200-year-old resort adjacent to the development.

The most desirable sites for new residential development usually are those near established or emerging employment centers, but this may be less important for conservation-based projects geared toward retirees, those intended as second-home communities or weekend retreats, or those that will include a commercial center or other employment opportunities. This consideration also might not apply in rural areas, where some conservation development projects seek to provide much-needed housing for people already living in the area.

If the target market includes families, the location and quality of public schools can play a critical role in site considerations. Some conservation development projects have included schools in their plans. Victoria Ranney, vice president of Prairie Holding Corporation, the developer of Prairie Crossing, says that the charter school there has played an important part in the conservation development's success. Likewise, the Hidden Springs development near Boise, Idaho, has benefited from the public school located on the property. The Galisteo Basin Preserve is planning a 400-student environmental education–based charter high school in its village center, in part to reinforce the continuous learning and environmental stewardship values of the larger project.

Parcels best suited for conservation development include those with significant amounts of natural lands of high ecological, agricultural, or cultural value. Preserved land in a conservation development also may provide important connective value, creating "missing links" within major riparian corridors, ridgelines, or wildlife migration corridors. A primary attribute of a conservation development community is a green infrastructure network of hubs and links. Hubs anchor green infrastructure networks, providing origins and destinations for wildlife, outdoor recreation, and ecological processes. Links include natural features at every scale, from a major river or ridgeline to a backyard swale, a community trail system, or a grove of trees. The interconnectedness of these elements is critical to the health of the green infrastructure system. A well-designed conservation development project can protect elements of green infrastructure, extending the benefits well beyond the conserved parcel.

One of the main attractions of a conservation development project is the common open space it provides. It stands to reason that people in the desired market will react favorably to a site where ample green space exists beyond the new development. Sites near national or state parks, forests, nature preserves, public beaches, and other recreational areas may be easier to market than those where the only preserved land lies within the conservation subdivision.

Conservation design principles require a project's protected open space to be connected. In master-planned communities, for instance, the design may include tot lots at the block level with trails that connect to neighborhood parks, which in turn connect to village, community, or regional parks. These green-space systems should be connected by walkways and/or multipurpose paths, as well as by street linkages.

Conservation development should be viewed in context. While many large rural parcels—particularly those in the West—offer opportunities for preserving open space, developers must take into consideration not only the ecological values of the land, but also the wide range of environmental goals that may affect land use decisions. The closer housing is to jobs and commercial centers, for instance, the smaller a new development's impact will be on the environment. Sustainable development goals may include locating new residential development near a major employment center, ensuring easy access to existing transportation networks, and/or providing schools, shopping, and employment opportunities on site.

Conservation developers also should take into account their project's impact on its surroundings, including viewsheds, land use patterns, and the ecosystem. Ecosystems are interconnected; what happens on one parcel of land sometimes has major downstream effects on other properties. The focus on nature requires developers to assess how changes to the landscape will affect water flow, wildlife movement, habitat health, and other ecological functions on—and beyond—adjacent parcels. A project adjacent to a wildlife corridor, for example, may provide the means to preserve that corridor in perpetuity. Incorporating working landscapes and resource-based industries such as agriculture and forestry into a conservation development might help a community support and protect a rural economy that is threatened by population growth. In addition, working landscapes may provide habitat for fish and wildlife, protect water resources (as aquifer recharge areas), and/or connect other natural features of the landscape.

The Regulatory Environment
Another consideration in site selection is the regulatory environment. As was discussed in Chapter 3, current zoning laws, subdivision codes and environmental regulations may make a site more or less conducive for conservation development. In some areas, obtaining building permits is a highly political process. Localities wary of growth may have placed limits on the number of permits they will allow in any given timeframe or area. On the other hand, a conservation subdivision might be well received by communities that have a strong land ethic and/or where the land is tied to the community's cultural history and identity. Residents of agrarian communities, for instance, may embrace a conservation development project that will help them preserve working farmland and maintain their traditional way of life. Bundoran Farm, for example continues to host the annual Albemarle County Fair. This would have been impossible if the site had been developed in a conventional manner.

A focus on nature requires developers to assess how changes to the landscape will affect water flow, wildlife movement, habitat health, and other ecological factors.

Developers who misjudge the local political environment or propose a project that does not fit the community's long-term plans can face difficulties even if the project technically meets the letter of the law. Even in areas where land conservation is part of the local comprehensive plan or the region's goals, the development team may have to educate officials about how the proposed project fits into these plans or goals. While these obstacles might not rule out conservation development on a potential site, the development team should be prepared to work closely with local officials and the community to ensure that desired goals can be achieved.

Site selection also requires careful attention to infrastructure needs, including water and sewer services, road access, and other issues. In Santa Fe, New Mexico, concerns about local water supplies almost derailed the Village at the Galisteo Basin Preserve. The development team had to demonstrate that the village's well field would not impair nearby aquifers and that a "business as usual" development pattern—large-lot subdivisions throughout the 12,800-acre (5,180-ha) ranch—would put a far greater strain on water resources than the proposed compact, conservation-oriented project. The team also had to educate residents about the village's anticipated impact on roadways, stormwater management systems, and other public infrastructure.

A final regulatory consideration is the local government's willingness and capacity to support a conservation development project. Do local government officials and staff have knowledge of and/or experience with unconventional types of development? Many municipalities and counties have adopted conservation initiatives, incentives, or programs that may tie into a new project. How likely are they to make changes to zoning and/or subdivision regulations to accommodate conservation development? What is the process for making such changes?

The availability of utilities and public services also must be carefully evaluated. In many localities, permission to develop a site depends on the availability of water and sewer lines. Developers not used to working in rural areas may be surprised by the inability of a small rural government to respond quickly to utility requests. If the proposed conservation development project is to be completed in phases, the future availability of utilities is another important consideration.

Charles Adams and Don Killoren experienced many unforeseen challenges working with the local government in Bath County, Virginia, a rural community that has no traffic lights and a population of roughly 4,800 people. The county lacked clear rules for how the county's volunteer firefighters would sign off on plans, for instance, and had always offered water and sewer services on a first-come, first-served basis, leaving the developers no assurance that they would have enough water or sewers for Homestead Preserve. Success depended on educating local officials and the community on a wide range of issues.

Even sophisticated local governments that are ready to embrace unconventional types of projects may need to go through a learning curve. Conservation development projects may require substantial interaction with and the involvement of various government bodies from the outset. If the public sector is recruited early in the development process and is fully committed to the concept, it is less likely to throw up time-consuming roadblocks as the process unfolds.

The Market

Market demand and demographics play a role in the types of conservation development best suited for

---

Land Acquisition and the Right of First Refusal

Some land acquisition programs include rights of first refusal. This guarantees an organization the opportunity to purchase important property, but does not obligate it to do so. By granting a right of first refusal, a property owner agrees to notify an organization that the property has been offered for sale and invites the organization to match an offer. This allows an organization to identify prospective buyers and negotiate an agreement to protect the property with the potential new owner. This right may be donated to an organization or sold for a nominal fee. Similarly, an option to purchase involves paying the landowner for the guarantee that he or she will reserve a property at an agreed-upon price for a set period of time, typically six months to one year.

The Guilford Land Trust in Guilford, Connecticut, used the right of first refusal concept as part of its strategy for protecting a major wetland. When the land trust approached the owner of a 54-acre (22-ha) parcel about selling, he was not interested, but the land trust persuaded him to sign a letter of intent to sell the property to the organization if and when he decided to dispose of it. Although a letter of intent is not enforceable, the land trust was confident that continued contact with the owner would remind him of this agreement. Eight years later, the owner decided to donate the wetland portion of the property to the land trust and sell the high ground to a developer. The land trust then was able to persuade the owner to donate the entire property rather than sell any of it.

Source: Mark A. Benedict and Edward T. McMahon, *Green Infrastructure: Linking Landscapes and Communities* (Washington, D.C.: Island Press, 2006): 155.

a region and/or particular parcel. Consumers in rapidly growing areas, for instance, may exhibit a higher interest in—and willingness to pay for—open space and natural amenities. Areas with higher-income demographics may be better able to support the lot premiums in high-end conservation development projects. In addition, conservation development projects may be particularly attractive to "green" consumers, who believe that protecting the environment is an important lifestyle choice.

Developers also must consider the market for higher-density projects. In many conservation-oriented projects, individual lots are smaller. New research by *Builder* magazine indicates that today's buyers are less likely to think of housing primarily as an investment and more likely to think about how the home will fit their lifestyle. What is more, for many buyers the character of the neighborhood is more important than the size of the house or lot. This should bode well for conservation developments, although some families might be less interested in such communities than would singles, empty nesters, or retirees who are willing to trade in yard work for other leisure activities.

Developers must take into account whether the prospective project has sufficient appeal to attract the desired market. Even where woodlands, meadows, or natural open space is viewed as a project's primary amenity, research shows that success depends on providing many of the other amenities that homebuyers in the market expect. Market research undertaken by the developers of the Santa Lucia Preserve in Monterey County, California—where 18,000 acres (7,285 ha) were set aside as a nature preserve—indicated that a golf course and other high-end amenities would be good investments and might be critical to the project's financial success. Focus groups showed that more than one-third of prospective buyers would not purchase at Santa Lucia unless it had a golf course. (Ironically, the same focus groups revealed that 10 percent of potential buyers would not purchase a site at Santa Lucia if it *did* have a golf course.) Similarly, Jim Chaffin's market research suggested that his Spring Island community might not succeed unless it offered a golf course in addition to the nature preserve and other amenities. "The golf course was our insurance," he says.

Still, conservation communities may be able to substitute natural amenities for some of the built features potential buyers have come to expect. The initial proposal for Spring Island included two golf courses; Chaffin offered only one, figuring that keeping 1,200 acres (486 ha) in its natural state would be more attractive than a second course. At Prairie Crossing, in Grayslake, Illinois, market research suggested a community pool was an important amenity. The development team found that the lake resulting from the community's natural water retention system would serve the same purpose in the summer and had the added benefit of providing an ice-skating rink in the winter. Other conservation communities include playgrounds, bicycle paths, equestrian centers, ponds stocked with fish, and other amenities designed to attract the target market.

Creating a Vision and Goals

Conservation development is more than just conservation *and* development. The approach requires a clear understanding of what is to be conserved and why. The principles of conservation development and the values on which the development is based need to be communicated to everyone involved in the project. Having a clearly defined vision, values, and goals can help keep the project on track.

In most places, local government officials and community leaders are far more involved in real estate projects that involve land protection than in conventional development projects. Where conservation development is unfamiliar territory, the development team needs to work closely with local officials and the community in an educational capacity. This may involve coming to consensus on a community vision and demonstrating how the conservation development project fits into this vision.

Vision and Values

Many communities, particularly those where growth is imminent, have used visioning exercises to clarify what residents want the community to look like 10, 20, or even 50 years in the future. The community visioning process may include mapping exercises in which stakeholders work together to discuss priorities for conservation and development. Consumer preference surveys may be used to help people understand the tradeoffs they are making. At best, a conservation developer could play a pivotal role in this process; at the very least, the developer must know about any visioning that has taken place before proposing a conservation development project.

One of the challenges of conservation development is that success depends on striking the right balance between the need to preserve valued land and the need to accommodate growth. Leaders of conservation development projects often find themselves caught between competing forces: some communities may want to keep

Myers Farm

Qroe Preservation Development LLC has been practicing an innovative method of land development it calls "farm preservation development" for more than 25 years. Qroe's approach on every project is to preserve at least 75 percent of the land in perpetuity. At Myers Farm, a 50-acre (20-ha) preservation development in Greenfield, Massachusetts, Qroe expanded this concept to include a mix of uses, including multifamily residences and educational facilities.

At Myers Farm, almost 40 acres (16 ha) of the site is preserved for agriculture. Qroe sold about 37 acres (15 ha) of the property to the Franklin Land Trust, which in turn sold an agricultural preservation restriction to the state of Massachusetts and then sold the protected land to a working dairy operation, Bree-Z-Knoll Farm. To complement the historic farmhouse, Qroe built a 39-unit condominium development and a charter school on the remaining six acres (2 ha). All of the buildings feature farmhouse-style architecture, providing residents with the charm and character of country living within walking distance of Greenfield Community College, to which Qroe donates a percentage of each home sale.

Myers Farm, a 50-acre (20-ha) conservation development in Greenfield, Massachusetts, includes multifamily residences, a working dairy farm, and a charter school on the same site.

things just the way they are even when it is clear that additional housing is needed. Moreover, conservation development projects are as different as the sites on which they occur. As a result, people have very different ideas about what conservation development means and what it should look like. Having a clear vision for its project can help the development team define and communicate expectations to local officials, conservationists, potential buyers, and interested citizens.

A vision statement and a set of development principles also should be used to help guide the planning process. These statements help keep a project on track by providing members of the development team with a goal toward which to work. An effective vision statement is short and actionable. The vision statement should be shared with everyone working on the project, including planning and design consultants, architects, lawyers, lenders, appraisers, landscape architects, builders, and marketing specialists, as well as with potential homebuyers. Some developers post a written vision statement where it can serve as a visual reminder to everyone of what the team hopes to accomplish.

A vision statement also can serve as inspiration for residents of the community. The vision statement for Serenbe, a 900-acre (364-ha), mixed-use conservation community in Fulton County, Georgia, describes the project as "a community where people authentically live, work, learn, and play in celebration of life's beauty, a place where connections between people, nature, and the arts are nourished." The statement goes on to remind people of the importance of committing to the vision: "This vision can only be achieved for future generations if we commit ourselves now to building a community that is a living part of its natural surroundings, not something built at nature's expense."

It is important to emphasize that a vision should not be developed in a vacuum. Effective visioning requires a group effort; only a vision statement that has been developed and agreed upon by the entire project team will have the buy-in needed to drive an effective planning and design process. Developers should set aside plenty of time to discuss and debate various options. They should test ideas with a broad range of people—staff, consultants, marketing and real estate professionals, local residents—and use their input to tweak the vision statement until it truly describes what they want to accomplish.

Values statements also may be incorporated into a project. Some developers have created a statement of values for all their projects; others choose to define a set of values for each specific project. These statements help articulate the principles on which a

Guiding Principles for Prairie Crossing

Ten important principles established by the community's founders have guided Prairie Crossing since its inception. Together, these guiding principles provide the framework for a way of life that respects the environment and enables residents to experience a strong connection between community and the land.

1. Environmental Protection and Enhancement. Prairie Crossing's land was purchased to safeguard its open spaces. Three hundred and fifty of its acres (142 ha) are legally protected from development. Prairie Crossing is part of the Liberty Prairie Reserve, more than 5,000 acres (2,024 ha) of publicly and privately held land that includes nature and forest preserves, farms, and trails. At Prairie Crossing itself, greenways have been constructed and houses placed to protect the environment, native vegetation, and wildlife of the Midwest.

2. A Healthy Lifestyle. More than ten miles (16 km) of trails, a stable, and a large lake with a swimming beach and a dock provide opportunities for healthy outdoor exercise. The farm supplies fresh organic vegetables, flowers, and fruits to the community. Individual garden plots are available at a small cost. Lake Forest Hospital has built a new facility at Prairie Crossing.

3. A Sense of Place. Prairie Crossing is squarely rooted in its central Lake County location. Landscape and architecture are inspired by the prairies, marshes, and farms of the area. Streets are named after prairie plants and early settlers who frequented the site. A palette of rich house colors derives from the warm tones of the native landscape. The community buildings—a historic barn, a schoolhouse, and a farmhouse—remind residents that others have lived on this land before, and that others, to whom residents have responsibility, will live here after them.

4. A Sense of Community. In the belief that community and conservation can go hand in hand, the trails and gardens of Prairie Crossing are designed to be places where people can meet to enjoy and care for the land. The homeowners association has taken responsibility for the community amenities, design review, and other aspects of community life at Prairie Crossing. Volunteer stewardship activities are organized by the Liberty Prairie Conservancy, which conducts environmental programs throughout the Liberty Prairie Reserve. From the outset, Prairie Crossing has sought to work collaboratively with its neighbors, seeking to achieve unusual synergies with homeowners associations, public officials, and local businesses.

5. Economic and Racial Diversity. Prairie Crossing welcomes residents of all races. Its founders believe that a mix of incomes and races is essential to the future of society. They have attempted to keep costs and prices down so that some homes will be within the range of families needing affordable housing in Lake County.

6. Convenient and Efficient Transportation. Prairie Crossing is approximately an hour from Chicago by train or car. There is commuter rail service to Chicago and O'Hare Airport from two stations adjoining the site. Prairie Crossing lies within a triangle of three major roads: Routes 45, 137, and 120. Trails lead to the train station, the College of Lake County, the University Center of Lake County, the Liberty Prairie Reserve, Grayslake High School, and local stores and restaurants.

7. Energy Conservation. Homes at Prairie Crossing have been constructed with techniques that reduce energy consumption by approximately 50 percent in comparison to new homes in the area. Communitywide recycling and composting programs are in effect. Prairie Crossing is designed to encourage walking and biking as alternatives to short trips by automobile. A wind turbine provides electric power to the farm. The new buildings of the Prairie Crossing Charter School are designed to Leadership in Energy and Environmental Design (LEED) standards.

8. Lifelong Learning and Education. The Prairie Crossing Charter School offers elementary education based on an environmental curriculum to children from two local school districts. Informal learning takes place at the Liberty Prairie Conservancy, the Prairie Crossing Institute, the farm, and the Byron Colby Barn community center. The College of Lake County and the University Center of Lake County are both located nearby.

9. Aesthetic Design and High-Quality Construction. Professionals who are highly accomplished in their fields have been responsible for land planning and architecture. High standards of design and execution throughout Prairie Crossing are a priority. Prairie Crossing has received national attention for its beauty and design that combines town and landscape planning.

10. Economic Viability. Prairie Crossing is being developed by families who wish to see the conservation community concept replicated elsewhere. They have made every effort to ensure that the project is economically feasible and have carefully budgeted for long-term success.

Source: Adapted from the Prairie Crossing website, http://www.prairiecrossing.com/pc/site/guiding-principles.html.

Conservation Values, Galisteo Basin Preserve, New Mexico

Through its carefully articulated design standards and development practices, the Galisteo Basin Preserve will exemplify the principles and practice of "restorative development"—a development practice that leverages the financial and technical capabilities of the real estate industry to reclaim and renew the ecological and hydrological health of sensitive landscapes such as the Galisteo Basin.

In combination with its community development goals, the Preserve will facilitate the permanent conservation and restoration of more than 13,000 acres (5,261 ha) of open space, the majority of which will be publicly accessible. Drawing on the professional experience and values of its staff and partners, the Preserve is designed to nurture deep and sustaining connections between land and people.

While it acknowledges architecture's capacity for artistry and transformation, the Preserve is a place where the *land* takes precedence. In this spirit, the design goals and development values of its four villages—the Village, Southern Crescent, New Moon Overlook, and the West Basin—are informed by the following principles:

- Love for the Galisteo Basin's precious scenic resources;
- Deference to the Galisteo Basin's rich cultural history;
- Stewardship of the region's animal, plant, soil, and water resources; and
- Respect for the complexity and creativity of social organizations.

Source: Adapted from the Galisteo Basin Preserve website, http://www.galisteobasin-preserve.com/gbpvision_conservation.php.

---

project is based and remind others on the project team what is important to the developer.

The developers of Hidden Springs, a 1,786-acre (723-ha) master-planned community built around a 130-acre (53-ha) working farm near Boise, Idaho, based their vision on eight principles, which guided the project's long-term planning and construction process. The principles emphasized the importance of the following values:

1. Maintaining rural character and farming traditions;
2. Creating a small-town atmosphere;
3. Respecting the natural environment;
4. Encouraging traditional home design;
5. Prioritizing quality of life and healthy living;
6. Maintaining high educational standards;
7. Pursuing demographic diversity; and
8. Establishing value and values.

Values statements may extend beyond the planning, design, and construction phases to include the values of the conservation community itself. Serenbe's values statement, for instance, identifies four values that focus on community quality-of-life issues: nature, passion, art, and community.

Articulating a shared set of values and goals allows residents—and prospective residents—to understand what it means to live in the conservation community, creating an authentic sense of place and reinforcing a sense of belonging. The values statement thus becomes a marketing tool, defining the community for consumers and attracting people who share these values. Having neighbors with shared values, in turn, builds a sense of community, which increases the project's desirability and home values.

Goals

Goals describe how the project team will achieve the desired vision. They define the team's basic agenda in specific terms. Effective goals are realistic and easy to understand. Some goals might take several months to accomplish; others may be relatively quick and easy to achieve.

A conservation development project may include conservation goals—such as "to provide sufficient habitat for gopher tortoises" or "to protect the viewshed from Route 88"—as well as

Conservation design principles require a project's protected open space to be connected. For instance, tot lots at the block level might connect by trail to neighborhood parks that, in turn, link to the larger green-space system.

more conventional development goals—such as "to create a diversity of housing options for a wide range of buyers."

Each goal in the project team's work plan usually has several objectives. While a goal identifies what the team would like to attain, objectives quantify the goal and, where possible, establish deadlines for completion.

Identifying Natural, Cultural, and Historic Features

Land often is thought of as simply the ground upon which uses are developed. But each site combines physical, ecological, and cultural characteristics that together impart a unique identity. Creating an inventory of natural, cultural, and historic features of the land and analyzing their relative importance are integral steps of conservation development planning and design. Careful analysis not only helps protect valued resources, it also provides the developer with an opportunity to establish a sense of place that builds value and fits the unique characteristics of the land. The process enables developers to

take advantage of special places on the property—for example, by situating homesites in the seams of the land, next to forested areas, or on knolls that offer views of ponds, meadows, and fields.

A site, properly selected and analyzed, yields a wealth of information about appropriate land use and spatial organization. It also provides insights into the essence and roots of the community. An understanding of both the site and the region's history, incorporated into the guiding principles of a project, is an integral part of "place making"—what gives a community its soul. Place making fosters a community identity that inspires pride among the people who live there. It requires attention to the form and look of the property, the buildings, and the surrounding landscape so that the design can anchor the project in its local and regional setting. Recreational and cultural resources, scenic views, vernacular architecture, and the like are often important attributes of rural communities. Protecting these features benefits the community and can help developers gain community support for their projects.

Criteria for Evaluation of Natural Sites

The following criteria should be considered when determining conservation values:
- **Size.** Importance to nature conservation increases with size; bigger is better.
- **Diversity.** Variety—that is, a range of species and habitats—is better.
- **Naturalness.** Less modification is better.
- **Representation.** Natural communities that are not well represented in existing protected areas should be priorities.
- **Rarity.** Sites that contain rare elements are better.
- **Fragility.** Fragile communities are more valuable and deserving of protection.
- **Typicalness.** Maintaining good examples of common species is important.
- **Recorded History.** Selecting well-researched and documented sites with a known presence of species and habitats is better than making suppositions.
- **Landscape Position.** The contiguity a site maintains with surrounding landscape elements—connectivity of habitat—is an important consideration, particularly for green infrastructure.
- **Potential Value.** Sites with diminished value but with restoration or enhancement potential are important.
- **Intrinsic Appeal.** The protection of certain conspicuous species may be appealing to society and may result in a greater overall appreciation for nature conservation—for example, preserving large specimen trees, like live oaks.

Sources: Adapted from Derek A. Ratcliffe, *A Nature Conservation Review*, Cambridge, UK: Cambridge University Press, 1977; and Tony Kendle and Stephen Forbes, *Urban Nature Conservation*, London: Spon, 1997.

Developers of conservation developments need to fully understand the quality and characteristics of the land's ecological framework. Ecological characteristics should inform the many decisions that are made about the size, use, configuration, and other characteristics of the built environment. Careful consideration of ecological characteristics and features helps ensure compatible uses and minimize activities that would degrade key ecological attributes. Building a recreational trail through sensitive habitat for rare plant or animal species, for example, would undermine the fundamental goals of a conservation development.

In particular, developers should carefully consider which attributes are most desirable—and the relative importance of each feature—since these decisions will have a profound impact on what the resulting open-space network will look like and the benefits it will provide. The list of desired attributes should reflect the vision for the developed community, as well as its conservation goals and objectives. The features identified at the outset will guide the community design, from identifying the attributes for which data will be collected to identifying and linking the network's elements, to evaluating and prioritizing the different parts of the network for restoration or conservation action.

Outdoor recreational opportunities are often important attributes for a conservation development. Factors such as access to passive and active recreational areas, trails and trailheads, public waters, and hunting and fishing opportunities can affect the project's design. Also of potential importance are the identification and protection of scenic vistas, overlooks, important wildlife corridors, scenic rivers and waterways, and other viewsheds. Viewsheds can be identified by walking the land and examining U.S. Geological Survey topographic maps, or calculated with the use of geographic information systems (GIS) from digital elevation data.

Cultural and historic resources also should be identified. These may include old buildings, stone walls, cemeteries or burial plots, archeological resources, and other historic sites. Some conservation communities in rural settings have preserved old farmhouses, stables, milking sheds, and the like, sometimes renovating them for use as community gathering places. The original farmhouses at Tryon Farm, a conservation community near Chicago, and at Serenbe, a mixed-use conservation community near Atlanta, have been renovated to serve as inns. Historic buildings also could be preserved as the owner's residence or as a sales center.

The Design Process

In *Design with Nature*, Ian McHarg suggests that a site analysis can be completed in a logical sequence: climate, geology, physiology, hydrology, soil, vegetation, wildlife, and land use.[2] He argues that each category of data follows from the preceding one. McHarg believes that the analysis of these elements reveals a particular site's degree of tolerance for development. Computer-driven and GIS data have simplified the use of this technique to evaluate a site's suitability for development. Overlaying the data in a matrix enables site designers to evaluate the overall suitability of a site for both development and conservation, as well as the suitability of particular areas within a site.

The site's physical configuration and dimensions influence the layout of homesites and supporting uses. The layout for any conservation development project must, as much as possible, respect the topography of the site and protect natural drainage patterns. Natural vegetation often is used as part of the stormwater—and sometimes the wastewater—management system. Streams, wetlands, and riparian areas may be priorities for protection and preservation in some conservation developments; other projects may seek to protect orchards, forests, farmlands, meadows, ridgelines, and other key resources. Most conservation developments use conservation easements to protect larger contiguous lands on one part of the parcel and cluster the built development on the remaining land. The built environment is planned in ways that create and preserve views, enhance community interaction or protect privacy. This may be particularly important in projects with clustered development.

Conservation development design involves the same steps as more conventional projects, but the order of the steps differs. In general, planners begin by identifying contiguous open space and then design the lots around that open space. In his seminal book *Growing Greener*, Randall Arendt outlines the following

Examples of Resources That Might Be Inventoried and Protected

Myriad resources on a particular site may merit protection due to their ecological, cultural, or historical value. Consider the following:
- Rare flora and old trees;
- Habitat for rare or endangered species;
- Ponds, meadows, marshes, and other wetlands;
- Riparian corridors, drainage ways and irrigation canals;
- Ridgelines;
- Views, including those from homes, public roads, and pathways;
- Old Native American trails, including footpaths used by tribes in the East and horse trails in the West;
- Civil War sites, including battlefields, earthen fortifications, and buildings used as temporary shelter for troops; and
- Old farmhouses, barns, stables, and other outbuildings, as well as chimneys and other remnants of demolished structures.

The first step in the conservation development design process is identifying conservation areas—that is, figuring out where *not* to develop.

four-step process for the design of a conservation subdivision: 1) identify conservation areas; 2) locate house sites; 3) align streets and trails; and 4) draw in the lot lines. Arendt compares the process to designing a golf course community, with protected open space replacing the fairways and putting greens.[3]

Step 1: Identify Conservation Areas

The first step consists of inventorying resources worth preserving. In addition to features that typically are designed around because they are daunting obstacles to development—such as wetlands, floodplains, and steep slopes—the list of features to be preserved will include resources that encompass special value-adding natural or cultural features that are extremely vulnerable because they are *not* located in unbuildable areas. Arendt divides the resulting lands into two categories: primary conservation areas, which comprise steep slopes, wetlands, floodplains, and unsuitable soils; and secondary conservation areas, which contain unique vegetation, wildlife, and cultural or agricultural resources that should be protected from clearing and grading.

Data derived from a GIS are extremely helpful in identifying the lands to be preserved, but experienced developers also emphasize the importance of walking the land. Ideally, the developer should do this several times, with individuals who have expertise in various disciplines. If particular species are to be protected, for instance, consultation with experts on the local ecology may be critical in determining which parts of the property should be preserved to provide the ideal habitat for those species.

In addition to ecologists, hydrologists, biologists, and other scientific experts, conservation developers sometimes walk the land with local residents. The input of landowners and other area residents can be particularly important when one is examining meadows and woodlands during seasons when special species are not in bloom or in residence. Arendt suggests walking the site with local officials and residents at the beginning of a community design process—as a sort of "charrette-on-foot."

Hydrology is often an important consideration in conservation developments. Understanding how water flows over the land will help a developer minimize the impact of stormwater on natural systems. The first step often involves mapping the natural hydrologic systems on the site and thoroughly assessing the water conditions of the site and its surroundings. This assessment should consider how much rainfall the site

After conservation areas are identified, the next steps are to locate homesites, align streets and trails, and, last, draw in the lot lines.

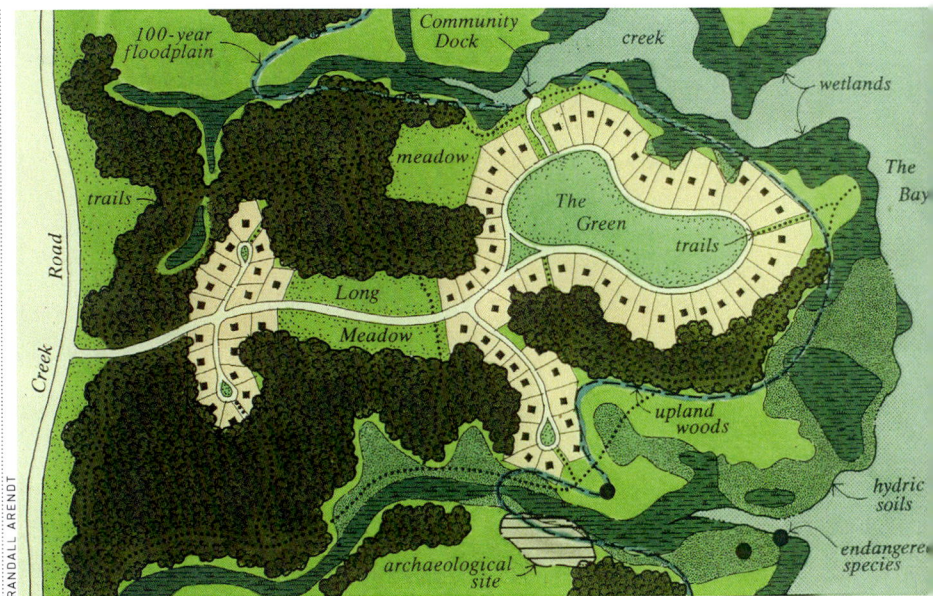

receives, where rainfall is absorbed into groundwater and aquifers, the natural drainage systems that are in place, and where and how water leaves the site. Conservation development involves taking advantage of these natural systems wherever possible, lessening the need for expensive built solutions and reducing the risk of flooding.

Aerial photographs also can help conservation developers select features to be preserved. Arendt describes a project in Florida, for instance, at which an aerial photo enabled him to spot the greatest concentrations of live oaks in a cow pasture and to design around them easily, creating a 13-acre (5-ha) park in the center of an 80-acre (32-ha) rural neighborhood. On a property in New England, where about half the land was vegetated with mountain laurel, a color aerial photo taken just after snowfall helped Arendt identify laurel stands and design the development around the most significant of them.[4]

Step 2: Locate Homesites

Once conservation areas have been identified, or "greenlined," the remaining land can be considered for the built environment. This next step involves locating the approximate sites of individual houses and other buildings. Arendt suggests placing homes at a "respectful proximity" to the conservation areas. Objectives for arranging development areas include screening them from public roads, providing them with access to and views of open space, and conserving as much undisturbed buffer between them as possible. Placing homes so they front or back up to protected open space enhances their value and marketability; situating them so they abut woodlands or water also may provide much-desired privacy. Conservation development design involves using the site's natural elements and protected features as focal points and design features. For instance, a cluster of homes may front on a hay meadow or other common open space that provides a passive and/or active recreation area for residents.

Step 3: Align Streets and Trails

The third step consists of tracing a logical alignment for streets to access the homes and other buildings, as well as for formal and informal trails to connect various parts of a neighborhood and to provide residents access to the common open space. Streets and trails are planned in a manner that minimizes stream crossings and disturbance to the site's woodlands, trees, and other natural features.

Following existing roads, trails, and footpaths wherever possible further minimizes disruption to the site and often reinforces the natural organization and flow of the landscape. For example, the site plan of Balsam Mountain Preserve, a conservation development project in western North Carolina, reuses old logging roads to minimize site disturbance. Tryon Farm in Indiana and Bundoran Farm in Virginia both built their road systems on old farm roads and cattle paths that led from one pasture to another, thereby preserving the beauty of the sites and reducing costs for grading and road construction.

Step 4: Draw In the Lot Lines

The final step is simply a matter of adding the lot lines. The developer needs to make sure that the lots are within the range of sizes identified during the goal-setting process. On large-lot sites, developers may further define the building envelope for each lot. Carefully situating the home, driveway, and other features of the built environment can help protect specific features, such as large trees or rock formations, and minimize interference with water flow and other ecological processes. Homes can also be sited to enhance benefits gained from natural elements, including solar heating and tree protection from winds in the winter, shade from trees and breezes in the summer, and natural sunlight all year round. Enhancing the development's sustainable features also will help attract environmentally conscious consumers.

Finally, the site design process should consider the property's relationship with the surrounding area. Planners should examine the map of potential conservation lands in the locality's comprehensive plan and explore how linkages can be created among resource areas on adjoining properties. "As each parcel is developed," explains Arendt, "the conservation lands network will emerge as a protected [green infrastructure] system, encompassing whatever features the community has identified in its plans and ordinances as being important to design around and save."[5]

Designing with Nature in Mind

Successful conservation design does not end with a map of the community. Many developers incorporate innovative sustainable development principles and practices to further "green" their conservation communities. Natural water management solutions are one example. Instead of constructing wide streets with curbs and gutters that carry water into a system of pipes and stormwater retention basins, conservation communities often use other, more environmentally friendly approaches in a stormwater treatment train that mirrors the way nature handles runoff and overflow. Bioswales—ecologically designed, shallow, wide channels—empty into natural retention basins. The development team for Jackson Meadow, a 64-house conservation subdivision near Marine on St. Croix, Minnesota, for instance, used roadside swales and an inverse crown on roadways to carry stormwater to open-space areas. Wetland grasses anchored in the inverse crowns further assist the absorption process.

Natural stormwater management systems have a number of advantages over conventional curb-and-gutter and underground pipe drainage systems. Natural systems typically cost far less to build. They also remove pollutants—through vegetative filtration, soil absorption, and plant assimilation—and decrease the rate of water flow. In piped systems, the concentrated flow of water at discharge points often causes downstream erosion and increases the risk of flooding. The features of a natural system also can provide a focal point for conservation communities. The lakes and ponds at Prairie Crossing and the meadows at Jackson Meadow serve as scenic, recreational, and ecological amenities.

Constructed wetlands are another aesthetically pleasing, relatively inexpensive way to provide ecological benefits to a conservation community

Designing in harmony with nature requires careful consideration of both building materials and landscaping materials, particularly the use of native plants and trees. Shown: Civano, in Tucson, Arizona.

of any size. Larger communities may have an obvious wetlands area, but wetlands also can be constructed at a very small scale and interspersed within a community. At Inspiration, a 245-acre (99-ha) conservation community in Bayport, Minnesota, a natural stormwater management system was designed as part of the land use plan. Fifteen on-site reservoirs direct surface runoff into biofiltration wetlands and rain gardens that store and infiltrate runoff into the groundwater. In addition, residents are encouraged to incorporate natural landscaping on their properties, including rain gardens, to help improve the water quality of rainwater runoff.

A constructed wetlands system usually consists of a shallow basin lined with an impermeable membrane and gravel or sand in which plants are rooted. As the water moves through the vegetation, it slows down, trapping sediments and pollutants. The millions of microorganisms in the wetlands help remove pollutants from the water. This naturally treated water then is recharged into underlying groundwater or the natural drainage system. Because this process occurs underground, most residents are unaware that the wetlands are anything other than an attractive design feature.

Designing with nature in mind also includes considering the needs of native plant and animal species. Sustainable landscaping often involves relying primarily on native species that will not upset the ecosystem, In areas where water is in short supply, native plants also tend to need less water. Natural and constructed landscapes can help reduce water and energy use. In addition to using native plants that need less water, designers may preserve or plant groves of trees to provide shade or protection from wind, reducing energy use. Green roofs, covered with grasses or plant material, are another popular option.

Conservation developers may also need to consider the needs of animals in their design. In addition to identifying and planning around wildlife corridors where possible, designing with nature may include constructing walls and fences to protect animals from humans and vice versa. Fencing along roadways may be needed to protect animals from cars, for instance, but this fencing may at the same time cut off animals from the corridors they use to travel between blocks of habitat. Designing with nature in mind requires considering the needs of species and looking for ways to meet these needs.

Another way conservation developers design with nature in mind involves considering the materials they use for buildings, walkways, walls, fences, and so forth. Some conservation developers look for opportunities to reuse the materials from one part of a site in another. Pieces of concrete from demolition sites can be used to form erosion-control systems on stream banks, for instance, or can be ground up further for walkways or retaining walls.

A final example is designing in a way that encourages sustainable building practices. The development team can create a master plan in which it is easier to design buildings

Inspiration, Bayport, Minnesota

Inspiration is a 245-acre (99-ha) conservation development subdivision near the St. Croix River. The Inspiration land plan was designed by ecologists, based on a scientific analysis of the land's ecological functions and topography. One hundred and seventy acres (69 ha)—70 percent of the site—is reserved as open space. Of this open space, 140 acres (57 ha) are being restored to native ecological communities, including tall-grass prairies, wetlands, savannas, woodlands, and forests. A large wildlife corridor on the eastern half of Inspiration connects the adjacent ecological areas in Minnesota's St. Croix Savanna State Natural Area to the south and the city of Bayport's Barkers Alps Park to the north. The wildlife corridor and other restored prairies provide important habitat for declining populations of grassland bird species and associated wildlife.

A natural stormwater management system ensures that Inspiration does its part to protect the water quality of the St. Croix River. Fifteen on-site reservoirs direct surface runoff into biofiltration wetlands and rain gardens that store and infiltrate runoff into groundwater resources. Residents are encouraged to incorporate natural landscaping—including rain gardens—on their homesites to help improve the quality of rainwater runoff. A new nature education center, designed as a community gathering place, will help make people aware of—and part of—the ecosystem in which they live.

For more information, see the project website, www.inspiration-bayport.com.

that optimize sustainable performance features. A design that orients the roofs southward, for instance, enables builders or homeowners to incorporate solar panels for heating water and/or providing solar energy.

The Project Team

The process of identifying the land to be preserved—and how it is to be preserved—works best when it is guided by an enlightened developer working in partnership with a landscape architect or land planner. The creative skills of a landscape architect or planner are essential to balance the technical training of an engineer whose expertise lies principally in designing streets and drains. "Designing with nature in mind is not easy," explains Jon Kohler, the managing partner of the Centerville Conservation Community in Tallahassee, Florida. "Laying out a conservation

Natural stormwater management systems have many advantages over conventional curb-and-gutter systems, including lower cost, improved function, and aesthetic appeal.

The Stakeholders of a Conservation Development Project

Conservation development often engages a broader coalition than conventional development. Success sometimes depends on forging a strong relationship among developers, neighbors, conservationists, and local officials. Consider the roles played by each of the following groups of people:
- Local elected officials;
- The local planning commission and/or other groups involved in land use planning;
- Councils of government or other regional organizations;
- Land trusts and other conservation-minded nonprofit groups;
- Farmland protection or historic preservation organizations;
- Real estate agents;
- Real estate developers;
- Homebuilders, lenders, and appraisers;
- Landowners;
- Neighbors and residents of the community and nearby area; and
- Other interested citizens who live, work, or play in the community.

community is a form of art, and many engineers are not artists."

In addition to the landscapers, architects, and engineers needed for conventional developments, the team for a conservation development project often includes professionals with expertise in ecology and environmental science. These experts can help analyze the land and its resources to ensure that the portion of the land with the highest conservation value is protected. In addition, natural resource managers and other land use experts can help identify restoration needs and management strategies for the preserved open space.

Marketing

The techniques for marketing a conservation community often differ from those used for more conventional developments. In some cases, conventional methods may be appropriate. The conservation aspects of a conservation community should be quantified and marketed as amenities, much like a golf course, a swimming pool, or proximity to a major commercial center. In most cases, however, the project's conservation aspects—its open space, nature center, hiking trails, and so forth—offer developers a clear market differentiator.

The housing in many conservation developments can command a higher price point than that in more conventional developments. But potential homebuyers may have to be sold on the concept that open-space amenities are worth the added cost. Doing so can be particularly difficult at projects in which the open space has been deeded to the local government or another public entity, so that citizens of the greater community may appear to benefit as much as those who purchase homes in the conservation development. Even in these cases, however, the conservation development's proximity to public green space can be marketed to potential homebuyers as an amenity. After all, the land adjacent to New York City's Central Park is some of the highest-priced real estate in the United States. This property benefits from a price premium even though the park is a public amenity. Pathways or trails that provide residents with easy access to public lands can make the open-space amenity even more valuable to them.

Some people, particularly those who can afford to live anywhere, enter the homebuying process with the mindset that they want *more* for their money—more property and more traditional amenities, such as swimming pools, golf courses, or tennis courts. A marketing campaign for a conservation community—particularly one with houses on relatively small lots and fewer traditional

The marketing of a conservation community may differ from that of a conventional development. For example, Bundoran Farm, as shown by this advertisement, emphasizes its shared amenities: homebuyers get 2,300 acres (930 ha) of open space, not just a homesite.

amenities—will need to address this thought process. Most conservation communities emphasize commonly owned features, giving homebuyers the sense that they are buying the entire parcel, not just the land within their lot lines. In fact, at Tryon Farm, a conservation community in Indiana, residents do not own any of the land on which their home sits; instead, they buy a share of the entire community. Such conservation-based projects may be particularly attractive to green consumers who strive to reduce their carbon footprints. Conservation developers can make their projects more appealing to this market by using green building techniques or by incorporating other design features, such as natural retention ponds, communal orchards, or organic gardens that appeal to an environmentally savvy market.

The housing market tends to be slow to change. Homebuyers may be predisposed toward homes in conventional developments that feel familiar to them. It may take considerable time and effort to highlight the

Balsam Mountain Preserve

Developers Jim Chaffin and James Light extended their "community within a park" vision with the development of Balsam Mountain Preserve, a conservation community set deep in the forests of North Carolina's Blue Ridge Mountains. This low-density development offers just 354 homesites within the 4,400-acre (1,781-ha) community, at a density of one home for every 12 acres (5 ha). The site plan situates homes for maximum privacy and provides spectacular views of the sweeping Blue Ridge Mountains. Care was taken to disturb the land as little as possible. In addition to careful site selection for homesites, the plan uses old logging roads to reach the new homes.

A majority of the land has been set aside for protection and preservation, with 3,000 acres (1,214 ha) under conservation easement. The development includes more than 50 miles (81 km) of trails for hiking or riding, as well as 38 miles (61 km) of streams for fishing or wildlife viewing. An on-site nature center, operated by the Balsam Mountain Trust, is committed to documenting and preserving the area's natural and cultural history. Staff naturalists educate residents and other members of the community and lead guided trips and fishing expeditions. Other amenities, including an Arnold Palmer signature golf course, equestrian facilities, and a sports camp facility with tennis, a swimming pool, and a fitness pavilion, are designed to appeal to the intended market.

JOHN WARNER/BALSAM MOUNTAIN PRESERVE

goals and benefits of a conservation-based community. Marketing a conservation development often involves telling the story of how the development came to be and what it intends to be in the future.

The developer of Marabou Ranch, a conservation development project on which just 55 homes will be situated on 1,717 acres (695 ha) west of Steamboat Springs, Colorado, has used some nontraditional techniques to reach affluent consumers. The developer has engaged nationally recognized entertainers to perform at marketing picnics and other events. The celebrities are selected carefully to ensure that their personalities and values are aligned with the properties at Marabou. "It's about telling a story," says Michael Richards, a member of the Marabou marketing team. "There's a whole strategy involved in establishing one of these projects, as we create awareness. It establishes value. It establishes credibility. It establishes substance."[6]

Measuring Success

The final step in the planning process is to determine how results will be measured. Many of the metrics used in conventional development are applicable to conservation-based projects, but it is important to consider how a conservation development project might differ. Experienced conservation developers caution that buildout and absorption sometimes take longer, for instance, because of the time needed for the market to grow accustomed to the new concept.

From a conservation perspective, one common indicator of success is the amount of land that is protected. But it is critical to keep in mind that successful conservation development also involves the *quality* of the conserved land. The age of plants, the number of species present, and the degree of connectedness among conserved areas are just a few of the measures of success that conservationists may use for a preservation or restoration project. A project's success also can be measured according to how well it accomplishes the following conservation goals:

- **Avoidance of edge effect.** Does the design protect interior forest or other natural areas? Is the open space contiguous? Does it have relatively regular or even borders?
- **Buffers.** Are buffers provided between conservation lands and developed areas? Do working lands have an adequate buffer from residential areas? For example, are vegetative buffers used to prevent conflict between active agriculture and homeowners?
- **Connectivity.** Does the design connect protected open space within the site to surrounding parks, woodlands, or natural areas?
- **Protection of riparian buffers.** Are riparian areas protected? Is there adequate space between waterways and the built environment?
- **Minimization of impervious surfaces.** Does the design seek to minimize the length and/or width of paved roads, sidewalks, and other impervious surfaces? Are pavers, gravel roads, and walking trails used where appropriate?
- **Protection of site-specific conservation values.** Are features incorporated into the design to protect the natural habitat of the animals that live on the site?
- **Land management.** Are sufficient measures in place to ensure that the conserved land will be appropriately managed in the near and distant future?

Perhaps the most useful measure of success is what the people who live in a conservation community have to say about it. Many people say that the quality of life in a conservation community is far higher than in conventional developments. Quality-of-life factors, such as the enjoyment one gets from a beautiful sunset or the health benefits of a daily walk through nature, are difficult to evaluate, but they often result in higher absorption rates, higher lot premiums, and better resale values.

Notes

1. Ian L. McHarg, *Design with Nature* (New York: Doubleday, 1969).
2. Ibid.: 105.
3. Randall Arendt, *Growing Greener: Putting Conservation into Local Plans and Ordinances* (Washington, D.C.: Island Press, 1999).
4. For these and other examples, see Randall Arendt, "Slideshow of 25 Cultural, Natural, and Restoration Features of Conservation Subdivision Design," http://www.greenerprospects.com/Terrain.org_RandallArendt_Cultivating_Issue18.pdf.
5. Randall Arendt, "Enhancing Subdivision Value through Conservation Design," *On Common Ground* (Summer 2001).
6. Tom Ross, "The New Look of Luxury: LPS Developments Changing Landscape," *Steamboat Today* (July 22, 2006), http://www.steamboatpilot.com/news/2006/jul/22/the_new_look/.

Management and Stewardship of Open Lands

CHAPTER 5

Although conservation development is a relatively new phenomenon, it is building on a long legacy of land conservation in America. Developers are incorporating many of the tools that have been used by conservationists, and conservationists are getting into the act of developing land for human use. A growing number of developers and conservationists are engaging in partnerships, recognizing that they can accomplish more by working together than when they are at odds with one another. These partnerships are building on lessons from early attempts to create neighborhoods that were designed to accommodate the natural features of the landscape and protect open space. Among the most important lessons learned is the need to plan for the long-term maintenance and stewardship needs of protected open space during the early phases of development.

Land conservation is a long-term strategy. Simply setting aside open space does not ensure its health or integrity. One cannot just buy land and forget about it; conservation land needs ongoing upkeep and maintenance. As conservation communities are designed, mechanisms must be put in place to ensure that commonly owned open space is protected permanently, maintained appropriately, and restored where necessary.

Experienced developers recognize that conservation development may require different approaches than conventional projects. For instance, natural landscapes have different monitoring and maintenance needs than do manmade systems. The maintenance requirements of a natural stormwater management system of swales and constructed wetlands, for example, differ vastly from those of conventional curb-and-gutter systems. Natural systems sometimes require less maintenance than manmade systems, but they still must be carefully monitored.

Strategies to protect desired community features must be developed at the beginning of the planning process, and education must continue unabated throughout the life of the project. Successful land stewardship programs depend on education and community involvement. Prairie Crossing has been successful not only because it was profitable, but also because it preserved 400 acres (162 ha) within the site, restored a previously degraded landscape, actively involved citizens in land stewardship, and led to a regional conservation initiative that has gone a long way toward preserving almost 2,000 acres (809 ha) of adjacent land.

Landownership

Who will own the conserved land is an important question. Different conservation development projects have taken vastly different approaches to ownership of

Simply setting aside open space does not ensure its health or integrity. Conservation lands need ongoing upkeep, management, and stewardship.

conserved land. In some conservation communities, individual homeowners own portions of the open space, while in many others it is owned collectively by the homeowners association (HOA). Still other conservation communities have donated or sold the conserved land to a local, state, or national land trust; to a local government; or even to a private business. How the open land is owned may affect the ownership structure for the developed portion of the property. All of the land at Bundoran Farm is owned by individual property owners. An easement dictates how the land can be used. At Tryon Farm, residents do not own the land on which their house is located; instead, they own a one-150th interest in the entire settlement. In most conservation developments, an HOA or land conservancy assumes ownership of the common areas that have been preserved for recreation or conservation.

Several ownership options exist for projects with agricultural open space. In some cases, the original

Rocking K Ranch, Pima County, Arizona

In eastern Pima County, Arizona, on the outskirts of rapidly growing Tucson, developers originally wanted to build a 21,000-unit resort and residential community on the 6,000-acre (2,428-ha) Rocking K Ranch adjacent to Saguaro National Park. The project was scaled back to 6,500 clustered units after opposition from the U.S. National Park Service and local environmentalists threatened to derail the development. As part of the agreement that allowed development to proceed, the most biologically important land was set aside as open space. Two thousand acres (809 ha) were sold to the National Park Service. The rest of the property is managed with input from Rincon Institute, a community stewardship organization supported by homeowners and businesses in the new development and visitors to the resort. The institute conducts long-term environmental research, helps protect neighboring natural areas, and conducts environmental education programs.

"Initially the developers were skeptical, but they now see that a legitimate commitment to conservation is good for marketing," says Luther Propst, director of the Sonoran Institute, which helped negotiate the arrangement. The developer agrees. "People will pay a premium for an environmentally well-thought-out community," says Chris Monson, president of the Rocking K Development Corporation. "Sometimes less is more, so we increased densities, clustered housing, and preserved open space. We think this makes our development look attractive. It also makes the units easier to sell."

For more information, see the project website, www.rinconinstitute.com.

Source: Adapted from Steve Lerner and William Poole, *The Economic Benefits of Parks and Open Space: How Land Conservation Helps Communities Grow Smart and Protect the Bottom Line* (Washington, D.C.: Trust for Public Land, 1999): 8.

Academy Village at Rocking K Ranch near Tucson, Arizona, blends seamlessly with its neighbor, Saguaro National Park.

landowner retains ownership of the farmland and continues to use it as it has been used in the past—for crops, grazing, and so forth. For example, a farmer can sell part of his or her acreage to a conservation developer and keep the remainder of the land to continue farming. In many conservation developments, homeowners own all the land, and restrictions are placed on portions of the contiguous land to ensure that it will be preserved as open space. Alternatively, a farmer can sell the development rights to a portion of the property while retaining ownership of it. This enables a farmer who is planning to retire to benefit from the development potential of the land's value while also enabling him or her to sell the fields to a younger farmer at an affordable price that reflects the land's market value as an agricultural operation. This, in turn, strengthens and protects the local farming economy.

The portion of the land to be preserved for agricultural use also can be sold "in fee" to the HOA, which then can lease it to local farmers or small commercial entities. Some conservation developments also include community gardens that residents maintain, either collectively or individually. Homeowners can use these garden plots to grow vegetables for their own use or engage in small-scale agricultural production.

One important consideration in determining the appropriate ownership structure is how the conservation land is to be used. Protected open space may be designed to be used for recreation, horseback riding, agriculture, timber management, or other activities. In other cases—where a fragile ecosystem serves the needs of rare species, for instance—the land may need to be protected from human interference. Conserved land also may provide water retention and/or other ecological services.

Much of the discussion in this book involves land that the developer owns or has an option to purchase, but it is important to keep in mind that many conservation development projects begin when a conservation organization has identified a parcel to be preserved. Conservation development may be a viable option if a local land trust or national nonprofit group such as the Conservation Fund, the Nature Conservancy, or the Trust for Public Land does not have sufficient funds to purchase the entire parcel. In such cases, the nonprofit group usually will partner with a developer by selling off the developable and/or less ecologically valuable portion of the land. The developer could purchase the land through a fee simple acquisition, or the sale could entail the acquisition of undivided interests, which involves the purchase of a percentage ownership in a property and allows the nonprofit group to maintain a legal interest in its management.

Land Protection Tools

Conservationists have developed many tools to ensure that protected land will remain forever free of development, and developers have adapted these tools to protect the open-space systems in conservation communities.

Conservation Easements

One of the most common tools involves placing the protected land under a conservation easement. This is a voluntary legal agreement between a landowner and a qualified land protection organization (often called a land trust) or a government agency that limits the type or amount of development on the designated property. The land itself remains the private property of the landowner. The land trust or government agency accepts the easement with the understanding that it must enforce the terms of the easement in perpetuity. Landowners agree to give up specific rights regarding how the land will be used, but otherwise can continue to use and enjoy the property.

One way of illustrating this concept is to consider landownership as a bundle of sticks. Each stick represents a landowner's right to do something with the property: to develop a subdivision, to build a house, to farm the land, to extract minerals, to cut timber, and so forth. With a conservation easement, a landowner sells or gives away some of these rights while still maintaining ownership of the land.[1]

Specific laws regarding easements vary from one state to another, but a typical conservation easement bars the property owner from altering the land's natural, scenic, or ecological features. Easements and other restrictions on the land can cover a wide range of land use issues. Two common types of easement are agricultural easements, through which landowners agree to keep their land in agricultural production, and scenic easements, the goal of which is to preserve desirable views. While the precise scope of an easement can vary depending on state law, the federal Uniform Conservation Easement Act expressly allows conservation easements that retain or protect natural, scenic, or open-space values of real property.

Conservation easements can be tailored to meet the specific needs of the landowner, but they often prohibit the subdivision of a parcel or the construction of structures on the land under easement. As already noted, conservation easements can allow certain types of uses to continue, such as agriculture, timber harvesting, or outdoor recreation. They also can restrict specific uses, such as hunting or the use of pesticides.

Most conservation easements are permanent. They "run with the land," meaning that the benefits and burdens of the land are passed along from owner to owner. If the land is sold, the easement applies to the new owner. This ensures permanent protection of the land's resources while allowing private ownership and traditional uses to continue.

One of the main advantages of easements is their flexibility. A conservation easement might prohibit industrial and commercial uses, restrict the number of residential units, or prohibit the construction of new roads. Alternatively, an easement might allow limited development by specifying which parts of the land can and cannot be developed or by setting a maximum number of acres on which development is allowed. In addition to prohibiting some uses, an easement can specify benefits of third parties, such as the right to cross property to access another property.

A conservation easement involves the actual conveyance of a portion of the property rights to a third party, usually a land trust or other nonprofit organization. Many landowners and developers donate easements to local, regional, or national land trusts, sometimes reaping measurable tax benefits in the process. In some cases, a new entity is formed to take on the responsibility of managing the conservation land. Easements also may be conveyed to government agencies.

In addition to assuring the seller that subsequent owners will maintain the land in a way that is consistent with his or her values and wishes, the main benefit of easements relates to taxes. It is important to point out, however, that tax benefits are only available to developers or landowners when the easement donation is not otherwise required as part of the development entitlement process. For example, if a local government requires landowners to set aside a certain percentage of a property as a condition of the approval process, the owner or developer cannot claim a tax deduction on that part of the property. Because this area of the law can be tricky, landowners should always seek competent legal advice when structuring conservation easement transactions.

The value of a qualifying easement can be deducted from federal income taxes as a charitable donation. To qualify for a federal income tax deduction, the easement must be 1) perpetual; 2) held by a qualified organization, either governmental or nongovernmental; and 3) serve a valid "conservation purpose," meaning that the property must have an appreciable natural, scenic, historic, scientific, recreational, or open-space value.

In addition, sometimes an easement can reduce the market value of the property, resulting in both estate and property tax benefits. By reducing the tax burden through an easement donation, landowners can help ensure that their heirs do not have to sell the family farm just to pay the estate taxes. A few states offer income tax credits for conservation easements, and these credits are transferable in Colorado, New Mexico, South Carolina, and Virginia. A landowner who donates all or a portion of a conservation easement valued in excess of his or her income can transfer (sell) any unused portion of the tax credit to another taxpayer. This enables a "land-rich, cash-poor" landowner to realize the development value of the land without actually developing it.

Land Transfers
Another tool to preserve land is the conveyance of fee simple title to a nonprofit organization, either by sale or as a gift. Small land parcels may be of particular interest to local entities, while larger parcels with high ecological value may be of interest to national nonprofit groups like Ducks Unlimited, the Conservation Fund, the Nature Conservancy, the Trust for Public Land, or American Farmland Trust. Although some national, state, and local conservation organizations may be willing to pay a substantial amount for certain properties, others may be willing to take ownership only if an endowment is attached to underwrite the land's ongoing maintenance and stewardship needs. In some cases, the developer may retain the right to use the land for recreational or stormwater management purposes.

Many developers have worked with local governments to transfer ownership of a portion of their sites. For example, U.S. Steel, which owned significant acreage in and around Birmingham, Alabama, sold 250 acres (101 ha)—now called Moss Rock Preserve—under conservation easement to the city of Hoover, which maintains almost ten miles (16 km) of walking trails and rock cropping that attract climbers from near and far. U.S. Steel Real Estate, a division of U.S. Steel, then planned and built the Preserve, an upscale traditional neighborhood development, on adjacent acreage. While leveraging its proximity to the public park, the developer further differentiated the Preserve by putting in place an interconnected system of walking paths—one of the elements of traditional neighborhood development—that connect to Moss Rock Preserve.

Restricted Conveyances
Another tool that can be used to protect land in perpetuity is a restricted conveyance that specifies how the land can be used in the deed and provides an enforcement mechanism, usually a fine or other damages. Restricted conveyances typically run with the land the way easements do. One of the limitations of restricted conveyances is that enforcement lies with the grantor; upon the grantor's death, the conveyance may be null and void.

Codes, Covenants, and Restrictions
Codes, covenants, and restrictions (CCRs) are a comprehensive set of tools that are used to detail allowable land uses on a particular property as well as to identify restrictions on those uses. They can be used to protect wetlands or wildlife habitat, as well as to identify the types of structures that are allowed. CCRs can be employed to encourage sustainable practices by owners, thus reinforcing a project's conservation aspects. CCRs can prohibit the use of groundwater in irrigation systems, for instance, requiring instead the use of graywater—recycled water that has been used in homes—or rain-barrel water harvesting. Similarly, CCRs can restrict the types of landscaping that can be put in place, for example, by prohibiting the use of nonnative

Conservation communities take different approaches to the ownership and management of conserved land. At Prairie Crossing, in Graylake, Illinois, conservation easements are used to protect open space and natural areas. The Liberty Prairie Conservancy, a land trust, manages the open-space easements.

plants. In addition, CCRs often go beyond describing specific land uses to identify what types of building will be allowed. They may specify one or more particular architectural styles for homes; prohibit attached garages, sheds, or fences; or prescribe standards for green building.

CCRs are enforceable by one neighbor against another. Often the HOA is charged with enforcement. Because all beneficiaries must agree to any proposed change to the CCRs, they are very difficult to update or revise. For this reason, it is important to consider all wording in the CCRs very carefully to ensure that it reflects the desired outcome. A restriction that requires all landscaping be indigenous, for instance, might mean that homeowners could not use *any* nonindigenous plants—even if they have grown on the property for more than a century. To avoid these issues, it is preferable to craft architectural and landscaping guidelines that provide prescriptive information about what *can* be used (such as a list of acceptable plants), as well as what the guidelines are intended to avoid (introducing nonnative species into the ecosystem).

The development team also should ensure that CCRs are flexible enough that they can be revised if conditions warrant. Changes to CCRs may be appropriate if a current strategy is not achieving the desired goal; they also may be required to accommodate new technologies and/or applications. Flexibility is best accomplished by including within the CCRs the standards that led to each restriction, so that proposed changes can be approved or denied according to whether or not they meet those standards. Flexible, adaptable CCRs are especially critical with respect to agricultural uses. Because farming is a business, it must adapt to changing technology and markets. CCRs for agricultural land, in turn, need to be flexible enough to enable farmers to accommodate and respond to such changes.

In some cases, changes in homeowners' priorities may also suggest that the CCRs need to be revised. For instance, homeowners might want to shift management priorities on preserved land to include restoration activities. It is critical to ensure that major programmatic changes are made only after careful study of how they would affect both the conservation land and the developed area. The CCRs in some conservation communities require input from the appropriate land management experts before a change can be made, while others require a vote of all homeowners, with a supermajority needed to change any regulations.

Over time, residents can easily lose sight of the intended purpose of restrictions. In suburban areas, HOA rules sometimes frustrate homeowners who cannot use the paint color of their choice or add an outbuilding for lawn equipment or garden supplies. In a conservation community, the main purpose of restricted conveyances, CCRs, and conservation easements is to ensure that the common open space remains in good condition, meeting the ecological and human use goals that led to its preservation. It is important to define these goals clearly at the outset. Still, adaptability should be built into the conservation community's programs and codes, to allow changes to be made while adequately protecting the land and ensuring its ongoing maintenance.

Financial Considerations

The benefits of conservation easements and other restrictions extend beyond protecting land; they also can offer financial benefits. Assume, for instance, that the owner of a 100-acre property decides to put 75 acres of it under conservation easement and clusters 50 homes on the remaining parcel, rather than dividing the parcel into 100 one-acre lots and building a house on each lot. In this scenario, the developer is building 50 homes rather than the 100 allowed under conventional zoning, resulting in a lower property assessment for real estate taxes. In addition, if the developer donates the easement on the open space to a local land trust or other nonprofit organization, he or she may be able to benefit from federal income tax deductions for charitable gifts or from state income tax credits.

Many states also offer reduced property tax assessments on working lands. The purpose of assessing such lands at reduced levels is to ensure that agriculture and/or forestry continues to be economically viable. In addition, some states assess open-space lands that meet specific criteria at reduced value. In Texas, for example, land that could meet criteria as agricultural land but instead is used for wildlife management can be appraised as agricultural land if participating landowners implement a wildlife management plan that meets state guidelines. Conservation programs often allow lands with agriculture- or forestry-related reduced assessments to roll over their reduced taxes, enabling landowners to participate in conservation practices without losing these tax benefits.

Federal, state, and local governments also may offer tax incentives to encourage the implementation of best management practices, such as the use of streamside buffers or roadside grass swales instead of conventional curbs and gutters. Some states allow income tax credits and deductions to reduce a landowner's state income tax burden with a credit for part or all of the costs of a conservation practice.

Additional benefits also could accrue to developers. Maintaining a green stormwater system, for instance, may allow a municipality to claim credits for nutrient reductions in a state nutrient-trading program that, in turn, may enable the municipality to expand its sanitary sewer without purchasing additional credits. The capital costs for stormwater or wastewater management systems may be reduced by aggressive maintenance of the green infrastructure or by water conservation requirements for a new conservation community. Building a natural wastewater system, for instance, may enable a utility company to avoid the costs of building and maintaining a costly sewer system for a new neighborhood.

Several options exist for projects with agricultural open space. A farmer can sell the development rights to part of or all the land, while retaining the right to farm. Alternatively, homeowners might own all the land, but deed restrictions would ensure that contiguous areas would continue to be farmed. This is the case at Bundoran Farm in Albemarle County, Virginia, where homeowners and cattle share the land.

In some cases, the use and maintenance of a community's green components can be negotiated with a municipality through a development agreement, which provides the developer with certain vested rights and outlines agreed-upon approaches to utilities over all or a portion of a development's buildout. The documents created in securing public financing and identifying community development areas can address the nature of the green infrastructure elements and their ongoing maintenance.

Another potential source of revenue is the capture of certain credits available for environmental characteristics associated with the preserved portions of the project or the operation of green infrastructure. For example, forested properties may soon be eligible for carbon credits because of their role in carbon sequestration. A conservation development project

The Preserve, Hoover, Alabama

The Preserve is an upscale planned residential community of 680 homes in a parklike setting in Hoover, a city just south of Birmingham. The Preserve's homesites are laid out so that no part of a neighborhood is more than about a quarter-mile (0.4 km) from its center, where a community hall, swimming pool, and eight-acre (3-ha) park are located. Front porches, classical architecture, and tree-lined streets are designed to create the authentic feel of the classic neighborhoods of decades ago.

But the most important feature of the Preserve is not what has been built there, but rather what has *not* been built there. A major element of the community's appeal is its location next to the Moss Rock Preserve, a 250-acre (101-ha) nature preserve owned by the city of Hoover. The city purchased the land from U.S. Steel Corp. in 1991 for $2.6 million; restrictive covenants ensure its permanent protection. The nature preserve features abundant trails, rock outcroppings, streams, waterfalls, wildlife, trees, and other unique features, including four rare plant species and a rare variant of sandstone glade. After U.S. Steel sold this parcel to the city, its real estate development company, U.S. Steel Real Estate, then focused on developing the remaining 311 acres (126 ha) of the property as the Preserve.

The Preserve at Hoover is a 680-unit traditional neighborhood development adjacent to a 250-acre (100-ha) nature preserve that was sold to the city of Hoover, Alabama, by the developer.

also may generate credits that can be sold when it sets aside wetlands, streams, or endangered species habitat. Additional credits may be generated through the construction of new wetlands or the restoration of environmentally compromised waterways. Setting aside areas as carbon sinks or using best management practices for nonpoint-source water quality credits may create new sources of revenue for operations. The reuse of wastewater may produce funds from the sale of the water as well as revenues from credits created through the reduction of nitrogen and phosphorous in the receiving waters. Developers must consider not just the availability of the programs, but also both the source of capital to take advantage of the programs and who will benefit from the revenue generated by them.

Restoration and Enhancement

In some cases, an easement or CC&R may specify restoration activities. Ecological restoration involves renewing a degraded, damaged, or destroyed landscape or ecosystem through active intervention. The practice of ecological restoration includes a wide variety of activities such as erosion control; reforestation, tree planting, or revegetation of disturbed areas; in-stream habitat restoration, nutrient and sediment load reduction, stream daylighting, and other stream remediation activities; and the reintroduction of native flora or fauna. Restoration projects might focus on removing blockages from waterways to allow fish passage; constructing road or railroad underpasses to permit wildlife passage, hydrologic continuity, and other ecosystem processes; closing roads or utility corridors; removing ditches; or removing invasive exotic species and weeds.

Ecological restoration activities may be included among the priorities for conservation communities. Restoration goals vary. In some cases, the goal is to return a landscape or an ecosystem to its original condition. In those cases, the tasks to be undertaken involve restoring land that has been cleared for agriculture or forestry to wetlands, prairies, or forests. One major component of the development plan for Prairie Crossing, for instance, was to restore portions of the site that had been used for soybean farming to native prairies and savannas.

The application of restoration ecology occurs along a continuum, from rebuilding totally devastated sites (such as those that have been mined), to ceasing degradation currently taking place on a site, to the limited management of relatively pristine sites. Some conservation efforts, particularly for heavily damaged sites, may stop short of complete restoration to remediate the site so it is useful for some purpose. In these cases, the goal is not to restore the site to its initial state but to improve the site to a predetermined condition. All restoration efforts aim to return the degraded system to some form of cover that is protective, productive, aesthetically pleasing, and/or ecologically valuable. A further aim is to develop a system that is sustainable in the long term.

Restoration of different types of landscapes requires different types of efforts. Much of what is involved depends on the condition, composition, and function of the land. For instance, it is more difficult to transform a landscape from grassland to shrubland than it is to convert it from one type of grassland to another.

Regardless of the effort required, restoration is a complex process that can take a considerable amount of time, money, and expertise. While no single process can turn any damaged ecosystem into one that is ecologically intact, the restoration process generally follows a natural sequence, from identifying restoration needs to monitoring success. Ecologists Richard Hobbs and David Norton have outlined the following steps of the restoration process:[2]

The land management and stewardship requirements for an organic farm, like the one at the South Village conservation community near Burlington, Vermont, are very different from the management requirements for a wildlife movement corridor.

Step 1: Identify processes leading to degradation or decline. Hobbs and Norton stress that too many restoration projects are undertaken without a complete understanding of the reasons that land has become degraded. "Such restoration projects are doomed to failure," they write, "because the degrading influences will continue to operate and work against restoration efforts."[3] In some cases, such as farmland or mine sites, the causes of degradation may be obvious. In others, it may be harder to uncover the reasons for declining ecological conditions. Moreover, the causes of degradation can include what Dan L. Perlman and Jeffrey C. Milder refer to as "missing pieces"—species or ecological processes no longer found at the site—and unwelcome additions, such as excess nutrients, pesticides, pollutants, or harmful exotic species.[4] Identifying the source of pollution or the reason why a particular species is dying out may require time and expertise, but doing so is essential.

The practice of ecological restoration includes a variety of activities, such as removal of invasive species, erosion control, reforestation, tree planting, reintroduction of native flora and fauna, and many other activities. Shown: Tessa Mesa, in Douglas County, Colorado.

The team must have a clear understanding of what is happening in order to address the problem.

Step 2: Define methods to reverse or ameliorate the degradation or decline. An initial restoration strategy may involve simply stopping whatever activity is harming the system, but many restoration processes will require further action. Simply excluding grazing activities, for example, may enable woodlands degraded by grazing to recover and reforest, but if the land's soil structure has been altered, restoration might not occur unless additional measures are taken. If components of the ecosystem—soil nutrients, plant species, water processes, and so forth—have been lost, success will depend on replacing these components. Conversely, excess nutrients, weeds, shrubs, exotic species, and other elements may need to

> ### Reasons for Restoration
>
> Richard J. Hobbs and David A. Norton have identified four fundamental reasons for restoration:
> 1. **To restore highly degraded but localized sites such as mine sites.** Restoration often entails ameliorating the physical and chemical characteristics of the substrate and ensuring the return of vegetation cover.
> 2. **To improve productive capability in degraded production lands.** Degradation of productive land is increasing worldwide, leading to reduced agricultural, range, and forest production. Restoration in these cases aims to return the system to a sustainable level of productivity.
> 3. **To enhance conservation values in protected landscapes.** Conservation lands worldwide are being reduced in value by various forms of degradation, including the effects of introduced livestock, invasive species (plant, animal, and pathogen), pollution, and fragmentation. In these cases, restoration aims to reverse the impacts of these degrading forces, for example by removing an introduced herbivore from a protected landscape.
> 4. **To enhance conservation values in productive landscapes.** In addition to the need for restoration efforts within conservation lands, there is also a need to increase the area of natural or seminatural vegetation in regions that have experienced extensive habitat loss and fragmentation. Restoration in this case entails returning conservation value to portions of the productive landscape, preferably by integrating production and conservation values.
>
> **Source:** Adapted from Richard J. Hobbs and David A. Norton, "Towards a Conceptual Framework for Restoration Ecology," *Restoration Ecology* (June 1996): 94.

be removed from the system before it can function sustainably.

Step 3: Determine realistic goals for reestablishing species and functional ecosystems. These goals should recognize both the ecological limitations of restoration and the socioeconomic and cultural barriers to its implementation. Success depends on a clear understanding of what is to be restored, which, in turn, requires defining why the restoration is being undertaken in the first place. Goals can address the physical, chemical, and/or biological properties of an ecosystem. Because these properties are interrelated, it is important to consider how goals in one area will affect those in another.

Complete restoration of a natural system is often unachievable, particularly where the land has been altered for decades or even centuries. Goals should take into account how the environment has changed, accommodating, for instance, the introduction of new species and the extinction of others. It is also important to consider the broader context of restoration. Changes that have occurred—and those that will occur—on land beyond the site under consideration, may affect restoration goals.

Goal setting can be a complex and contentious process, but having clear goals is critical because these goals will influence the scope and cost of the restoration project. Goals also influence priorities and the sequence in which restoration activities are completed. Not everyone agrees about what "success" looks like. To some people, restoration means returning a site to its pristine state. In most cases, this goal will be unrealistic, and the team will have to search for a more achievable goal. For this reason, stakeholders should be included in the goal-setting process.

Step 4: Develop easily observable measures of success. A further aspect of knowing what is to be restored is recognizing when goals have been reached. For each ecosystem attribute, the team should specify a set of clearly defined goals and objectives that will make it easy to determine whether the strategy is working. Collecting baseline data at the outset of the restoration project will provide a benchmark against which progress can be measured. It is also important to realize that it may take years for natural processes to regenerate. Success builds on success, so it is important to recognize success as it occurs. Intermediary goals can help. A plan that focuses on revegetation, for instance, can specify that 25 percent of the restoration area is to be covered by vegetation within six months of seeding.

Step 5: Develop practical techniques for implementing these restoration goals at a scale commensurate with the problem. The methods chosen will depend on the specific ecosystem and the factors that have contributed to its degradation. Restoration experts typically combine a variety of techniques to reach each restoration goal.

Step 6: Document and communicate these techniques so that they can be more broadly included in land use planning and management strategies. While this step is critical for efforts taking place at the landscape level, it also can be important in smaller initiatives. Sharing a project's restoration goals and techniques can help build local support for such efforts. This is particularly important when the site is of interest to the broader community.

Step 7: Monitor key system variables, assess progress relative to the agreed-upon goals, and adjust procedures if necessary. The monitoring process should begin at the start of the project and continue routinely throughout. Ongoing monitoring should be used to assess progress toward goals, identify problems, and change strategies if circumstances warrant.

The development team at Prairie Crossing followed these steps to identify and implement landscape restoration activities. The specific goal of its restoration activities was to re-create the prairie and savanna ecosystems that once existed in the area. Perlman and Milder point out the challenges involved in this restoration project.[5] The land on which Prairie Crossing is located had been in agricultural use for decades, and the intensive farming had altered the soil. Chemical fertilizers, pesticides, and herbicides had created a hostile environment for many native species. Viable seeds for most native prairie species were no longer in the soil. The prairie restoration required the introduction of seeds and seedlings from other locations. A final challenge was to replicate the natural process of the landscape in a residential area. In nature, frequent fires contribute to the health of the prairie. The restored grasslands at Prairie Crossing were situated in the midst of a 362-house residential development, raising obvious fire management issues.[6]

To address these challenges, the Prairie Crossing design team embarked on an ambitious program, gathering information about the ecology of the site (past and present), educating residents, and engaging experts to analyze, prioritize, and implement appropriate restoration activities. Today, Prairie Crossing residents play an active role in the annual controlled burn of the community's prairie grasses. In fact, this event is one of the highlights of the year for Prairie Crossing residents.

Even less ambitious restoration projects will have many layers, as the physical, chemical, and biological facets of a site interact. The physical aspects of a site will react to chemical and biological changes, for instance, and vice versa. Developers and others who have no experience with restoration should be prepared to hire outside experts to spearhead the project.

Land Management

Even when restoration requirements are minor—and long after they have been completed—conservation land will require ongoing management. Human habitation inevitably changes the natural environment. Invasive species, soil erosion, overuse by residents or visitors, and water pollution are some of the potential negative impacts of growth infringing on once-undeveloped or restored areas. Residents often replace native plants with exotic species that they find more aesthetically pleasing. These species may migrate from landscaped backyards to nearby woods, competing with native plants and disturbing habitat for wildlife and the natural processes of the land. Pets also may scare away or kill wild animals, while cars on newly constructed roads may kill wildlife crossing from one part of their habitat to another.

Even without human interference, the land's character and health may change through natural processes. Over time, these minor changes can become profound, affecting the land itself as well as the plants and animals that live there.

Management Goals

Developing an appropriate land management strategy requires a clear understanding of the land's natural features and their condition. The management of open-space lands—particularly those with high conservation or ecological values—will vary according to the type of land and its intended use. The open-space set-aside in a conservation community may include parks, playgrounds, lawns, farmland, forests, grasslands, and/or wetlands, each of which has different maintenance requirements. These maintenance requirements also vary according to the size of the protected area. Some open-space lands have ongoing landscaping needs; others may need intensive restoration activities at the outset.

Just as clearly defined goals are a critical part of restoration, so are they important to the ongoing maintenance of protected land. The development team must determine not only what it is protecting these resources *from*, but also what it is managing them *for*. Open space in a conservation development may be managed for active or passive use. Depending on the project, the open space may be managed for recreation, wildlife habitat, or agricultural production. Where protecting species is among a project's conservation goals, for instance, habitat restoration or the creation of new habitat may be needed to connect disparate areas and buffer the conservation land from development. Where the land is to be used for passive or active recreation, the management plan will need to include activities such as trail maintenance, mowing, and debris removal.

A number of special issues arise when land is managed for agriculture. These include cropping practices, fertilizer use, manure management, irrigation, water use, or the movement of livestock. In projects that include ranching or farming, houses need to be sited in ways that minimize conflicts with the agricultural uses. In

Landscape restoration activities provide an opportunity both to involve the residents and to conduct environmental education activities.

109

other projects—such as those with pastures, orchards, or vineyards—the agricultural lands can become a visual amenity for homeowners. Most conservation communities that include an agricultural component hire a farm or ranch manager to oversee the agricultural operations.

In the broadest sense, land management starts with answering many "why" questions: Why are we protecting a certain area? This leads into a discussion about the purpose the land is to serve: Will it protect biodiversity or habitat for animals or plants? Will it protect groundwater or surface waters? Will it be part of a natural water system, providing water retention or wastewater management solutions? Will it be used for nature-based recreation? Will it support agriculture or forestry? Depending on the size and nature of the protected land, one or all of the above may be appropriate goals for a conservation development.

In general, the management approaches for conservation lands should enhance landscape connectivity (by reducing fragmentation) and contiguity (by reducing the edge-to-interior ratio). Wherever possible, land management also should foster and reinforce a sense of place that is consistent with cultural values and beliefs, and should work toward achieving the desired future as identified in community visioning and network goal-setting processes.

Land management sometimes needs to replicate natural processes. Controlled fires are one example. The land management plan for the Centerville Conservation Community on the Florida Panhandle, for instance, includes the use of prescribed fire. Landowners throughout the Red Hills area use this natural land management tool to maintain the health of the ecosystem and reduce the risk of wildfire. Centerville's land management plan also requires the planting of native plants, shrubs, and trees, including the restoration of longleaf pine and wiregrass.

Management activities need to be directed toward one or more outcomes, such as increasing the number of migratory birds or providing walking trails that connect residents to adjacent parkland. Goals often are defined in ways that make them relevant not only to the residents of the proposed conservation development but also to the community as a whole. This generates goodwill in the community and can serve as a valuable marketing tool. Goals thus should deal not only with ecological restoration, but also with the ways in which the conservation development will meet the broader community's housing and recreation needs, enhance the quality of life of local residents, and support the local economy.

Monitoring

Ongoing monitoring of conservation land is needed to enable the management team to quickly identify and respond to problems that occur in natural areas. Monitoring does not need to be expensive or cumbersome. Some conservation projects use easily identifiable indicators, such as the numbers of a particular type of species that are present or the amount of ground cover. These indicators should be linked to the management goals. It is important to establish these indicators and monitoring procedures at the outset of the project. Indicators can be used to measure baseline conditions or trends, and/or to predict future conditions or qualities.

An effective monitoring program tests major assumptions and makes possible changes in management approaches when warranted. The information that results from monitoring must be used to refine management actions. Information about whether planned actions have been accomplished, whether assumptions that were made have proven correct, and whether management objectives have been met then can be used to reassess the situation, alter decisions, adjust implementation plans, or maintain current management practices.

While many land management goals focus on ecology and biodiversity, it is important to remember that land management also has implications for people. Reforestation intended to provide habitat for birds and other wildlife, for instance, purifies the air and protects against soil erosion, nonpoint-source pollution, and other environmental problems. Likewise, riparian management to preserve streamside habitat helps improve water quality and protect human settlements from flooding.

Stewardship and Funding

Few developers plan to continue overseeing the maintenance of common space or paying a development's operating costs after buildout. Exit strategies typically depend on when the HOA, land trust, or other organization can assume management and stewardship responsibilities and costs. Although an HOA's creation documents can assign it the burden of operating and funding the maintenance program for conservation lands, this structure runs the risk that the HOA will choose to reduce or eliminate the funding needed for appropriate land management or that it will run out of money to do so. Strong language should be written into the community's covenants to make it difficult for the HOA to eliminate maintenance requirements, but finding a means for funding these activities is also important.

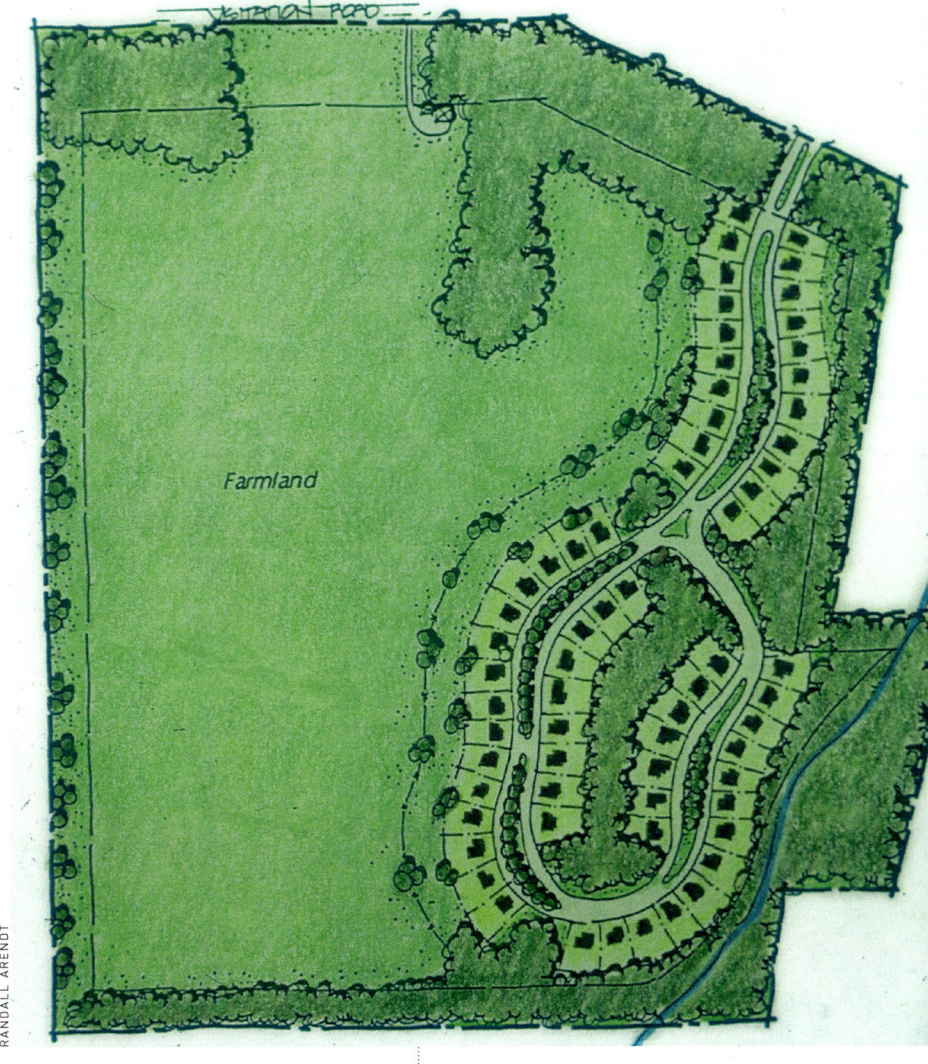

This site plan illustrates a simple, density-neutral approach to conservation development on an agricultural property.

Stewardship in High Plains Village, Colorado

Like many conservation developments, High Plains Village, a conservation development in Loveland, Colorado, began when developer Tom Hoyt started to experiment with the idea of merging development with land conservation. Hoyt, the president of McStain Neighborhoods, believed that developers could build a better world by rethinking the very nature of community. They could create places where people feel more of a connection to each other and to the natural environment. They could create places where enduring value is more important than conspicuous consumption—not just places where people live, but places where their lives become richer. "We believe there is a model to integrate development and conservation," Hoyt explains, "and we've struggled since our inception trying to figure out exactly what that meant. How do you go, 'We're conserving over here and we're developing over here,' when we really need to be thinking about them in the same sentence?"

Hoyt worked with the developers of the master-planned community in which High Plains Village is located to set aside 275 acres (111 ha) of open space and create a nonprofit organization to assume stewardship responsibilities for the preserved land. The High Plains Environmental Center (HPEC) is a permanent, independent, nonprofit organization that the developers believe creates a "living laboratory" dedicated to exploring and teaching the concepts and practices of environmental stewardship. It is charged with protecting wetlands and uplands, offering programs to the northern Colorado community, and supporting local developers, planners, and other consultants with information about sustainable design and development. The HPEC also serves as a neighborhood amenity, conducting a variety of environmental education and hands-on programs for children and adults on topics ranging from bird identification to fine-art painting to alternative vehicle technology. McStain created another nonprofit group, the High Plains Foundation, to assume ownership of the environmental education center and open space and to manage the endowment. Separate boards of trustees govern each of these nonprofit organizations.

Source: Cari Merrill, "Environmental Center Chief Helps Maintain Way of Life," High Plains Environmental Center News, http://suburbitat.org/drupal/node/6. See also McStain Neighborhoods, http://www.mcstain.com/Default.aspx?tabid=829.

Third-party nonprofit organizations sometimes are established to take on stewardship responsibilities, implement community educational programs, and suggest changes in how the land is managed as new technologies become available. These entities often are funded by charges imposed on the sale and resale of property within the community. At the Santa Lucia Preserve, for example, a conservancy was established to manage, restore, and enhance the lands that are permanently protected as a nature preserve. All lots share in ownership of the preserve. The conservancy receives guaranteed funding for its management through an endowment established by the landowner from a dedicated portion of the sales price of each residential parcel.

Conservation developers, particularly those undertaking major restoration activities, need to plan carefully to ensure that revenues are sufficient to cover costs. Some conservation communities successfully fund ongoing maintenance and management activities through transfer fees and HOA dues. Others use the revenues from leasing land or selling timber or produce grown on the site for land management activities. Additional potential funding sources include grants from government agencies or land trusts. Developers also may be able to partner with conservation organizations to care for ecologically valuable land.

In conventional developments, the HOA typically pays for the maintenance of common areas. In conservation developments, this maintenance may extend beyond lawn mowing and tree pruning to include a wide range of restoration, monitoring, and management activities. The added cost can lead to higher HOA fees, increasing the risk that conservation development will be affordable only for a wealthy few.

Where it is in keeping with the goals of the conservation community, agricultural pastures or forestland may be leased for farming, equestrian activities, or sustainable timber production, with the proceeds used to support the community's conservation and restoration needs. In order for these types of opportunities to be fully realized, working lands should be contiguous and of adequate size. In addition, it is important to consider the tax ramifications; the HOA may be required to report the revenues from leasing working land as income.

Some conservation communities also may benefit from government programs. McStain Neighborhoods—the developer of High Plains Village, a mixed-use community in Loveland, Colorado—created the High Plains Environmental Center to manage the community's lakes, wetlands, and open space. The team then set about ensuring that the center would have sufficient funding, by convincing the city of Loveland to dedicate some of its building permit revenues to support the center. The Loveland City Council was instrumental in ensuring funding for the center by approving development agreements that stipulated that some building permit revenues from the development would help fund the center.

Conventional cost/benefit analysis can be extended to take into account the benefits of protecting land, including social and environmental factors. For example, the Land Evaluation and Site Assessment (LESA) system developed by the USDA Natural Resources Conservation Service is designed to determine the quality of land for agricultural uses and to assess sites for their agricultural economic viability. LESA initially evaluates a site's soil quality and suitability for cropland or forest. It also evaluates a site's compatibility with relevant plans and zoning, access to public infrastructure, and so forth.

The Environmental Team

In most conservation communities, the HOA is actively involved in the upkeep of traditional parks, playgrounds, bike paths, and walking trails, but few HOAs have experience or expertise in maintaining or restoring fragile ecosystems or agricultural land. A conservation nonprofit group with experience in land management generally is better equipped to take on a conservation easement and assume responsibility for property management.

Ensuring the ecological stability of conserved land requires that resources—both funding and talent—be devoted to provide day-to-day management, monitoring, and stewardship. Success depends on ensuring that the people who assume these tasks have adequate experience, funding, and community support.

Conservation Managers

The development team for a large-scale conservation development should include an environmental manager. Some developers enlist environmental management firms to fulfill this role, but an environmental manager also can be hired as a consultant or as a full-time employee. The environmental manager plays an integral role during the design and construction of the conservation development to ensure that houses and other infrastructure are situated and constructed in ways that minimize their impact on the land and disturbance to the ecosystem. The environmental manager or environmental team leader also typically spearheads environmental education, recycling and restoration,

Sand Creek Ranch, Buffalo, Wyoming

The Sand Creek Ranch conservation community sits on about 850 acres (345 ha) of Wyoming foothill prairie near the Bighorn Mountains and between the towns of Sheridan and Buffalo. Owner John Jenkins wanted to protect the ranchland, but the cost of conservation seemed daunting. He knew that the ranch, like hundreds of others across the Mountain West, was worth far more with people on it than with only cattle and alfalfa.

Sand Creek Ranch evolved from a sense that the working ranches of the American West are rapidly becoming an endangered species. Jenkins lamented not only the loss of the acreage to rural sprawl, but also the loss of the values and the ranching lifestyle that have made the West so desirable. He aimed to preserve these values and the ranching lifestyle, which he accomplished by putting 500 acres (202 ha) of the 850-acre ranch under conservation easement and committing the entire property to the creation of a "ranch conservation community" that would be productive, sustainable, and, as he puts it, "a good way for folks to live in the country without destroying the country." After researching various options, Jenkins decided he liked the idea of conducting a thorough analysis of the qualities of the land, which would then drive the placement of homesites and protective easements. He added another dimension to the project by transforming the ranch's agricultural operations into a nonprofit undertaking, giving each homeowner a share of the business.

The idea behind Sand Creek Ranch, says Jenkins, is to give buyers the reality of owning an 850-acre ranch without the price tag or the upkeep. "People want to live out there," he says. "If you want to serve both masters, you've got to find a way to give people a wonderful real estate value without destroying the natural resource and wildlife values."[1]

After nearly three years of study, planning, analysis, and feedback, the working design for Sand Creek Ranch evolved to create and preserve something special and of sustainable value. The community has been designed to preserve the qualities of a fine western ranch forever and to maintain the ranch's agricultural productivity for future generations. While conserving and enhancing substantial wildlife habitat, the master plan also protects the ranch's open spaces, viewsheds, and mountain vistas. State-of-the-art irrigation and other farm and ranch improvements made possible by a community of new owners provide efficiency that actually increases Sand Creek's historic hay-producing capacity by a factor of seven.

Sand Creek Ranch, an 850-acre (345-ha) cattle ranch near Buffalo, Wyoming, integrates farm and ranch operations with a community of 99 homesites, thereby preserving the working landscape and benefiting the project's rural neighbors.

Consultants worked closely with a team of mapping and geographic information systems (GIS) experts and other professionals with expertise in range management, soils, wildlife habitat, engineering, real estate development, and law. This group worked for nearly two years to create a comprehensive plan. The challenge was to generate a practical, sustainable plan that protects the ranch while also providing homeowners lasting value and an enjoyable, genuine western lifestyle. The master plan, which informs all decisions, emerged from a commitment to optimize the unique combination of views, landforms, habitat, and history that define the property.

Each ranch neighborhood has been master planned to maximize the visual separation between itself and other neighborhoods nearby while preserving individual viewsheds for each homesite. Designated building envelopes on each of the 99 one-acre (0.4-ha) homesites have been carefully sited to optimize the privacy and intimacy created by a unique combination of topographic relief, native vegetation and planned vegetative enhancements, view distance, and view angles, while providing efficient access to and from the community's primary road network. As a result, each of Sand Creek's ranch neighborhoods—and the homesites within each neighborhood—feature permanently protected views to preserved open space, adjacent working ranchlands, and the Bighorn Mountains, which rise dramatically just four miles (6 km) to the west.

The ranch seamlessly integrates farm and ranch operations within the conservation community. This sustainable agricultural activity maintains the ranch setting for owners and generates revenue to help offset upkeep and maintenance costs. Practical management plans for recreation, agriculture, and wildlife across the ranch allow for sustainable agricultural operations and on-ranch recreation and fitness pursuits. By preserving the working landscape with a conservation-based limited development strategy, Sand Creek Ranch also benefits its rural neighbors and the community as a whole.

The ranch includes a wide range of amenities appropriate for a rural lifestyle, including equestrian facilities, barns, a 4-H program, a community garden and picnic shelter, nine miles (15 km) of equestrian and hiking trails, and a community headquarters where neighbors can socialize. All of these facilities, and the activities they support, promote community interaction within an authentic rural atmosphere. A set of design review guidelines was created to help owners plan homes of lasting architectural character, authenticity, and value.

For more information, see the project website, www.sandcreekranch.com.

1. Quoted in David Frey, "Have Your Ranch & Develop It, Too," *The New West* (Spring 2008), http://www.newwest.net/magazine/article/having_your_spread_and_developing_it_too/C555/L555/.

and landscape management activities after the design phase is complete. In addition, the manager's tasks may include educating residents about eco-conscious living, sustainable landscaping principles, pest management, wildlife ecology, the appropriate use of trails and common areas, and so forth.

Depending on the goals of the conservation community, additional expertise may be required. The development team at Bundoran Farm, for instance, includes a natural resources manager, a sustainability manager, and a farm manager. The natural resources manager is responsible for the community's natural resources management plan and serves as a liaison between those who live on the property and those who work the land, promoting careful stewardship and the use of the land and its resources. The sustainability manager works with individual residents, design professionals, and builders to incorporate energy efficiency and sustainable development practices into residences as they are built. The farm manager maintains Bundoran Farm's cattle herd and pasturelands, keeps the farm equipment and facilities in good working condition, and looks after the forest trail system.

Depending on the nature of the community, sustainability and land management activities may be part of a broader mission. At Sand Creek Ranch, an 850-acre (344-ha) conservation development

Land stewardship activities are a popular and effective way to get people involved in their communities. Farmers markets, like the one at Prairie Crossing, in Grayslake, Illinois, are another way to engage the residents of a conservation community.

that includes a working ranch in Wyoming, an on-site association manager and contract operators provide security, wildlife management, and general maintenance services. These services include operation of the community's irrigation system and its hay farming and weed control operations, as well as management of the community's 4-H horse program.

It is important to ensure that environmental stewardship continues past the build-out phase. This usually is accomplished by having the HOA assume responsibility for environmental activities, but clear management guidelines and an ecological framework are needed to help guide decisions. Some conservation developments also include a nature center staffed by one or more naturalists to provide ongoing education programs and stewardship activities.

The Role of Residents

Regardless of who assumes ownership of the protected land in a conservation community, its residents will play an important role. Most conservation communities rely on a combination of homeowner stewardship and maintenance agreements. Maintenance costs typically are added into the cost of homeownership in such communities through a tax on the sale and/or resale of a home, through HOA fees, or through some combination of these. When management systems are designed correctly, homeowners perceive the natural systems as value-added amenities and actively participate in their maintenance. In some conservation communities, required fees have been supplemented by voluntary donations from residents who want to expand the environmental protection programs already in place.

Residents should be encouraged to assume environmental stewardship responsibilities. Environmental stewardship embodies three concepts: responsibility, care of the land, and management of the land for the benefit of future generations. Stewardship also can include management practices that recognize the benefits of the land—including ecosystems that support biodiversity, flood control, scenic views, and so forth—and maintain the land in ways that protect these benefits for future generations.

Stewardship goes beyond these communal efforts when community residents are encouraged to look for ways to reinforce environmental principles on their own property. For instance, homeowners should recognize that how they care for their yard can affect their neighbors and the natural environment of surrounding areas. Even where CCRs do not require doing so, homeowners can be encouraged to avoid cutting down large trees, put in place landscaping that minimizes water usage, engage in green landscaping practices, and/or avoid using harmful fertilizers and pesticides.

Land stewardship activities are a popular and effective way to get people involved in their community. Tree-planting ceremonies, river or stream cleanup efforts, and trail maintenance programs can provide residents with opportunities to become actively involved in their community. Residents also can be involved in monitoring activities, perhaps by routinely counting the number of a particular species found in a defined area. In areas where residents are moving from urban to rural settings, these stewardship activities can forge critical links between people and the natural environment in which they live. For instance, the environmental education center at Spring Island, a conservation community off the coast of South Carolina, provides a variety of programs designed to teach residents about the environment and connect them with nature, including a summer camp for children, sea kayaking and bird-watching trips, daily trail rides, and visits to an on-site nature center. A full-time naturalist runs the preserve and its programs, which are supported and managed by the Spring Island Trust. Funding for the trust comes from a 1.5 percent fee on the initial sale of each lot and a 1 percent fee on subsequent sales.

Community education is an important aspect of any stewardship program. Sometimes simply informing citizens of the benefits of land or water resources can drastically reduce the impact of human activities on natural resources. Many people, for example, do not understand the repercussions of cutting down a large shade tree or using nitrogen fertilizers to make their lawns greener. They also may be unaware of what happens when exotic plants are introduced into an ecosystem. Educational seminars, workshops, nature walks, brochures, and pamphlets all can be useful elements of a strategy to educate the community. Conservation communities often provide literature for residents about how to live with nature. In rural areas where farming or ranching is to be continued, this literature may include tips to help people understand how to live in harmony with working land.

Educating residents about how they can become better environmental stewards—for example, through recycling, composting, or natural mulching—can help residents recognize that they are part of a larger community and that the land they own is part of a larger ecosystem. These educational opportunities help bridge the gap between community residents and the land on which they live. Human involvement with the land is part of the landscape's ecology, and stewardship programs can help people better understand the relationship between man and nature. Encouraging a love of the land may be one of a conservation developer's greatest marketing assets.

Notes
1. When prospective developers consider obtaining an easement, it is important for them to verify that the landowner does indeed own all relevant rights to the property. If a third party—such as the state or federal government, or a private individual—holds mineral rights, for example, the easement could not prohibit oil and gas exploration.
2. See Richard J. Hobbs and David A. Norton, "Towards a Conceptual Framework for *Restoration Ecology*," Restoration Ecology (June 1996): 95–96.
3. Ibid.: 96.
4. Dan L. Perlman and Jeffrey C. Milder, *Practical Ecology for Planners, Developers, and Citizens,* (Washington, D.C.: Island Press, 2005): 172.
5. Ibid.: 172.
6. Ibid.: 172.
7. Quoted in David Frey, "Have Your Ranch & Develop It, Too," *The New West* (Spring 2008), http://www.newwest.net/magazine/article/having_your_spread_and_developing it_too/C555/L555/.

Conservation Development Case Studies

CHAPTER 6

Changing U.S. demographics are fueling new approaches to residential development. Two-parent families with young children are no longer the nation's primary homebuyers, so developers are looking to appeal to a much wider group of buyers. Throughout the country, people are searching for alternatives to the faceless, unappealing sprawl that is swallowing up the places they call home. Developers have responded to market trends with innovative approaches that merge people's need for housing and their desire to preserve land and natural resources.

Land use professionals' interest in designing and developing sustainable communities also is growing. Nearly 70 percent of developers surveyed recently said that there is an inadequate supply of alternative developments such as conservation communities. These developers think that between 10 and 25 percent of the households in their market areas would be interested in alternative development forms. In some regions, they say, the market for innovative types of development exceeds 50 percent.[1]

Developers, conservationists, planners, and other land use professionals are joining forces to explore alternatives to conventional zoning and land use regulations. Bringing together conservationists and developers with a variety of experiences and perspectives can help foster innovative solutions to land conservation and development challenges, providing a better option for communities and the people, plants, and animals that live in them.

Of the millions of housing units that will be developed in the coming years, only a small percentage will be in conservation communities. As the market proves that it is ready for new approaches, this percentage will gradually grow, and conservation communities will make their way into more of America's rural and suburban areas.

The cases profiled in this chapter vary widely in terms of acreage, number of homes, amenities, and approaches. They include examples of conservation subdivisions, limited development projects, and large master-planned communities. Yet the development teams' goals and strategies are often complementary, although uniquely executed. Their motivation for pursuing this work ranges from protecting working landscapes to preserving scenic beauty, to protecting fragile ecosystems and the species that live there. Notwithstanding their unique points of emphasis and practice, the developers of these diverse projects regard the permanent protection of significant landscapes as a defining purpose of their work. It is our hope that these case studies will offer an intriguing glimpse into the realm of the possible, and that they will inspire others to explore this extraordinarily dynamic and quickly evolving sector of the real estate development industry.

Note
1. O'Neill, David J., *Environment and Development: Myth and Fact* (Washington, D.C.: ULI–the Urban Land Institute, 2002).

Bundoran Farm

Albemarle County, Virginia

CASE STUDY

Special Features

- Approximately 1,000 acres (405 ha) of productive pastureland with 300 head of cattle.
- Two working apple orchards totaling 154 acres (62 ha).
- More than 20 miles (32 ha) of trails ranging from single-track hiking trails deep within forests to carriage trails for horseback riding.
- Several lakes that host a variety of aquatic life and provide a source of drinking water for livestock and other wildlife, as well as fishing and other recreational opportunities for the community.
- More than 1,000 acres (405 ha) of managed forests, some of which are contiguous to several thousand acres of off-site forests. One tract has been designated a "minimal management zone" that will be allowed to revert to old-growth forest.
- Site of the annual Albemarle County Fair, which highlights the Charlottesville-Albemarle area's natural and agricultural resources.
- The Baldwin Center for Preservation Development, providing a central repository for information regarding preservation development and sustainable agriculture.

Bundoran Farm is a 2,300-acre (931-ha) conservation community in Albemarle County, Virginia, roughly 15 miles (24 km) southwest of downtown Charlottesville. The working farm was purchased in 2005 by Qroe Preservation Development LLC and Celebration Associates, which partnered for the first time on this venture.

The project combines a high-end residential development with extensive land conservation, including a working farm with more than 1,100 acres (445 ha) of cattle pastures and several apple orchards. The working farm is central to the design of the project; it is seen as a productive, industrial enterprise that will continue to evolve and improve. Bundoran Farm's master plan is further guided by principles of environmental sustainability and the protection of natural features and rural viewsheds. The site plan allows for a maximum of 108 homesites, significantly fewer than the 163 that were allowed under existing zoning. All of the houses, as well as the roadways and other infrastructure, will be carefully tucked into the seams of the land between forest and pasture, preserving the rural character of the landscape.

Origins

Bundoran Farm evolved over many years from several large landholdings that have been used to grow tobacco and apples, as well as to raise cattle. The Bundoran Farm landscape is an iconic place in Albemarle County. It has served as the site of the annual county fair since 1988 and is one of the largest single property holdings in the county. The farm includes about 1,100 acres (445 ha) of cattle pastures, 1,000 acres (405 ha) of managed forest, and more than 150 acres (61 ha) of apple orchards.

Fred Scott's family had owned Bundoran Farm for more than 60 years. By the early 1980s, he was preparing to retire, and his children had no interest in continuing to farm. Still, he was reluctant to sell the property to the tract homebuilders who came knocking on his door. Instead, he wanted to find a way to cash in while maintaining the integrity of the farm and its rural landscape. After reading about the work of Qroe Preservation Development LLC, which had developed several farms into conservation communities in New England, he contacted Qroe to explore whether it might be a good fit for his property. Subsequently, Scott visited Robert Baldwin, Sr., Qroe's president, and toured a number of the company's projects. A few years later, Baldwin contacted Scott with an offer to purchase Bundoran Farm, and the two men settled

Bundoran Farm is a 2,300-acre (931-ha) conservation community outside Charlottesville, Virginia. The project includes a working cattle farm and apple orchards, and it serves as the site of the Albemarle County Fair. The innovative nature of the project has led to positive stories in the national, state, and local press, resulting in free publicity.

All the homesites take advantage of Bundoran Farm's exceptional physical attributes. These include creek and woodland frontage, sloping hillsides, solar orientation, and desirable views.

on the details of the sale of the property in a series of e-mail messages.

Before founding Qroe in 1981, Robert Baldwin, Sr., had a successful career in manufacturing and had served on several local planning commissions. He believed there was a better way to develop farmland than to divide it all into house lots and streets, so he set out to find a way to give farmers more influence over what would happen to their land after they sold it. Qroe created a novel "preservation development" concept, which provides innovative and workable answers to the ecological and economic sustainability questions facing rural landowners. The concept combines conservation, farming, and residential development. Central to Qroe's development concept is the permanent preservation of farmland and open space as a key residential amenity.

Baldwin met Charles Adams and Don Killoren, the principals of Celebration Associates, a nationally recognized developer of award-winning master-planned mixed-use communities in the eastern United States, through his involvement with the Urban Land Institute. The three often discussed collaborating, but they had not found the right project—until Bundoran Farm. Qroe and Celebration Associates quickly settled on a partnership agreement, put together a team, and threw themselves into the planning process. Building upon the foundation of Qroe's planning and governance model, the two firms have shared development responsibilities as co-managers of the project.

The Vision

As in other Qroe communities, preservation development is at the heart of the Bundoran Farm project. Baldwin's plan was to use limited residential development to preserve the farm's rural character and agri-

Roads, driveways, and other infrastructure are carefully situated in order to protect water quality, minimize site disturbance, and maintain rural character. Wherever possible, existing farm roads and cattle trails were incorporated into Bundoran Farm's road system.

cultural landscape. This approach resulted in plans for a low-density community of roughly 100 homesites, with 90 percent of the farm's acreage put under a proven system of easements and deed restrictions designed to ensure the beauty, character, and vitality of the land in perpetuity. The approach to development at Bundoran Farm can be described as a "three-legged stool" in which farming, environmental protection, and residential development serve as the three legs. Each leg represents a different activity and constituency, and plays an equal role in the use and management of the land.

Working land is at the heart of the preservation development concept at Bundoran Farm. This is not just a residential community for families who are attracted to a rural lifestyle. It is a working business, a "factory" whose factory floor is the topsoil. The farmland will remain a contributing part of the community, a living example of the true definition of sustainability.

The second leg of the development approach is environmental protection. Bundoran Farm seeks to protect the site's land, water, wildlife, and natural resources. To help achieve this, Audubon International, a nonprofit organization that supports environmental stewardship and sustainability, has engaged in a partnership with the developers to help protect the farm's natural resources. While Audubon International already was well known for its work on golf course communities, this was the first time that the group had become engaged with an agricultural project. Audubon International's consultants helped the developers shape the development plan and provided expertise regarding stream crossings, forest preserves, and habitat restoration. The organization, which has personnel located on the property, continues to conduct research, provide ongoing analyses, and make recommendations that will help the farm, orchard, and timber managers protect water quality and prevent topsoil erosion.

The final leg of the stool is the development of residential homesites. Plans call for the development of 93 to 108 homesites over several years. The residents who call Bundoran Farm home will become stewards of the working farm and protected land.

Reaching Out to the Community

Fred Scott introduced Bundoran Farm's new owners to his neighbors and allowed them to explain their novel approach. The development team believes that Scott's involvement helped pave the way for unprecedented community support. Albemarle County is growing rapidly, and many county residents were worried that the area's rural character would be compromised by the farm's development—as had happened in other parts of the county. Local farmers and large landowners were equally concerned that "no growth" zoning initiatives were too blunt an instrument, essentially stripping them of their financial security. The development team was proactive in addressing both these concerns early on.

"We got to know our neighbors and listened to them," says David Hamilton, the Qroe employee who oversaw the development process. Hamilton moved to the site to serve as Bundoran Farm's project manager, and spent considerable time and effort building relationships with the farm's neighbors. "The things we addressed from the very beginning at Bundoran Farm were things the neighbors had never heard addressed by a developer. . . things like viewshed protection and maintaining the rural character of an area." The neighbors liked what they heard and were pleased with a plan that included fewer homesites than the 163 allowed by Albemarle County's zoning laws.

"It is really impressive to watch the Bundoran planning crew at work," says Scott. "They have put in a lot of thought, a lot of time, and—I'm quite sure—a whole lot of money into thinking things out ahead of time. They spent time interviewing people, learning about local history, how cattle and forestry operations work, and all the other things that are important to me and my neighbors. When they showed us plans of how the development might look, it looked right to us. We really appreciate the fact that the project is going to sit very lightly on the land."

Planning

The Bundoran Farm development team engaged in a planning process that included comprehensive, multi-disciplinary studies of every aspect of the land. The team identified, catalogued, and evaluated ecologically rich areas and viewsheds. They looked to identify and preserve large, contiguous open-space areas—including forested areas—in order to protect wildlife habitat, riparian areas, and water quality.

The developers realized that protecting large, contiguous areas of productive farmland was integral to maintaining an economically viable agricultural operation. Bundoran Farm's large pastures and orchards not only enable more efficient agricultural operations, they also provide the farm's primary public viewsheds.

In addition to preserving the ecology of the land, the developers wanted to protect the visual character of the landscape. They undertook a series of studies to help them fully understand what people would see and experience as they traveled through the pastures and meadows of Bundoran Farm and along the country roads surrounding the property. To protect the scenic beauty of the rural landscape, the design team also walked and drove the roads within and around the farm to consider the views. Through a comprehensive and holistic analysis, areas generally appropriate for the placement of homesites began to emerge.

Walking the land helped the design team further refine the location for each home. Key selection criteria for individual homesites included views, privacy, access, and ease of building. Homesites were strategically situated to be out of the public viewshed and to maintain large tracts of viable working land and contiguous natural habitat. Most of the homesites were set along the seams of the pastures and forest, where they could be tucked into the landscape.

About 90 percent of the land at Bundoran Farm will remain as undeveloped, protected landscape.

The next step was to provide access to each of the homesites. Roads, driveways, and other infrastructure were carefully situated to protect water quality, maintain the site's rural character, and minimize site disturbance. Wherever possible, existing roads, footpaths, and trails were incorporated into the development's road system. The development team successfully petitioned the county government for permission to build private roads within the development. In an effort to preserve the parcel's rolling pastures and forests, the developers of Bundoran Farm also were granted waivers to various zoning rules. For example, they were allowed to build a road with a nonasphalt surface and with grass along the shoulder rather than standard curbs and gutters.

Farmland and Natural Resource Management and Protection

The character and use of the pastures and forests are preserved through a series of easements that overlay the farm and greenbelt areas. The easements allow common passive use of and access to these portions of the property. The developers believe that homeowners, acting as land stewards, will diligently monitor these uses, so they set up the Bundoran Property

Owners Association as the principal holder and enforcer of the easement provisions. During the entitlement process, the county asked for and was readily granted a position as coholder of the easements.

Bundoran Farm uses natural resource management practices that have a positive impact on the ecosystems that sustain life. The Bundoran Farm Natural Resource Management Plan serves as a blueprint for the long-term operation and management of the property in accordance with the best environmental stewardship practices. As an Audubon International Gold Signature Sanctuary, Bundoran benefits from Audubon International's initial design and resource management expertise, a rigorous certification process, and ongoing advice.

The farm's streams, ponds, and wetlands are valued, sensitive resources. In addition to providing water for Bundoran Farm's agricultural and recreational activities, the waterways feed into the Hardware River, the James River, and, eventually, the Chesapeake Bay. Ongoing water-quality testing is underway to fully assess the impacts of the development and its natural resource management practices.

In order to effectively balance the long-term interests of Bundoran Farm's residents with the needs of a successful farming enterprise, the developers established a farm management committee to oversee farming operations. This five-person committee is composed of two Bundoran Farm residents, one nonresident environmental expert, one nonresident agricultural expert, and a fifth member jointly selected by the others. The committee manages farmland leases and/or directs farming activities, supervises farm personnel, and sets long-term policies and goals. The homeowners association's board of directors has final authority on major business decisions, but it can reject the committee's recommendations only though a supermajority vote.

Homesites

All of the homesites are designed to take advantage of Bundoran Farm's unique physical attributes. This includes careful consideration of solar orientation, prevailing winds, creek frontage, sloping hillsides, and desirable views. The lots vary in size, from 2 to more than 100 acres (0.8 to 41+ ha). Homesites also vary in location; some offer open meadow views, some are on forested sites, and others lie along the wooded edges of pastures.

Each site delineates the parcel of land that will be owned by the homeowner and further defines a smaller portion of land where a home can be built. "In most cases, your lot line is not very meaningful," says Hamilton. "You have about a half acre you can build on, and outside of that you have a two-acre box which is really your private domain, with no trails or agriculture running through it. Beyond that delineated box, agricultural operations and cattle are allowed to go back and forth across any landowner's property. Every homeowner also has a right to use the 20-mile network of trails and take advantage of all of the many recreational amenities on Bundoran Farm's 2,300 acres."

In most cases, the homeowner's parcel will include pastureland, trails, or land designated for other community uses. "We did this for a very specific reason," explains Hamilton. "We wanted to give people a sense of ownership—stewardship—over the land. We didn't want people to think they should call someone else if they saw someone using the land in an inappropriate way. We wanted homeowners to feel as though they have the responsibility to watch out for the land. If they see someone who is doing something they shouldn't, we want them to ask them to stop."

Sustainable Design and Construction

A thorough understanding of the unique characteristics of each site at Bundoran Farm lays the groundwork for the design of a home that will complement the landscape and make the most of its natural features. Lot portfolios established for each homesite provide basic site information to help prospective buyers select the lot that best meets their needs and build a home that will capitalize on the unique features of the land. While landowners have significant flexibility in the design of their homes, architectural guidelines help ensure that all homes at Bundoran Farm maintain the agrarian feel of the community. An architectural design guidebook helps buyers understand the architectural styles and details that are best suited to the community.

The design of the homes at Bundoran Farm generally falls into one of two design categories: traditional vocabularies, which draw from the architectural vernacular that has emerged over time in the Virginia Piedmont and the rural area around Charlottesville, and individual vocabularies, which are contemporary interpretations of traditional rural buildings that complement more traditional homes. The common threads that weave these traditional and individual vocabularies together include site relationships, basic building forms, materials, and colors.

Project staff members emphasize that the purpose of the architectural design book and guidelines is to inspire, encourage, and inform homeowners, architects, and builders, not to dictate exactly what can and cannot be built. The developers offer a list of prequalified architects and builders to help ensure that each home is constructed in a manner consistent with Bundoran Farm's overall goals.

Bundoran Farm also has a sustainability manager, whose job is to help develop and implement sustainable building practices and operations and to educate residents, builders, architects, and the general community about sustainability concepts and how to apply them. To this end, the sustainability manager has developed an environmental stewardship manual (dubbed the "Green Book") that focuses on the sustainable design and development of homes at Bundoran Farm. The manual helps residents understand how to incorporate sustainable design principles to increase energy efficiency, water conservation, and the use of best practices in siting, design, construction, operation, maintenance, and waste management.

Marketing

Bundoran Farm does not necessarily appeal to a traditional market, and the development team believes that standard marketing techniques are insufficient to reach the target market. The marketing approach focuses more on education than advertising. Marketing efforts use a "beauty shot" of the farm in its pristine state and the guarantee that 90 percent of the land will remain "as is" to capture the attention of the target market. Most of the team's marketing efforts have taken place in and around the state of Virginia. The developers have capitalized on the natural appeal of Charlottesville, which *Money* magazine named one of America's "Best Places to Live" in 2006.

Above all, the developers say, Bundoran Farm has benefited from the general goodwill in the community and beyond. Several early buyers are the result of ongoing communication within Albemarle County—people who were drawn to the idea of preserving the county's rural lifestyle. Another early buyer was familiar with Qroe's preservation developments in New England and happened to be planning to relocate to the Charlottesville area. The innovative nature of the project has led to positive stories in the state and local press, providing free publicity for the development.

Results to Date

Bundoran Farm homesites range in price from $350,000 to more than $1 million. The lots went on the market in October 2007; 11, representing the full range of lot types, sold within the first

Bundoran Farm is the site of the Baldwin Center for Preservation Development, which was established to advance state-of-the-art practices in rural land use planning, including agricultural preservation, environmental stewardship, and conservation development.

The Baldwin Center for Preservation Development

On June 14, 2006, Robert Baldwin, Sr., and Qroe Companies regional director David Brown were killed in a private plane crash near Bundoran Farm. Robert Baldwin, Jr., who had worked with his father for many years, assumed the position of CEO of Qroe and now directs the Bundoran Farm project. Until the day of the crash, he had never set foot in Albemarle County, but he had been hearing about the project for years. "My father was more excited about this project than anything he had ever done," Baldwin says. "It was very exciting for me to get down there and get involved, to see what he saw and talk to the people he had spoken to, and to help make this legacy a reality."

One element in the effort to preserve the elder Baldwin's legacy is a center dedicated to advancing state-of-the-art practices in rural land use planning and development, including agricultural preservation, environmental stewardship, and conservation development. Named the Baldwin Center for Preservation Development, the center is housed in a state-of-the-art green building at Bundoran Farm. The mission of the Baldwin Center is to share the lessons and experiences of Bundoran Farm well beyond its boundaries. The center also is envi-

nine months, netting approximately $7 million. Construction of the first houses began in July 2008; at the end of 2009, four were occupied and several others were under construction.

The property's working farm is leased to Adventure Farm and managed by Carl Tinder, president of the Albemarle County Farm Bureau. There are currently about 300 head of cattle on the property. The farm also leases its apple orchards to the region's leading commercial apple enterprise. The continued presence of these agricultural operations has helped ensure the economic viability of the Bundoran Farm community.

sioned as a gathering place for local citizens and farm-related entities. The center will work to enlighten, encourage, and inform others about preservation development and the practical aspects of sustainability, environmental stewardship, and the role of farming in modern life.

Challenges and Lessons Learned

As in any innovative land development project, the development team faces significant challenges in making its dream a reality. Perhaps the greatest challenge is explaining the concept to prospective buyers. It takes significant time to educate people about the philosophy behind Bundoran Farm and how the community differs from conventional developments. The development team members estimate that they spent at least ten hours with each of the first prospective buyers before they began the purchasing process. One early prospect came with 80 questions, some of which the team could not answer. "We knew the answers to most of them," says Bob Baldwin, Jr., "but we had to follow up on a few of the questions." From these meetings with early prospects grew the "founding stewards" concept. These early buyers helped the development team formulate solutions to some of the unique problems faced at Bundoran Farm. "The founding stewards have helped us unravel some perplexing problems," says Hamilton. "They have also given us insight into some of the ongoing concerns of the community and prospective buyers."

Of course, not everyone is attracted by the idea of living on a working farm. The target market is a higher-end consumer who truly appreciates the rural, agrarian environment. Many potential homeowners have never lived on a farm, however, and may not be aware of what this means. Farming is sometimes messy, and not all prospective purchasers of million-dollar homes are attracted to the idea of cattle grazing on their property. The developers take special care to ensure that homeowners fully understand how the farm works and that owning a home there means living in proximity to farm animals. The community represents a series of compromises. For instance, allowing cattle to graze across the fields naturally would create a hazard for drivers, so roads were fenced off from the land on which cattle graze.

In addition to explaining Bundoran Farm's overall principles and practices, identifying the appropriate lot for each interested buyer also is challenging. Every lot is different, and it would take many hours to show prospective buyers all of the homesites by touring the entire farm. To minimize the amount of time required for these tours, the development team prepared a fact sheet for each lot that provides basic facts about the site. This helps the team narrow down the options for prospective buyers before heading out over the farm to explore the various sites with them.

Another challenge has involved balancing land management principles with homeowner desires. Homebuyers—especially wealthy homebuyers—are used to making decisions about where and what to build without much outside interference. Bundoran Farm's developers are sensitive to providing as much flexibility in decision making as possible, but complete autonomy flies in the face of the community's goals and objectives. Some potential buyers bristled at the idea of having any of their land used for farming; others did not like the idea of trails running across their land. "It can be hard to stick by your principles when someone is ready to write a million-dollar check," says Bob Baldwin, Jr. He describes one interested buyer—a successful corporate executive—who appeared to be just the kind of person they were hoping to attract to the farm. "He didn't like some of the ideas at the farm, though," Baldwin continues. "He asked, 'What if I don't want the cattle in the pasture behind my house?' He was used to getting

Site plan.

his own way and thought he could negotiate on this issue. It was hard to say no because we knew we'd lose the sale. But it's important to stand behind the vision and principles that you've set for such a community. He just wasn't right for Bundoran Farm."

Figuring out the best way to ensure that farming will continue to be at the core of the community in the years to come has been another challenge. Effective farm management is essential to a successful enterprise. Making sure that the farm will remain economically viable required a mechanism for reviewing and renewing contracts for cattle farming and apple operations, and for ensuring that current and future farmers abide by the tenets of the community. Recognizing that the needs of Bundoran Farm will change over time, the team looked for a way to enable current land uses to evolve according to the needs and desires of the community, while also ensuring that such uses will be consistent with a working farm. Baldwin offers one example: "If someone comes to us with the idea of growing grapes for a winery, we needed to have a way for the community to decide whether this was a good idea."

These and other issues were addressed through establishment of a farm management committee and a homeowners association. The farm management committee makes recommendations on the use of the agricultural land. While the committee has considerable latitude in operating the farm, the homeowners association has the final say. For most matters, a simple majority vote is required, but if an issue involves any measure that would alter the fundamental nature and spirit of the farm, a super majority of all the landowners is required.

The homeowners have a fair amount of latitude to run the farming operations in a way that balances economics and sustainability, but CCRs ensure that they cannot cease all farming operations or add to the number of homes on the property.

Replicability

While the Bundoran Farm conservation community concept is replicable in other areas, Bob Baldwin, Jr., emphasizes that it cannot be easily translated to any farm. One of the things that contributed to Bundoran's success, he says, is that the Scott family was ready to retire. In Baldwin's experience, owners who stay on the land and continue farming it often are unwilling to cede adequate control of farm management and operations to the developer and, ultimately, to community residents. This can make it difficult to implement the concept of the farm as an integral part of community life. "Fred Scott has been really great," says Baldwin. "You can sometimes imagine him saying, 'That's not how I'd do it,' but he stays out of things . . . . unless we ask his opinion. And he plans to live here, so he has a stake in what happens."

Baldwin also emphasizes that topography plays a critical role in the success of conservation developments. The hills of Albemarle County proved ideal for "hiding" homes and other infrastructure from view, so the rural landscape is maintained. In addition, the concept of a truly working—industrial—farm requires a piece of property of sufficient scale to support the selected agricultural endeavor. This amount of acreage can be difficult to find in many areas.

BUNDORAN FARM

LAND USE INFORMATION

Site area	2,300 ac/931 ha
Open space under easement	90%
Number of residential units planned	92–108
Number of lots sold	11
Percentage of residential development complete	10%
Gross residential density (units per ac/ha)	0.05/0.12 (average 21.3 ac/unit, 8.6 ha/unit)

LAND USE PLAN

	Acres/ Hectares	Percentage of Site
Residential	100/41	4
Roads	20/8	1
Working open space: (active farming and recreation)	1,275/516	55
Undeveloped open space (natural open space)	900/364	39
Community facilities	5/2	1
Total	**2,300/931**	**100**

RESIDENTIAL INFORMATION

Lot Type	Lot Size (ac/ha)	Range of Initial Sales Prices
Single-family homesites	2–100/0.8–41	$300,000–$1,000,000

Unit Type	Unit Size (sq ft/m²)	Range of Initial Sales Prices
Existing estate homes (2)	5,000–7,000/465–650	$2,000,000–$3,500,000

DEVELOPMENT COST INFORMATION

Site Acquisition Cost	**$30,000,000**

Site Improvement Costs

Road Construction	$6,500,000
Sewer/water/drainage (wells)	50,000
Landscaping and common area	450,000
Telecom/power	1,300,000
	$8,300,000

Construction Costs (Amenities)	**$500,000**

Soft Costs

Master planning and design	$1,400,000
Engineering	1,500,000
Project management & administration	2,900,000
Marketing and sales (excl. brokerage)	2,050,000
Legal/accounting	850,000
Taxes/insurance	800,000
Town association and Foundation	1,700,000
Construction interest and fees	5,000,000
Licenses, bonds, permits	200,000
	$16,400,000
Total Development Cost	**$55,200,000**

DEVELOPMENT SCHEDULE

Planning started	2003
Site purchased	2005
Sales started	Fall 2007
Construction started	Summer 2008
Project completed	2014 (projected)

DEVELOPMENT TEAM

Owner

Edge Valley Preservation LLC (a partnership among Charlotte, North Carolina–based Crosland; Fort Mill, South Carolina–based Leroy Springs & Company, Inc.; and Qroe/CA LLC) Charlottesville, Virginia

Developer

Qroe/CA LLC (a partnership between Qroe Preservation Development LLC of Boston, Massachusetts, and Celebration Associates of Charlottesville, Virginia)

Site Planners
Qroe/CA LLC
Charlottesville, Virginia
www.qroefarm.com

McKee/Carson
Charlottesville, Virginia
www.mckeecarson.com

Open-Space Protection/Preservation/Management
Edge Valley Preservation LLC
Charlottesville, Virginia

Audubon International
Selkirk, New York
www.auduboninternational.org

Real Estate Sales and Brokerage
McLean Faulconer
Charlottesville, Virginia
www.mcleanfaulconer.com

Project Website
www.bundoranfarm.com

Galisteo Basin Preserve

Santa Fe, New Mexico

CASE STUDY

Special Features

- Of the 13,522-acre (5,472-ha) parcel, 96 percent permanently preserved as open space.
- All preserved land to remain open and accessible to the public.
- Four small conservation neighborhoods, plus a mixed-use village that will provide 965 homes, a café, a post office, a chapel, offices, and a school.
- Mixed-use village to include a high percentage of workforce and affordable housing.
- Proceeds from the sale of large conservancy lots to be used to pay for the planning of the village.
- Model water conservation measures and green buildings.
- Stewardship at the forefront of community life: the village school will include an Outward Bound curriculum, and the village plan includes an environmental education center where residents can learn about land conservation and restoration.

The Galisteo Basin Preserve is a 13,522-acre (5,472-ha) conservation development located 13 miles (21 km) southeast of Santa Fe, New Mexico, in the central Galisteo Basin watershed. Spearheaded by Commonweal Conservancy, a Santa Fe–based nonprofit organization, the Galisteo Basin Preserve represents an innovative approach to land conservation and community building in which traditional neighborhood development is being used to fund the acquisition and preservation of a vast and fragile landscape. Unlike many other conservation development projects in the American West, the Galisteo Basin Preserve was conceived, first and foremost, as a publicly accessible open-space conservation initiative.

The Galisteo Basin Preserve master plan includes four conservation neighborhoods and a mixed-use village in which 965 homes will be clustered within a dramatically framed 380-acre (154-ha) valley. Roughly 30 percent of the planned village homes will serve income-qualified households. Through its proximity to a proposed commuter rail line, aggressive water conservation and reuse infrastructure, solar-oriented site plan, and "healthy building" construction standards, the proposed village aspires to demonstrate the efficacy of green development in a mixed-use, mixed-income, landscape-scale conservation development context.

The Galisteo Basin Preserve's open space will be overlaid with conservation easements, guaranteeing that 96 percent of the project's land resources will be permanently protected for future generations. The project embraces the values and principles of "regenerative land development"—a practice of land healing and habitat restoration that will involve more than 19 square miles (4,921 ha) of grasslands and forests, along with approximately 12 miles (19 km) of arroyos and stream corridors for the benefit of wildlife and groundwater aquifer recharge. Another critical planning objective is the development of a regional trail system that will include approximately 50 miles (81 km) of publicly accessible hiking, biking, and equestrian trails. Real estate transfer fees from sales of properties within the Galisteo Basin Preserve will help fund the stewardship and educational programs in perpetuity.

Origins

The Galisteo Basin is renowned for its spectacular scenic, cultural, and wildlife habitat values and its ecologically significant land and water resources. The scattered remains of obsidian tool making, petroglyphs, and shallow pit houses

The Galisteo Basin, located 13 miles (21 km) outside Santa Fe, New Mexico, is renowned for its spectacular scenic, cultural, and wildlife habitat values.

The West Basin consists of four ranch homesteads ranging in size from 125 to 263 acres (51 to 106 ha). Three other large-lot conservation neighborhoods were laid out to raise capital for the high-density conservation village.

offer glimpses into the 7,000-year human history of this wild and open landscape. Rich in Native American, Spanish, and American history, the Galisteo Basin reflects the scars and ambitions of more than 350 generations of ancient and modern people.

Following the land rush of the early 1900s, the Thornton family assembled a 21-square-mile (5,439-ha) ranch for cattle grazing in the basin. Pieced together from 160-acre (65-ha) homestead patents issued to aspiring ranchers and miners during the Territorial Period, the Thornton Ranch brought a measure of stability and coherence to an otherwise disjointed pattern of landownership. Reflecting the patchwork quilt history of the region, several parcels of public land owned by the U.S. Bureau of Land Management and the state of New Mexico adjoin and fit within the ranch boundaries.

Ted Harrison—who later became president of Commonweal Conservancy—was introduced to the spectacular scenic and cultural resources of the Thornton Ranch when he served as the Southwest regional director for the Trust for Public Land (TPL), a national land conservation organization. In this capacity, he directed TPL's purchase of approximately 1,500 acres (607 ha) of archaeologically significant rock outcroppings on the southwestern part of the ranch—an area known as Petroglyph Hill—for the benefit of Santa Fe County. "After completing this transaction," says Harrison, "Santa Fe County's planning director acknowledged the good intention of the public land purchase, but also included a disclaimer. He wondered whether the 1,500-acre acquisition would merely serve as a 'museum piece' for future generations—evidencing what this landscape *used* to be after the surrounding Galisteo Basin was developed in accordance with the county's general plan (i.e., 40-acre ranchettes)."

"The critique of TPL's work as 'curatorial conservation' inspired me to rethink the land conservation practice I had pursued within TPL for 18 years," Harrison said. "It prompted me to reimagine the need and importance of community building in a comprehensive, integrative, humanist approach to park-making and land conservation."

Santa Fe County's zoning classification for the Thornton Ranch included 40-acre (16-ha) minimum "Homestead" properties and 12.5-acre (5-ha) minimum "Basin Fringe" lots. At the time of the Petroglyph

Hill transaction, the Thorntons were actively marketing the ranch to "business as usual" developers. Harrison felt that breaking the property into 40- and 12.5-acre ranchettes posed a serious threat to the area's scenic, historic, cultural, and ecological resources. He believed the only way to protect the land would be to "reframe the conversation" between those who sought to develop the land and those who hoped to preserve it.

After completing the Petroglyph Hill acquisition, Harrison tried to engage TPL as the facilitator of a large-scale conservation initiative that would also accommodate a mix of community-serving development—an approach with which TPL had some experience. In cases in which the lands TPL was acquiring for open space, scenic, and/or wildlife values were not entirely appropriate or necessary for public land management purposes, TPL occasionally sold a portion of the parcel to a developer and used the proceeds to fund the acquisition and preservation of environmentally sensitive areas. Usually, the part that was sold—what Harrison calls the "sacrifice area"— was conveyed without major restrictions on the land's development. Harrison believed that TPL could play a more active role in guiding the development process on lands that adjoined a conservation acquisition, thereby ensuring that the environmental and development values of a property or region could be more mutually supportive.

Uncomfortable with the risks and financial responsibilities of managing a large-scale and potentially controversial development program for the 13,000-acre (5,261-ha) Thornton Ranch, TPL judged the Galisteo Basin Preserve concept promising but believed it was inconsistent with TPL's long-term business strategy. Intrigued by the opportunity that the Thornton Ranch presented, Harrison founded Commonweal Conservancy in 2003 with the express purpose of integrating the practices of community development and land conservation, of demonstrating a new model of environmentally responsible community development wherein development would help finance landscape-scale conservation initiatives.

As Commonweal Conservancy's president, Harrison negotiated an agreement with the Thornton family to purchase the ranch in five phases. The first acquisition phase occurred in 2005; the last is targeted for 2011. As a nonprofit organization, Commonweal Conservancy secured the property at a "bargain sale" price. At the time the transaction was negotiated, the estimated fair-market value for the property was approximately $40 million; the negotiated purchase price was $19,833,000.

Initially, community development was envisioned as a means to an end—a way of generating funds to underwrite the acquisition, preservation, and restoration of the Galisteo Basin's northern rim. Soon after launching the initiative, however, Harrison recognized that the Thornton Ranch presented a unique opportunity to articulate a resource-efficient development plan and to establish a community of land stewards who would be intimately connected to, deeply knowledgeable about, and actively invested in the landscape they called home.

Conservation and Development

In collaboration with representatives of Santa Fe County, conservationists, archeologists, professional planners, and neighborhood groups, Commonweal Conservancy embarked on an ambitious plan to conserve the vast majority of the Galisteo Basin Preserve—more than 12,800 acres (5,180 ha)—as publicly accessible open space.

While Commonweal Conservancy's overarching goal was land preservation and restoration, the group also had a vision for creating a diverse and authentic community as a complement to the conservation program. Harrison recognized that the development plan would require a great deal of skill, not only in engineering and site planning, but also in traditional neighborhood development practices and community building. Careful attention to the community program, urban design, landscape architecture, and use of water and energy resources would be critically important to Commonweal Conservancy's vision of creating an "intimate, enlivening, deeply knowledgeable, and active stewardship community."

"The puzzle-making quality of traditional neighborhood development has proven both fascinating and maddening," says Harrison. "Like a Rubik's cube, the block faces need to be organized in exactly the right pattern and in the correct sequence. Invariably, many of our early puzzle-solving attempts were painfully deficient. But iteration after iteration, the plan moved closer to our vision of a connected, respectful, and vital community design."

Initially, Commonweal Conservancy viewed its responsibility as the "articulator of a vision," says Harrison. "To advance the project, we expected to join forces with a 'real' developer—someone who had substantial financing and long experience in town building." But the group's early efforts to attract an outside developer to the project proved unsuccessful. "Developers with credible experience in conservation development lacked a presence in Santa Fe or were busy with projects in other parts of the country," Harrison says, and local developers "viewed us as naive, idealistic, and romantic. They believed our vision was out of sync with the large-lot settlement pattern that was common at the suburban fringe."

After assembling a planning team of landscape architects, land planners, geographic information systems (GIS) professionals, engineers, architects, ecologists, and hydrologists, Commonweal quickly witnessed its role evolve from "articulator of a vision" to master developer. After 20 years in the "white-hat world of the conservation profession, I woke up one morning to the sobering truth that I had inadvertently become a developer," Harrison says. "We had crossed an exciting and somewhat terrifying threshold, and there was no going back."

Site Planning

To understand the development opportunities and constraints involved in the areas to be developed, Commonweal Conservancy used sophisticated GIS and physiographic modeling technology to carefully analyze the property's topography, scenic qualities, and cultural and ecological resources. Analysis of the GIS information and other data identified appropriate locations for the village site and the conservation neighborhoods.

Sales of conservation neighborhood lots have been used to help underwrite the acquisition of the Galisteo Basin Preserve. The West Basin consists of four equestrian or ranch homesteads, 125 to 263 acres (51 to 106 ha) in size, along the western boundary of the preserve. New Moon Overlook, which is situated on a ridge overlooking the village, includes 20 large homesites, ranging in size from 13 to 52 acres (5 to 21 ha), set back from the ridge to preserve the viewshed while giving homeowners spectacular views of the surrounding basin. Southern Crescent is designed to support 22 homesites between approximately three and nine acres (1.2 and 3.6 ha) in size. Each of the homesites and building envelopes are carefully tucked within the property's hills and valleys to preserve the area's visual, natural, and cultural resources. A fourth conservation neighborhood, Lyra Crossing, will include four equestrian parcels of 32 to 185 acres (13 to 75 ha).

Each of the conservation neighborhoods takes its cues from the surrounding landscape; the *land* takes precedence in the design. In this spirit, the design goals and development values of the proposed village, as well as the Southern Crescent, New Moon Overlook, West Basin, and

This Galisteo Basin residence is powered by a solar photovoltaic system, but its architectural character draws on northern New Mexico's traditional pueblo revival style.

Lyra Crossing neighborhoods, are informed by the following principles:
- Love for the Galisteo Basin's precious scenic resources;
- Deference to the Galisteo Basin's cultural history;
- Stewardship of the region's animal, plant, soil, and water resources; and
- Respect for the complexity and creativity of social organizations.

Commonweal Conservancy proposed a large-scale, tightly clustered development approach in its master plan for the mixed-use village. The village is designed to support 965 homes at full buildout in 2020. Within the village, a range of home sizes, types, and price points is planned to accommodate a variety of household sizes, types, and financial capabilities. Designated affordable and workforce housing options include cottages and studios that will be priced at $95,000, and 1,350-square-foot (125-m^2), four-bedroom homes priced at $235,000. Market-rate cottages and large custom homes are projected to sell at prices ranging from $190,000 to more than $900,000, respectively.

"Serving the full range of incomes and lifestyle needs in the area is fundamental to our community-making strategy," says Harrison. "Santa Fe's demographics don't mirror the national averages. Our community includes a disproportionately high percentage of single moms, divorcees, and widowers—a segment of the housing market that is poorly served by the community's spec and production builders." The residential program also includes a multigenerational cohousing neighborhood of 25 to 35 units, as well as a mix of homes and neighborhood designs that will serve the needs of Santa Fe's "elders and wise ones," Harrison adds.

The village design includes commercial, civic, and educational development as elements in the larger goal of facilitating a dynamic, integrated, and walkable community. The design team anticipates that the village center will include a café, a post office, a nondenominational chapel, and live/work space for local artisans and community-based businesses.

Fundamental to the community's vision and values is the role of education and continuous learning. Toward that end, Commonweal Conservancy has been working with a charter high school that combines instruction in Spanish and English with an environmentally focused curriculum. An elementary school will be included in a later phase of the village plan. Harrison believes institutions of learning are inseparable from the village concept because they will "anchor the community's sense of ownership and commitment to place. Programmati-

Design Guidelines

To accomplish the goals identified during the site planning phase, Commonweal Conservancy identified a series of design guidelines, including:
- Build structures that fit gently and inconspicuously within the property's hills and valleys;
- Protect public viewsheds from light pollution and rooftop "sky-lining" effects;
- Restore the productivity and ecological diversity of grasslands and riparian corridors;
- Enhance the water storage capacity of alluvial soils and minimize erosion;
- Utilize the sun, wind, land, and trees to facilitate heating, cooling, lighting, and ventilation;
- Maximize the use of locally produced benign building materials, waste reduction techniques, and green design practices; and
- Utilize highly efficient water conservation, rainwater catchment, and wastewater reuse design strategies and technologies.

cally, schools can supercharge the flow and energy of the community's daytime population and enhance the viability of otherwise nascent commercial enterprises."

Conservation and Environmental Stewardship

Stewardship is at the forefront of life in the Galisteo Basin Preserve. The village's high school will include an Outward Bound–certified curriculum in which students use the open space as an outdoor classroom. In addition, the design team has set aside five acres (2 ha) of land for a green burial program. The green cemetery is designed to lay lightly on the land, with no headstones and with cremation and burial practices that conform to national green burial standards. The village design also includes parks and footpaths that connect neighborhoods to one another, to open space, and to the larger basin.

In addition, the village plan includes an environmental education center at which residents can learn about land conservation and become actively engaged in stewardship and restoration activities. "We have an opportunity to create something more than a great place to call home," explains Harrison. "In our most romantic, ambitious vision of this work, we aspire to create a stewardship community—one in which village residents will be deeply knowledgeable about this remarkable landscape. If we are successful, community members will be the experts of this place—actively engaged in species monitoring, such as cataloguing bird species as they migrate through the region, and working hand in hand with the preserve's anticipated community stewardship organization and local land trust in restoration activities."

A real estate transfer fee on the sale and resale of lots and houses will fund the preserve's ongoing stewardship and restoration programs. Commonweal Conservancy currently is overseeing these responsibilities but plans to establish an independent community stewardship organization to oversee the long-term management of the preserve's open space. In addition to Galisteo Basin Preserve residents, this group will include representatives from surrounding communities and the county to ensure that management activities reflect the intentions and desires of the broader community.

Financing, Marketing, and Sales

Commonweal Conservancy's land purchase agreement with the Thornton family involves a long-term option at a "bargain sale price"—as defined by the U.S. Internal Revenue Service

(IRS)—that affords the organization the exclusive right to purchase the property in five phases over an eight-year period. The bargain purchase price is a unique aspect of the deal structure—one that leverages the conservancy's nonprofit status to create an opportunity for tax savings for the Thornton family, while concurrently containing its land acquisition costs. The acquisition structure also has enabled Commonweal Conservancy to generate funds from property sales in its conservation neighborhoods, as well as to secure development financing from commercial and nonprofit lenders.

When Commonweal Conservancy made its initial purchase, the ranch was entitled with 130 legal lots of record that derived from the property's original homestead patents. Commonweal reconfigured 25 of the homestead lots into two flagship conservation neighborhoods. After two years of word-of-mouth marketing, the conservancy had sold four of the five large lots in the West Basin (the first neighborhood offered for sale) and all 20 lots in New Moon Overlook. Many of these lots were sold to local residents. Funds from the initial sales provided seed capital for further acquisitions and allowed Commonweal Conservancy to develop the master plan.

Commonweal Conservancy expects to begin marketing the village after its initial development phase is approved by Santa Fe County. The village's Phase I plan includes 149 residential units and 37,500 square feet (3,500 sq m) of community and educational facilities. Subdivision approval for the first phase is anticipated in 2010. The first homes in the village are expected to be available for purchase in 2011, depending on the strength of Santa Fe's housing recovery following two painful years of deep economic recession.

While the large-scale protected areas and network of trails that surround the village and conservation neighborhoods will be an important driver for lot sales, Harrison emphasizes that the vision of the project differs significantly from other conservation development initiatives. "The people who have purchased lots within the first round of preserve neighborhoods like the fact that they are challenging the typical standards of rural and suburban development. This isn't about private open space, golf courses, or lavish amenity packages. It's about being connected to the land, being deeply connected to the earth in a way that allows people to

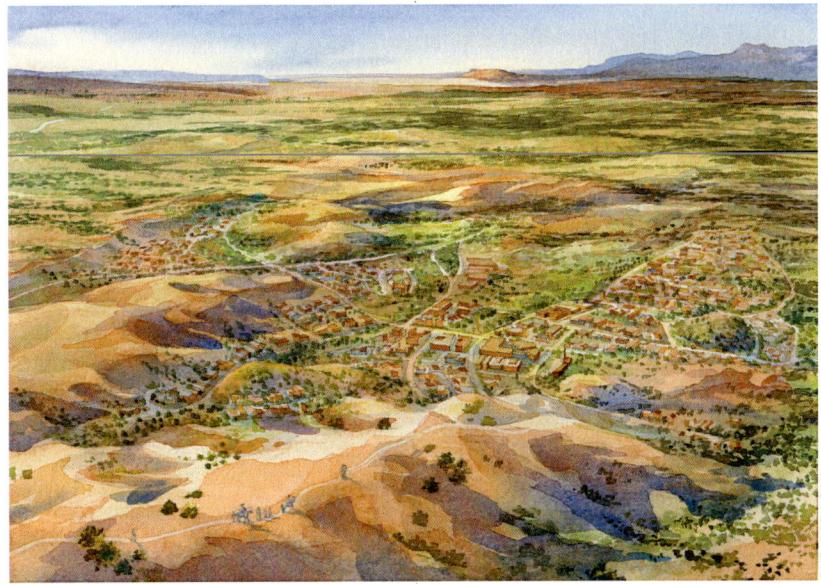

Galisteo Basin's developers have proposed a tightly clustered mixed-use village of 965 homes at full buildout. The village design includes residential, commercial, civic, and educational elements.

celebrate the pure and simple beauty of the place we call our home."

In contrast to other conservation developments that promote exclusivity and private open space, the Galisteo Basin Preserve celebrates *public* access to previously inaccessible natural areas. Building on Harrison's experience with TPL, most of the preserved land will be accessible by the public via an extensive trial network. Commonweal Conservancy views the land as a resource both for residents of the Galisteo Basin Preserve and for the people of the nearby communities of Lamy, Galisteo, and Santa Fe.

To that end, many of the developer's early marketing efforts have focused on creating opportunities for Santa Fe residents and visitors to explore the preserve using the 15 miles (24 km) of trails that Commonweal Conservancy developed in advance of the village approvals. The organization also has co-branded its work with other local nonprofit groups, ensuring that the values commitments of the organization and the project are clearly presented and consistently demonstrated.

Challenges and Lessons Learned

The Galisteo Basin Preserve project is deeply rooted in the values and ethics of land conservation. As conservationists immersed in a development process, the project principals have experienced a steep learning curve and "paid a good bit of tuition" as they embarked on this far-reaching community-making enterprise.

Concurrent with the planning and program discussions that have informed the village development effort, Commonweal Conservancy and its consultants have devoted considerable time and energy to the Galisteo Basin Preserve open-space plan and program. Eschewing the predilections of preservationists, the developer believes that the history and ecology of the preserve can be well served by allowing an actively managed, quick rotation grazing program to be tested within healthy, resilient areas of the preserve. But ranching is hard on the land and takes considerable space, and many local conservationists are skeptical about the compatibility of land restoration and ranching. Similarly, Commonweal Conservancy is committed to creating an active farming program within the preserve, one that includes community gardens, an orchard, greenhouses, a tree nursery, and perhaps limited row crops. To environmentalists who fear that agricultural operations will demand too much water from northern New Mexico's semi-arid climate, Harrison argues that "by bringing our food sources closer and making their production more visible, I think we advance more of an environmental protection and sustainability message than if we ignored the interconnections among food and nature."

The project's early success has largely been defined by the strong relationships that Commonweal Conservancy has forged with the community. "It's been a significant challenge to manage the community's needs and expectations as to how land can accommodate a mix of development and conservation uses," says Lauren Whitehurst, Commonweal Conservancy's director of marketing and communications. "Not everyone is on the same page. There is some hesitation and mistrust—both on the conservation side and on the development side. But engaging with people respectfully, listening well, and responding to their concerns has allowed us to build strong bridges among a wide range of community stakeholders."

The project has received significant local scrutiny. The Galisteo Basin is a well-loved area that has been relatively untouched for centuries. Residents of nearby towns were concerned about the land being developed, fearing not only the impact on the landscape itself but also on their water resources. "Commonweal spent a lot of time communicating to neighbors and leaders within the environmental community that we were not here to disrupt this land's complex

Stewardship is at the forefront of life at Galisteo Basin Preserve. The village plan includes an environmental education center, green buildings, and low water use.

ecology and its quality of open space," says Whitehurst. Citizens also worried about an increase in traffic and demands on public services.

One tool that helped illustrate the Galisteo Basin Preserve vision early on was a set of maps that compared what the land would look like if it was overlaid with "business-as-usual" development patterns versus what it would look like if the county adopted Commonweal Conservancy's clustered-development plan. "The power of content-rich maps and superb GIS modeling cannot be overstated," Whitehurst says. "Once we moved past the protests that 'time should stop and nothing should change' into the realm of 'How do we manage the *inevitability* of change?' we got to a much more productive place in the dialogue."

The early relationship-building efforts helped. More than 50 people attended the 2007 public hearing in which the Santa Fe Board of County Commissioners voted on Commonweal Conservancy's master plan for the village. Remarkably, despite the project's size and potential impact, not a single person spoke against it. "Admittedly, it helped that we are a nonprofit conservation organization instead of a traditional developer," Whitehurst says, "but it also spoke to values of the project and to the substantive dialogue Commonweal pursued with the surrounding communities and elected officials."

In the three years leading up to its public hearing schedule, Commonweal Conservancy representatives spent countless hours in community meetings, explaining what they intended to do and what they saw as the project's array of public benefits. Through this process, says Harrison, the Commonweal Conservancy staff became deeply committed to carrying out the vision—to doing what they have said they would do. Although the organization had not intended to play the master developer role when it first conceived the project, it is no longer looking to divorce itself from its substantial development responsibilities. "If we were to hand the project off to an outside developer at this stage, it would be a terrible violation of trust, given the relationships, history, and commitments we've forged with community members and decision makers," says Harrison.

Despite the project's remarkable early success, Commonweal Conservancy is reluctant to put the Galisteo Basin Preserve and the village forward as a replicable conservation development model. "By definition, conservation development is site specific," cautions Whitehurst. "It needs to attend to the unique attributes of climate and ecology, as well as to the evolving needs and desires of the local government, community organizations, and citizens. This isn't about formulas. It's about being attentive to a broad range of needs and concerns, and responding to those needs with a mind and spirit of creativity and respect."

"First and foremost, the preserve is intended to be a landscape-scale conservation effort," Harrison explains. "But the project economics have to be compelling too. This is an important test of the 'doing good and doing well' ambition. If we fail in our efforts to generate good returns to our investors, this will be a philanthropic exercise that doesn't move the needle of the larger industry. To be successful, the preserve needs to inspire the mainstream toward this practice."

Harrison also emphasizes the importance of actively engaging conservation-oriented organizations in the land planning and development process. "The nonprofit sector—and conservation organizations particularly—no longer have the luxury of ignoring or vilifying the development industry. We have a responsibility to play an active and constructive role in guiding the land use process so that it serves the needs of people *and* the land on which we are dependent," says Harrison.

"In a world that is too easily divided between 'good guys' and 'bad guys,' the conservation community has missed an opportunity to identify shared interests and forge common ground," Harrison says. "In my experience, the only hope of protecting the scenic landscapes, wildlife habitats, farmlands, water, and cultural resources that define our sense of place demands a coming together of heretofore disparate interests. We need to address the complex economic, social, educational, and health care needs of the population while simultaneously ensuring the permanent protection and regeneration of the natural systems and processes on which we depend for our survival."

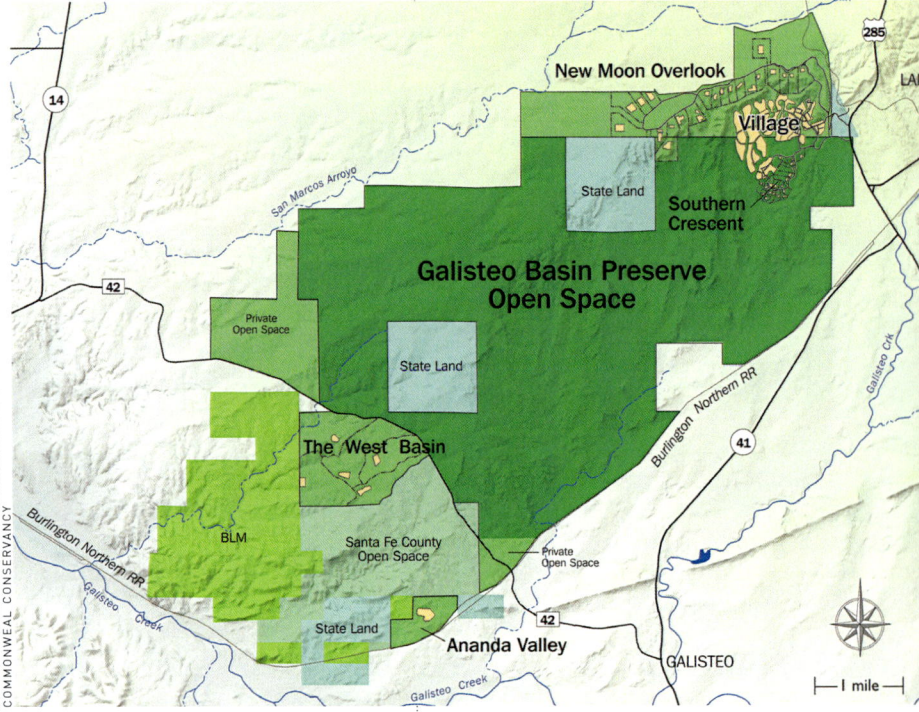

Site plan.

GALISTEO BASIN PRESERVE

LAND USE INFORMATION

Galisteo Basin Preserve (entire project)

Site area	13,522 ac/5,472 ha
Number of residential units planned	1,015
Number of lots sold	39 (all in the conservation neighborhoods)
Percentage of residential development complete	0.4%
Gross residential density (units per ac/ha)	0.076/0.188[1]
Average net density (units per ac/ha)	
West Basin	0.006/0.015
New Moon Overlook	0.017/0.042
Southern Crescent	0.23/0.57
Lyra Crossing	0.025/0.062

The Village at the Galisteo Basin Preserve

Building envelope	306 ac/224 ha
Number of residential units	965 (planned)
Percentage complete	0
Gross residential density (units per ac/ha):	3.2/7.9

LAND USE PLAN

	Acres/ Hectares	Percentage of Site (Village)	Percentage of Site (GBP total)
Village residential	151/61	49.3	1.1
Village roads	25/10	8.2	0.2
Developed open space (Village parks, common areas)	100/40	32.7	0.7
Protected Preserve open space (natural open space)	13,090/5,297	N/A	96.8
Town center/ mixed-use/school	24/10	7.8	0.2
Sewer and power facilities	6/2.4	2.0	0.04
Other residential development (conservation neighborhoods)	126/51	N/A	0.9
Total	**13,522/5,472**		

RESIDENTIAL INFORMATION

Conservation Neighborhoods

Neighborhood/ Lot Type	Lot Size Building Envelope (ac/ha)	Range of Initial Sales Prices
West Basin: equestrian/ranch homesteads	125–263/51–106 3.5–4.5/1.4–1.8	$525,000–$899,000
New Moon Overlook: rural homesites	13–52/5–21 1.0–4.0/0.4–1.6	$232,815–$612,750
Southern Crescent: rural homesites	2.9–8.8/1.2–3.6 0.23–0.73/0.09–0.30	$179,500–$409,000
Lyra Crossing: equestrian/ranch homesteads	32–185/13–75 0.5–3.2/0.2–1.3	$350,000–$475,000

Conservation Neighborhood Sizes	Acres/ Hectares	Number of Units
West Basin	680/275	4
New Moon Overlook	1,258/509	20
Southern Crescent	96/39	22
Lyra Crossing	349/141	4

Village Homesites[2]

Lot Type	Lot Size (sq ft/m²)	Range of Initial Sales Prices (Projected)
Studio/cottage lots	1,200–2,000/112–186	$50,000–$70,000
Condo/stacked flats	1,200–2,200/112–204	$50,000–$80,000
Townhome/semiattached home lots	1,900–4,000/177–372	$65,000–$85,000
Single-family detached courtyard home lots	1,300–6,000/121–557	$80,000–$100,000
Single-family detached semicustom home lots	4,500–15,000/418–1,394	$100,000–$250,0000
Single-family detached custom home lots	5,500–50,000/511–4,645	$125,000–$300,000

Village Homes

Home Types	Home Size (sq ft/m²)	Range of Initial Sales Prices (Projected)
Studio/cottages	750–1,100/70–102	$200,000–$310,000
Condo/stacked flats	750–1,350/70–125	$200,000–$325,000
Townhomes/semiattached homes	1,100–2,200/102–204	$300,000–$400,000
Single-family detached courtyard homes	1,300–2,400/121–223	$350,000–$450,000
Single-family detached semicustom homes	1,500–2,800/139–260	$400,000–$600,000
Single-family detached custom homes	1,700–3,200/158–297	$500,000–$1,200,000

DEVELOPMENT SCHEDULE

Planning and sales started (West Basin)	2003
Planning started (Village)	2004 (master plan initiated with Santa Fe County)
Site purchased	2005–2011 (phased acquisition)
Construction started (West Basin)	2005
Construction started (Village)	2010 (projected)
Sales started (Village)	2010 (projected)
Phase I completed	2012 (projected)
Project completed	2022 (projected)

DEVELOPMENT TEAM

Owner/Developer
Commonweal Conservancy
Santa Fe, New Mexico
www.commonwealconservancy.org

Site Planners
Site Workshop
Seattle, Washington
www.siteworkshop.net

Civitas Urban Design & Planning, Inc.
Vancouver, Canada
www.civitasdesign.com

Civil Engineers
Magnusson Klemencic Associates
Seattle, Washington
www.mka.com

Bill Zeedyk (low-impact road design, planning)
Santa Fe, New Mexico

Architects
Trey Jordan Architecture
Santa Fe, New Mexico
www.treyjordan.com

The Miller Hull Partnership
Seattle, Washington
www.millerhull.com

Open-Space Protection/Preservation/Management
Earth Works Institute
Santa Fe, New Mexico
www.earthworks.com

Regenesis
Santa Fe, New Mexico
www.regenesisgroup.com

Dryland Solutions
Santa Fe, New Mexico
www.drylandsolutions.com

Development Advisers
Jeff Kingsbury, Greenstreet Ltd.
Denver, Colorado
www.greenstreetltd.com

Jim Heid, UrbanGreen
San Francisco, California
www.urbangreen.net

Landscape Planning
Site Workshop
Seattle, Washington
www.siteworkshop.com

Tim Blose, Native Earth Landscaping
Santa Fe, New Mexico
www.nativeearthlandscaping.com

Project Website
www.GalisteoBasinPreserve.com

Notes
1. Because the majority of the preserve is planned as protected open space and the bulk of residential development is clustered in the village, this number does not accurately reflect the actual density of residential development as planned.
2. These figures are for market-rate homesites only. Affordable lot prices are dependent on Santa Fe County predetermined product pricing and the contract structures with local nonprofit agencies involved in the construction and/or financing of each home. Workforce and affordable lot prices will range from $10,000 to $75,000. Affordable home prices are keyed to area median income (AMI) and are dependent on Santa Fe County predetermined product pricing and the contract structures with local nonprofit agencies involved in the construction and/or financing of each home. Commonweal Conservancy estimated that the average affordable and workforce home prices in the Village will range from $122,000 to $202,800.

Hidden Springs

Ada County, Idaho

> **CASE STUDY**
>
> ### Special Features
>
> - More than 1,000 acres (405 ha) of natural open space.
> - Community-supported organic farm.
> - Extensive network of sidewalks and trails that reduces dependence on the automobile.
> - Innovative, smart wastewater reclamation system that irrigates the organic farm and common areas.
> - Community programs that connect residents to the natural environment.
> - A K–7 elementary school, a village store and café, a library, a community mail center, and a local heritage museum that is on the National Register of Historic Places.
> - A total of 850 homes clustered in five neighborhoods; the original zoning would have allowed one home per 40 acres (16 ha), or roughly 45 houses.

Hidden Springs is a 1,756-acre (711-ha) master-planned community built around a 130-acre (53-ha) working farm in the Dry Creek Valley, about 20 minutes northwest of downtown Boise, Idaho. The community—which at buildout will contain 850 residential units and a mix of retail, recreational, and educational facilities—includes more than 1,000 acres (405 ha) of open space dedicated to a variety of uses, including preserved lands, hiking trails, agriculture, wetlands, and wildlife preserves, as well as landscaped greens and playing fields. The majority of the open space—more than 800 acres (324 ha)—is under conservation easement; the rest is protected by underlying zoning. In contrast to conventional subdivisions in the area, the site plan for Hidden Springs preserves environmentally and visually sensitive slopes as open space by clustering homes in a village on the valley floor or tucked within hidden side valleys, where they do not dominate the landscape. The project also features an innovative wastewater reclamation system, community-supported agriculture, an elementary school, a public library, a village store and café, and comprehensive design guidelines.

Origins

Located ten miles (16 km) northwest of Boise, Hidden Springs sits in a rural setting in the Dry Creek Valley. An agricultural area, the valley was once home to Basque farmers. For a semi-arid, high desert climate, the site is relatively well irrigated; the development gets its name from several subsurface springs located on the property. The site is bisected by Dry Creek, which is fed by melting snow from the foothills.

By the mid-1990s, the owner of the land, Grossman Company Properties, began planning to develop the site, but wanted to preserve the integrity of the land as it did so. In 1995, Jim Grossman, president of Grossman Company Properties, visited Prairie Crossing and took part in a ULI symposium on environmentally responsible development practices. "His preliminary vision for Hidden Springs was similar to what we were doing at Prairie Crossing," says Frank Martin, president of Shaw Homes, who was then Prairie Crossing's development manager. Grossman hired Shaw Homes as a development and financial consultant to help him refine his plans and shepherd the project through the entitlement phase. In 1997, Grossman hired Martin to step in as project manager, and Martin moved to Idaho to oversee development.

Aerial view of Hidden Springs, a 1,756-acre (711-ha) master-planned community northwest of Boise, Idaho.

At buildout, Hidden Springs will include 850 homes in five neighborhoods, retail space, schools, and recreational amenities. More than 1,000 acres (405 ha) of open space will be preserved.

Core Values and Guiding Principles

Hidden Springs was envisioned as a sustainable community in the design tradition of Idaho's small towns. The developers based their vision on eight principles, which guided the long-term planning and construction of the project:

- **Rural character and farming traditions.** Hidden Springs will maintain the rural traditions of the property by incorporating older outbuildings into the landscape designs where practical, and by dedicating land to appropriate agricultural and open-space uses.
- **Small-town atmosphere.** Traditional neighborhood design will serve as the foundation for Hidden Springs's small-town lifestyle.
- **Respect the natural environment.** The developers and residents will respect the natural environment.
- **Traditional home design.** The developers will encourage the design and construction of homes that are comfortable and durable, using energy and other resources efficiently and responsibly.
- **Quality of life and healthy living.** The developers have set aside, and will care for, large and diverse areas for outdoor living and recreation.
- **High educational standards.** The community will support neighborhood schools and lifelong learning opportunities.
- **Demographic diversity.** Builders will offer a variety of houses, so that people of many ages, incomes, and backgrounds can live at Hidden Springs.
- **Value and values.** The community of Hidden Springs will provide enrichment, enjoyment, and value for many generations to come.

These principles have helped ensure the continuity of the vision, despite changes in ownership, development staff, vendors, and consultants.

Hidden Springs's rural character is being preserved. Open space is maintained by the homeowners association using transfer fees from residential sales.

Master Plan

The original zoning provisions would have allowed one home per 40 acres (16 ha)—or roughly 45 homes, but a planned community ordinance adopted by the county in 1997 would have allowed Hidden Springs's developers to build up to 1,035 homes. The final site plan includes 850 homes, a number determined by the characteristics of the site and the market.

Land preservation was a primary goal from the outset. The development team studied the site to identify the land with the highest resource values for conservation. The protected land preserves wildlife habitat for pronghorn antelope, mule deer, coyotes, badgers, raptors, and other animals that make their home there. In addition to the preserved wildlife habitat, Hidden Springs includes a community-supported organic farm. Homeowners buy shares in the farm, which grows a variety of vegetables and other produce. The shares entitle the homeowners to a portion of the produce that is grown on the farm.

The developed portion of the land is divided into five distinct neighborhoods, each with its unique design theme. The diversity of housing types ranges from condominiums in the town center to custom homes on 1.5-acre (0.6-ha) lots. A network of 24 trails winds through the development, connecting amenities, neighborhoods, and foothills.

The town center, located near the community's main entrance, features a fire station, preschool, library, and a mixed-use building that houses a small convenience store, a café, business offices, and a community mail center. Set around a traditional village green, the town center serves as a gathering place for community activities. To further encourage community interaction and a sense of community, Hidden Springs does not have postal delivery. This forces residents to visit the town center daily to get their mail and thereby provides an opportunity for people to meet and get to know their neighbors. Other community amenities include parks, playing fields, tennis courts, two swimming pools, a clubhouse, an elementary school, and a community barn where events such as weddings and parties are held throughout the year.

Architecture and Building

The homes at Hidden Springs emphasize resource efficiency, four-sided architecture, and authentic design, with variation in size and price to foster a diverse community. The architecture

The community is built around a 130-acre (53-ha) working farm.

uses a variety of traditional styles on fully landscaped parcels to enhance neighborhood streetscapes. A design review board oversees the implementation of strong architectural and landscape guidelines. Massing, architectural authenticity and consistency, building height, exterior colors, roof pitch, and how a home is sited on its lot are some of the topics reviewed. The guidelines include detailed illustrations showing encouraged and discouraged design solutions.

Green building guidelines are also in place. In the first phase, the developers partnered with local builders to set the stage for high-quality design and model energy-efficient construction practices. The development team encouraged builders to participate in the U.S. Department of Energy's Building America Initiative or the U.S. Environmental Protection Agency's Energy Star program. "This was initially tough going," says Martin. "We built the first 25 homes to get the development going, and all of these complied with these programs, but we were not able to convince other builders to do so. They didn't see any value—they felt they could sell the homes regardless." In the sixth phase of the seven-phase project, the developers mandated that all homes meet Energy Star requirements. Martin says he wished they had been able to do this earlier.

Ongoing Stewardship Activities

The Hidden Springs Open Space Council, a group of resident volunteers, organizes a variety of stewardship and education programs and publishes a monthly newsletter, *Habitat Happenings*, which features articles on wildlife sightings in the community and educational programs on wildlife, conservation, and environmental stewardship.

As houses and lots are sold and resold, a transfer fee of 0.25 percent of the sales price funds trail improvements, landscape restoration, wetland and open-space enhancements, and educational programming. In fall 2008, the development team turned over the homeowners association—the Hidden Springs Town Association—to the residents and included approximately $600,000 in transfer fee funds to support the management of the community's open space. The association employs a town manager who implements the open-space plan and oversees related programs.

Going Green

One of Hidden Springs's early challenges resulted from its distance from municipal sewer services. Average annual rainfall of just 12 inches (31 cm) posed an additional challenge for the development team. To help address these problems, the development team

A town center is located near the main entrance and includes a fire station, a preschool, a library, offices, and convenience retail.

built a sustainable wastewater reclamation system that recycles Hidden Springs wastewater through a two-step process. The wastewater travels from each neighborhood to a series of ponds, where it undergoes intensive aeration and natural filtration. The treated water then is pumped out to irrigate farm fields and common areas and returned to the aquifer.

Another resource-saving effort is the community's traffic management plan, which was designed to encourage residents to walk or bike rather than drive within the development. The plan carefully ensures pedestrian access to all of the community's amenities, including the town center, library, and elementary school.

Financing

Hidden Springs initially was developed as a partnership between an entity of the Carlyle Group of Washington, D.C., and an entity of Grossman Company Properties of Phoenix, Arizona. Carlyle Realty contributed the initial equity, while Grossman contributed the land, which it had owned for many years. The development performed below expectations during the early phases, however, which led both entities to exit the partnership in 2001.

The current owner, Developers of Hidden Springs LLC, an entity of Minneapolis-based GMAC ResCap, turned the financial situation around. With lessons learned, creative thinking, and some help from the market, Hidden Springs grew from less than 1 percent area market share in 2002 to more than 7 percent in 2006, while attaining an average home sales price 37 percent above the area average. From 2007 to 2008, as the area market fell 35 percent, Hidden Springs commanded a 4 percent market share at an average sales price 61 percent above the local market price. By the end of 2008, Hidden Springs had generated pretax profit of $2.8 million plus $3.8 million in development and asset management fees, after recovering $6.8 million in loss reserves. The developer expects the sale of remaining assets to net additional profits in 2009.

The Boise market has seen an influx of investors in recent years. To facilitate community building, Hidden Springs has prohibited builders from knowingly selling to investors. In addition, each home must be started within six months of the lot closing and completed within 12 months. If construction does not commence within this time frame, the community's speculation-discouraging buy-back provision kicks in.

Marketing and Sales

Hidden Springs was developed in seven phases. Martin emphasizes that phased development can help keep cash flowing in a fragmented market like Boise.

An early effort to position the community as a latter-day Mayberry failed because consumers perceived the marketing effort to be contrived. A more authentic and sophisticated marketing strategy subsequently was put into place. The current creative pitch is "The Antidote to Anywhere, USA," which contrasts the community's unconventional design and features with the rest of the relatively undifferentiated Boise market.

To ensure a higher degree of professionalism and control of on-site sales and marketing, the developer initially established an in-house brokerage entity dedicated to Hidden Springs properties. This action was counter to the local trend of developers and builders using established real estate offices to sell new homes. The initial result was confusion, skepticism, and resistance from the brokerage community, which adversely affected sales rates in a market that has a high degree of broker co-op sales. After the developer listed Hidden Springs with a well-established local brokerage, co-op sales quickly aligned with the market.

The initial product offering at Hidden Springs was relatively limited and was targeted primarily to families with

Lifelong learning opportunities are among the community's core values. Hidden Springs Charter School is one of the educational facilities.

school-age children. The pricing was also narrow, competing at the top of the Boise market. The marketing program later was expanded to include one- and two-person households. Although the majority of residents are middle to high income, the more affordable units on smaller lots near the pool and clubhouse have helped diversify the product types and buyers. Today, Hidden Springs is an intergenerational community with more diversity than most other communities in the area. More than half of the buyers have come from outside Idaho, compared to about one-quarter of those in other new-home developments.

The Hidden Springs website has proven to be the community's most effective marketing tool. Special events also have helped attract potential buyers. A targeted program of events attracts people to Hidden Springs and allows them to experience the benefits of living in a community with trails and natural amenities. Hidden Springs also has used more traditional marketing tools, such as newspaper, magazine, TV, and radio advertisements. Sponsorship announcements on the local National Public Radio station were used to reach the psychographic and demographic profile of targeted buyers.

The community's location was another challenge in early phases of the development program. During the first phases, potential buyers said they believed the community was too far from Boise. New development soon sprawled to bedroom communities west of Boise, however, and since then Hidden Springs has enjoyed the

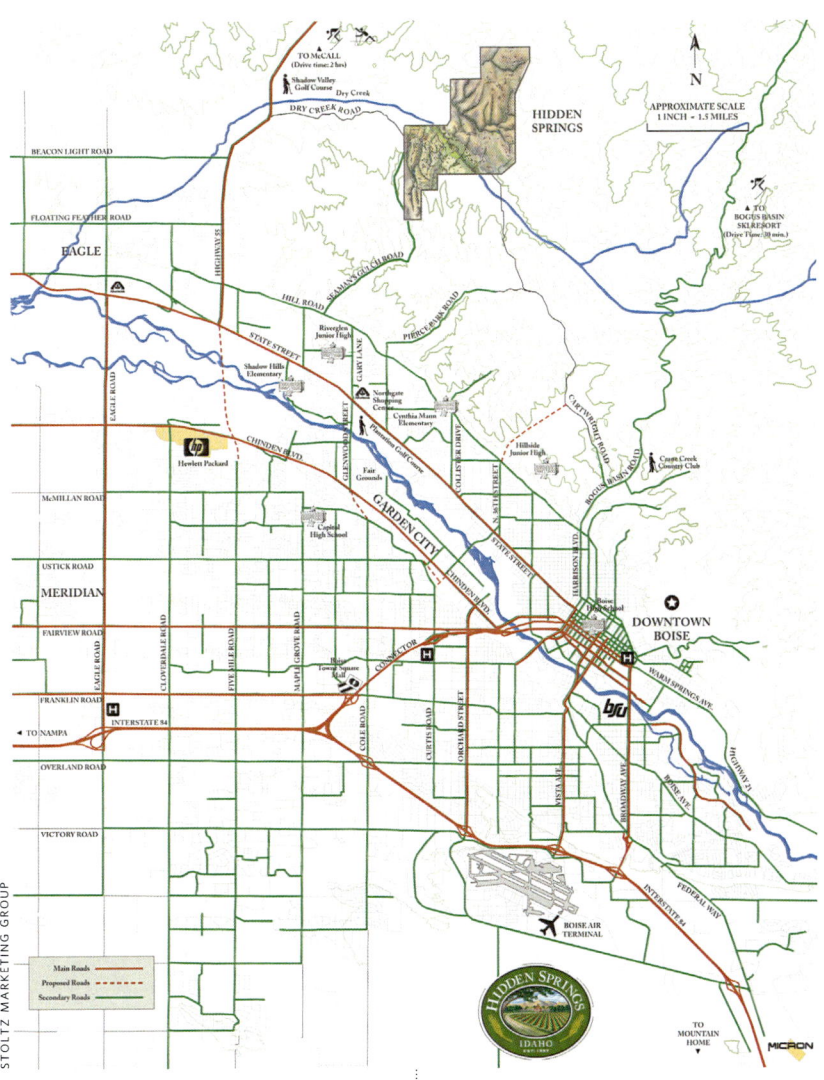

Location map.

Master plan.

advantage of being "close in." Later phases also benefited from strong word of mouth. Community-building events and programs helped to differentiate the development and build community loyalty. This translated into referrals for new lots coming on the market.

Despite the nationwide cooling of the real estate market in 2006, Hidden Springs posted its second-highest single-year home sales in its eight-year history that year: 163 homes were sold in 2006, compared to 192 in 2005 and 112 in 2004. Current lot pricing ranges from $80,000 to $315,000, and unit prices range from $335,500 to more than $1 million, selling at a premium in the market. By fall 2009, all 850 lots had been sold and the project was complete. A comparison of Hidden Springs's absorption rates and prices per square foot to other communities in the area validates the developer's belief that people are willing to pay more for a community that includes trails and preserved open space.

Challenges and Lessons Learned

The novelty of the community posed several challenges throughout the development process. Because Ada County did not have a master-planned community ordinance in place, the entitlement process took two years. In 1997, Hidden Springs became the first community approved under the Ada County Planned Community Ordinance, the first of its kind to be adopted by an Idaho jurisdiction. The ordinance allows for the development of new communities under the guidance of a specific plan based on smart growth principles.

The lack of similar master-planned developments in the area set the stage for Hidden Springs to be a cutting-edge community. However, the innovative land planning, architecture, and premium pricing initially proved to be ahead of the market. Early phases performed in line with the market, given the relatively narrow product offering and price point. The pro forma, however, required a greater sales velocity to ensure the project's solvency, because of the significant upfront development costs. The rural location presented several development challenges, including a lack of infrastructure and paved access roads, which increased development costs.

Hidden Springs also was the first community in Idaho to impose a transfer fee on home sales and resales. At Prairie Crossing, the transfer fee was set at 0.5 percent. "The concept of a transfer fee was new, and I was reluctant to go that high," says Martin. The developers instead imposed a 0.25 percent transfer fee—a decision Martin regrets. "We could have imposed a 0.5 percent fee without losing business," he says. "It is an expensive process to program and maintain open space at that scale. Hidden Springs relies upon sales in terms of money coming in." Martin also wishes he could have done more to preserve open space beyond the boundaries of Hidden Springs, as was done at Prairie Crossing, but the idea met with too much resistance from the community.

Small homebuilders dominate the Boise market. The Hidden Springs builder program struggled initially, as most local contractors were reluctant to abandon their existing house plans in favor of investing in redesigns to fit the vision of the community. The developer had to educate builders about the merits of green construction practices and siting homes in an alley-loaded configuration. Over time, however, the community has proven to be highly desirable and profitable for several local builders.

Hidden Springs also received a lot of attention from its own residents and those in the adjacent community. When the development team proposed reducing the farmstead from 100 to 30 acres (41 to 12 ha) to accommodate a shift to higher-density development on the valley floor in response to market demands, it was met with strong resistance from some Hidden Springs residents. Throughout the planning and construction phases, a set of guiding principles helped align all stakeholders with the community vision. In addition, the developers emphasize the importance of establishing a clear ownership structure, management control, and decision-making process to ensure empowerment and accountability.

The development team cites several reasons for Hidden Springs's ultimate success. Foremost is the project's ability to differentiate itself from other new developments in the area, most of which are single-product subdivisions. By conserving open space, Hidden Springs has been able to capitalize on its rural setting and the beauty of its surroundings. The community's unique architecture, sense of community, and overall sensitivity to the land are also key selling points.

"Open space can be part of the palette of community-building programs that engage residents and connect them with each other and the natural environment," says Martin. "Prairie Crossing and Hidden Springs draw together like-minded folks who care about the community. This enhances the sense of community—a sense of community that people want to be part of."

HIDDEN SPRINGS

LAND USE INFORMATION

Site area	1,756 ac/711 ha
Number of residential units	850 (830 single-family and 20 multifamily units)
Gross residential density (units per acre/ha)	0.48/1.19
Average net density (per acre/ha)	1.41/3.48

LAND USE PLAN

	Acres/ Hectares	Percentage of Site
Residential	594/240	34
Roads	91/37	5
Developed open space (parks, common areas)	42/17	2
Undeveloped open space (natural open space)	1,005/407	57
Town center/mixed-use/ school	17/7	1
Sewer and power facilities	7/3	<1
Total	**1,756/711**	**100**

RESIDENTIAL INFORMATION

Unit Type	Unit Size (sq ft/m²)	Range of Initial Sales Prices
Cottage	1,600/149	$170,000s
School Ridge	1,800–2,200/167–156	$170,000–$220,000
Village	2,200–2,600/204–242	$240,000–$270,000
Foothills	2,400–3,000/223–279	$265,000–$300,000
Cottonwood	1,650–2,700/153–251	$335,000–$525,000
Maple	2,200–3,700/204–344	$435,000–$620,000
Aspen	2,600–4,000/242–372	$580,000–$689,000
Marketplace	1,835–2,420/171–225	$300,000s
Custom	3,000–6,000/223–557	$800,000–$1,000,000

DEVELOPMENT COST INFORMATION

Site Acquisition Cost	**$8,750,000**

Site Improvement Costs

Excavation/grading	$9,425,000
Sewer/water/drainage	10,300,000
Paving/curbs/sidewalks	4,920,000
Landscaping/irrigation	2,810,000
Telecom/power	1,700,000
	$29,155,000

Construction Costs

Office and retail	$1,400,000
Amenities	3,200,000
Fire station	600,000
	$5,200,000

Soft Costs

Architecture/engineering	$3,180,000
Project management	4,800,000
Marketing and sales	5,900,000
Legal/accounting	1,015,000
Taxes/insurance	1,500,000
Town association	500,000
Construction interest and fees	3,800,000
Licenses, bonds, permits	460,000
	$21,155,000
Total Development Cost	**$64,260,000**

DEVELOPMENT SCHEDULE

Planning started	January 1995
Site purchased	February 1997
Construction started	November 1997
Sales started	September 1998
Project completion	December 2009

DEVELOPMENT TEAM

Owner
Developers of Hidden Springs LLC, an entity of GMAC ResCap
Minneapolis, Minnesota

Developer
Frank Martin, Martin Community Development LLC
Boise, Idaho
www.hiddensprings.com

Site Planner
Hart Howerton
San Francisco, California
www.harthowerton.com

Architects
Mithun Partners, Inc.
Seattle, Washington
www.mithun.com

Nagle Hartray Danker Kagan McKay Penney Architects Ltd.
Chicago, Illinois
www.nhdkmp.com

Glancey-Rockwell & Associates
Boise, Idaho
www.glanceyrockwell.com

Other Key Team Members

Legal
Givens Pursley LLP
Boise, Idaho
www.givenspursley.com

Engineering
RiveRidge Engineering
Boise, Idaho
www.rvrdg.com

Marketing
Stoltz Marketing Group
Boise, Idaho
www.stoltzgroup.com

Group One, Inc.
Eagle Idaho
www.groupone.com

Project Website
www.hiddensprings.com

Homestead Preserve

Bath County, Virginia

CASE STUDY

Special Features

- 10,185 acres (4,122 ha) under conservation easement with the Nature Conservancy and the Virginia Outdoors Foundation.
- Homesites hand-selected to protect the integrity of the landscape.
- Green orientation and building principles, including EarthCraft-certified homes.
- Award-winning restoration and reuse of the Old Dairy Barn, a community icon.
- Membership in the historic Homestead resort's golf and tennis club, as well as access to its other world-class amenities.
- At buildout, a maximum of 450 homesites disturbing less than 300 acres (121 ha) in seven neighborhoods.
- A clear commitment to preserving the best of the land, leading to support from the local government and neighbors.

Homestead Preserve is a conservation-based community located adjacent to the historic, world-class Homestead resort, in a rural area between Warm Springs and Hot Springs, Virginia, surrounded by the Allegheny Mountains. The community design incorporates green building principles and capitalizes on Homestead Preserve's unique location adjacent to the resort and the George Washington National Forest.

Immediately upon acquiring the 11,561 acres (4,679 ha) surrounding the Homestead Resort, the developer, Celebration Associates, sold 9,250 acres (3,744 ha) to the Nature Conservancy, which christened this natural area the Warm Springs Mountain Preserve. This is one of the largest privately owned and managed natural areas in Virginia. The critical forest habitat contains three rare plants, eight rare invertebrates, and three rare natural communities, including a globally rare montane pine barren. The developer later donated a conservation easement on another 950 acres (385 ha) to the Virginia Outdoors Foundation, a state-chartered land trust. Much of the remaining acreage also will remain as open space, since the site design clusters a maximum of 450 homes in seven neighborhoods. Homesites are hand-selected to accommodate the landscape and to maximize views and the protection of natural features. The community's primary market is affluent second-home buyers who benefit from Homestead Preserve's many amenities, including membership in the Homestead resort's golf and tennis club.

Origins

The Homestead was founded in 1766 as an inn with hot mineral spring–fed spas and soon became known as one of the country's finest resorts. For more than two centuries, the Homestead has hosted some of the nation's wealthiest and most influential citizens. Its guests have included 23 U.S. presidents—beginning with George Washington, who once owned portions of the 3,000 acres (1,214 ha) of land on which the resort sits. Today, the resort offers vacationers three championship golf courses, snow skiing, a shooting club, a tennis club with six courts, a large pool complex, a full-service spa, shops, and restaurants, as well as fishing, horseback riding, and falconry—all amidst the scenic rural beauty of Bath County, Virginia.

Surrounding the Homestead resort are 15,000 acres (6,071 ha) of land that initially had been acquired by the Virginia Hot Springs Company, a public firm funded by J.P. Morgan, during the late 1800s and early 1900s. For many years, resort visitors have used the 90 miles (145 km) of trails crisscrossing

The Homestead, a world-class hotel and resort, was founded in 1766 as an inn.

this land. Robert E. Lee once said of the surrounding countryside: "The views are magnificent, the valleys so beautiful, the scenery so peaceful."[1] When Celebration Associates developers Charles Adams and Don Killoren came upon this land in the late 1990s, they agreed with Lee's assessment. They knew they had found something special.

The Inspiration

Adams and Killoren had worked for the Walt Disney Company, where they oversaw its community development efforts in Celebration, Florida. In 1997, they left Disney to form their own company, Celebration Associates. Although Disney was their first client, Celebration Associates soon moved on to work in North and South Carolina. Adams and Killoren committed themselves and their company to ensuring the character and quality of the buildings and landscapes within each of their communities.

In the mid-1990s, Adams moved his family from Florida to North Carolina. He was attracted by the rolling terrain and viewsheds of the Southeast, as well as by the lifestyle and educational opportunities the state's universities would offer his children. But he soon realized that the land was changing. "After we got there," says Adams, "we saw the erosion of the very landscape that had drawn us there. And we saw that one of the main problems was that conventional development gobbled up the countryside." Adams and Killoren thought there must be a better way to develop. "We asked ourselves: Is there a way to build homes and not sell the family farm?"

Celebration Associates hired land development consultant Todd Olsen to do primary research and to seek out precedents. What Adams and Killoren found was that although some examples of conservation communities—such as Prairie Crossing—existed, these developments typically were one-off deals. Through their involvement with the Urban Land Institute, they discovered one person who was replicating the conservation development model on a broader scale: Robert Baldwin, Sr., who, as president of Qroe Preservation Development LLC, had developed several conservation communities in New England. Adams met with Baldwin and toured some of his projects. Baldwin explained how he was handpicking lots and working with the farmers who owned the land to enable them to sell part of their land while continuing to farm the rest. "The relationship quickly blossomed," says Adams. "I immediately understood Mr. Baldwin's approach."

Adams established a division of Celebration Associates, which he called American Farm Estates, to look into replicating Baldwin's model in the Charlotte and Chapel Hill, North Carolina, areas. He found that the price of properties in the suburbs close to Charlotte or Chapel Hill would require a much higher density than he wanted. Even with clustered development, the economies of scale were tough to meet in these markets. He also knew that he needed a fairly sizable piece of property so the houses could be tucked into the countryside.

In 1999, Adams met the principals of ClubCorp, which owned several resort properties, including the 3,000-acre (1,214-ha) site on which the Homestead sits. ClubCorp sought to buy the Virginia Hot Springs Company, which owned 11,561 acres (4,679 ha) surrounding the resort, and courted Celebration Associates as a potential development partner. When the ClubCorp deal fell through, Adams and Killoren set about purchasing the Virginia Hot Springs Company themselves to acquire this unique parcel of land.

Acquisition

The purchase was more complicated than an outright land purchase, but Adams and Killoren believed the land was special enough to warrant the extra effort. It required purchasing 580,000 shares from shareholders around the country and spinning off the assets that Adams and Killoren

Homestead Preserve is surrounded by a 9,250-acre (3,744-ha) nature preserve owned and managed by the Nature Conservancy.

did not want. The developers formed a new entity, Virginia Hot Springs Land Company, and worked with lawyers and accountants to make the purchase happen. "We met with divisions and departments of the law and public accounting firms that I didn't even know existed," says Adams.

Acquiring a public company was a risky venture. Fortunately, says Adams, Celebration Associates's equity partner—Springs Company—was not a typical real estate investment company; it had experience owning many other types of firms. Adams and Killoren also were fortunate that there was other interest in the land. The Nature Conservancy sought to acquire a portion of the land because of its inherent ecological value.

The Nature Conservancy performed an analysis to determine which land was most suitable for conservation, based primarily on its ecology and biodiversity. "There couldn't have been a better marriage," says Adams. "They were interested in untouched land. They were excited about the wetlands on top of the mountains where the water stood in saucerlike pools. They were not as interested in the land in the valley that had been cleared for pasture and was better suited for development."

On the same day Adams and Killoren bought the Virginia Hot Springs Company, they sold 9,250 acres (3,744 ha) to the Nature Conservancy for the below-market price of $6 million. In addition to the tax benefits that the sale offered to investors, the $6 million in cash helped lower the cost basis on the remaining property.

Decisions about the land remained, however. ClubCorp, the owners of Homestead Resort, wanted to make sure that its guests could continue to use the trails on the surrounding conservation land, while Adams and Killoren wanted to make sure that the new homeowners also would have access to the land. The three parties with interest in the land formed a tri-party agreement spelling out issues involving the maintenance of and liabilities on the land. "I never saw as many documents lined up on a table as on the day we closed," says Adams.

In October 2003, Celebration Associates and Crosland—a diversified, Charlotte, North Carolina–based real estate firm—formed an investment company, Warm Springs Investment Company LLC, to purchase 2,222 acres (899 ha) from Virginia Hot Springs Land Company. Additional land was added to the holdings through assemblage, taking the project acreage to 2,300 acres (931 ha). Warm Springs Investment Company LLC later sold member interests through a private placement offering to 35 founder investors.

Land Conservation and Preservation

Adams and Killoren set about evaluating the 2,300 acres (931 ha) under intense scrutiny from the surrounding community. They used several overlays to map the land and decide how it should be used. Under existing county zoning regulations, the parcel could have supported 2,700 homes, but Adams and Killoren believed such a high density would dramatically degrade the character of the landscape and undermine their marketing approach. At the same time, the mapping analysis identified an additional 935-acre (378-ha) parcel that the developers believed should be preserved. They approached the Nature Conservancy, which indicated that it was not interested in this parcel but suggested several other options. In 2004, the Virginia Outdoors Foundation, a state-chartered land trust, accepted the donation of a conservation easement on this property.

Adams and Killoren emphasize the importance of their land preservation efforts in facilitating the development of the rest of the property. "The fact that over 10,000 acres of the initial parcel would never be developed was a huge selling point, not only for those who bought from us but also for state and local legislators," says Adams. "They were very leery of outsiders, and our decision to preserve the land absolutely helped us as we got into this process."

To further support local preservation initiatives, the development team established a mechanism whereby a portion of every property sale at Homestead Preserve (2 percent of land sales and 1 percent of transfer fees) goes to the Virginia Hot Springs Preservation Trust. To date, the trust has raised more than $1 million to be used for historic preservation and restoration, environmental conservation and stewardship, agricultural cultivation, and other worthwhile efforts aimed at preserving the rich heritage of the region.

Celebration Associates also hired several valuation experts to determine the land's potential and the value of the conservation easements. This was not an easy process. As Adams says, "It is hard to find a

The historic dairy barn was converted into a community center, recreational facility, and swimming complex.

precedent for land associated with a 200-year-old resort where 23 presidents had slept."

The conservation easements provided $17.5 million in federal tax benefits. The development team could not take advantage of all of these benefits, so they passed 30 percent of them on to 35 founder investors. In addition to the $150,000 each founder received from the portion of the federal charitable deduction, the founders benefited from Virginia state income tax credits.

Site Plan and Neighborhoods

Adams and Killoren set about developing the site plan for the remaining parcel. Throughout the site planning process, the developers sought to protect the integrity of the landscape and preserve its history. "There's the rich history of the hotel, the springs, the physical beauty of the place. There's so much that makes it attractive," Adams says. "We want to make sure that when we ultimately lay in the pieces—the homes, the redevelopment of the village—we do so in a way that they all feel comfortable in this setting, like they're at home."[2]

Rather than establishing a grid of roads and then blocking off the lots of houses, the development team hand-selected each lot, identifying the best locations for homes based on the characteristics of the landscape. The team then figured out how to provide access to these sites, laying the roads where they would have the least impact on the landscape. This approach resulted in a site plan in which the homes and infrastructure lay lightly on the land. At buildout, a maximum of 450 homesites will disturb less than 300 acres (121 ha). The homesites will be clustered in seven neighborhoods, each of which takes its name from the agrarian function the land once served.

Each of the first four neighborhoods—Sheep Meadow, the Old Dairy, Delafield Rise, and Warm Springs Farm—is distinguished by its own unique characteristics:

- The Sheep Meadow neighborhood, which was the first to be built, includes 103 homesites. Some are situated to offer residents spectacular views of the nearby mountains; others create a "home in the woods" feeling and provide visual access to the Homestead and the Old Course, a golf course at the resort that was built in 1892.

As of the end of 2009, 95 of the 103 homesites had sold.

- In the Old Dairy neighborhood, the land has been divided into 39 parcels ranging in size from one-half acre to ten acres (0.2 to 4 ha). The historic dairy barn was restored as a community and recreation center for homeowners. It houses a swimming pool, a fitness center, a spa, a children's activity center, a retail market, foundation offices, and the property owners association.
- The Delafield Rise neighborhood features 112 homesites. Its homes will reflect the architectural heritage of the Virginia Highlands. Most sites provide wooded settings with Homestead, meadow, or mountain views.
- The homesites in the Warm Springs Farm neighborhood tend to be a bit larger, ranging in size from 1.9 to 13 acres (0.8 to 5 ha).

To further ensure that viewsheds and natural features of the landscape would be protected, the developers delineated proposed development zones (PDZs) for each site that specify where on the lot the home should be situated. Like the lot sizes, PDZs vary in size to accommodate the natural landscape, but they range from 6,500 to 30,000 square feet (604 to 2,787 m²), depending on lot size. Within each PDZ there is a maximum building and grading envelope (BGE) that limits land disturbance to between 8,000 and 15,000 square feet (743 and 1,394 m²). The PDZ allows flexibility of home placement, while the BGE minimizes land disturbance. The homeowners association and an architectural review board enforce the PDZs, BGEs, and other design principles.

Architecture and Green Building

Complementing the site plan is a set of carefully crafted design guidelines that consider and reinforce the area's architectural and design heritage while accommodating a "green" community. The design team painstakingly researched the characteristics of the Virginia Highlands to develop architectural standards that would adhere to the traditions of the region. These standards dictate that the houses will be designed following one of four traditional architectural vocabularies: Highlands Classical, Highlands Farmhouse, English Romantic, and Highlands Arts and

EarthCraft Homes

The EarthCraft House program is a voluntary green building program that serves as a blueprint for healthy, comfortable homes that reduce utility bills and protect the environment. The program was created in 1999 as a partnership between the Greater Atlanta Home Builders Association and Southface Energy Institute. It became a statewide program in Virginia in 2005.

All EarthCraft builders must be trained and certified, and all EarthCraft homes must undergo a formal evaluation and blower door test by a third party in order to receive EarthCraft designation. EarthCraft House technical guidelines often exceed the minimum requirements of a product manufacturer, installer, or building code. The guidelines are flexible enough to allow for a variety of approaches to environmental construction. EarthCraft gives homebuilders great flexibility by providing a point system. Builders can earn the necessary points by choosing the measures most practical for their specific homes.

EarthCraft promotes diligent air sealing of the building envelope and its mechanical systems, resulting in homes that are more energy efficient, less costly to maintain, and more durable overall. EarthCraft also encourages the use of resource-efficient materials, including concrete with fly ash, cellulose insulation, and carpeting that contains recycled materials. In addition, EarthCraft encourages water conservation measures and the use of Energy Star–rated appliances.

All the homes at Homestead Preserve meet EarthCraft House green building standards.

Crafts. Homestead Preserve's pattern book provides a useful resource for owners, architects, landscape architects, and builders, giving everyone a sense of the elements important to the design of sites and houses. The pattern book guides each home's style choices, proportions, and architectural details. The guidelines and illustrative examples presented in the book provide the foundation for ensuring the character and quality of buildings and landscapes within Homestead Preserve. These patterns reinforce a sense of place that is unique and distinctive.

A guild of preferred architects and builders ensures the quality and integrity of the homes at Homestead Preserve. Each of these architects and builders is dedicated to green building principles and practices. Many Homestead Preserve homes feature green construction components, including geothermal heating and cooling systems, use of Forest Stewardship Council–certified lumber, and strict construction guidelines for building materials and recycling. In addition, all the homes are equipped with high-efficiency, Energy Star–rated appliances. In 2008, Homestead Preserve became the first community in the Allegheny Highlands to certify a home under the EarthCraft House program, a formal green building certification program designed to promote the construction of homes that use less energy, make use of sustainable building materials, and provide a healthy living environment for residents. "We decided to become part of the EarthCraft Virginia program because its green building tenets complemented our long-term commitment to the landscape of the Allegheny Highlands," says Killoren. "Most of our owners are already environmentally committed individuals. That's why they chose to buy at our conservation community in the first place. We wanted to provide them the additional opportunity to not only live in a community committed to landscape stewardship but also committed to building in ways that decrease our environmental footprint."

Other aspects of the community have been carefully designed to provide an old-world feel with modern conveniences—a fact that is not lost on residents. "We felt strongly about the developers' commitment to the environment," says Tom Regnell, who built an EarthCraft-certified home at Homestead Preserve for himself and his wife. He also appreciated the architectural integrity of the development. "For us, that's very important. The buildings look like they've always been here. Even the creek crossings—

most people would do them in concrete," he adds. "Here they made them out of real stone."

Building Restoration and Renovation

The Homestead resort originally was designed to be completely self-sufficient. The Old Dairy Barn provided resort guests with fresh milk, butter, cheeses, and other dairy products. Built in 1928, the barn had become a Bath County icon. When the operation was abandoned in the 1970s, the Old Dairy fell into disrepair.

The developers of Homestead Preserve saw the Old Dairy Barn as an opportunity to help link the new development with the land's agrarian past and decided to restore it rather than tear it down. In May 2005, restoration of the barn began. It took almost two years and $6 million to restore and renovate the barn as a 20,000-square-foot (1,858-m^2) community center for Homestead Preserve. The building now houses an Olympic-size swimming pool, a spa, a fitness center, meeting rooms, and other amenities. The Old Dairy has since been listed in the National Register of Historic Places and named a Virginia Historic Landmark, ensuring its preservation for generations to come. In March 2008, it received the Outstanding Adaptive Use Award from the Virginia Department of Antiquities. The Old Dairy also includes the preserved Milk House, renovated as a one-stop convenience market, offering fresh food items and information on the development. Plans are underway to provide space for a small farmers market at which local farmers can sell their goods and produce.

Marketing and Sales

Homesites, which range in size from one-half acre to 13 acres (0.2 to 5 ha), are priced from $300,000 to more than $1 million; homes are priced from $750,000 to $3 million. The developers have used many of the same tools as those at more traditional developments, including a sales launch model in which they release roughly 50 properties at a time. In addition, they have a story center in Hot Springs where potential clients can learn more about the development and available properties.

Central to the marketing efforts is the Homestead resort. "The fact that the existing resort came with so many amenities has been key to our success," says Killoren. "Target market–wise, the Homestead lined

Land preservation is a key feature at Homestead Preserve.

up perfectly with what we were trying to do with Homestead Preserve." The developers have leveraged the resort's loyal guest base for sales leads and provided sales information at the resort itself. Not surprisingly, most of the interest has been regional in scope, with many buyers coming from Virginia, North Carolina, and Maryland.

The first lots went on the market in 2005. Sales during the first couple of years were brisk, but tapered off in 2007 and 2008. Adams and Killoren believe this is due primarily to the downturn in the real estate market, which has hurt the market for high-end vacation homes. As of January 2010, 159 homesites have been sold and 26 houses have been built. In the Sheep Meadow neighborhood—the first to be built—95 of the 187 lots have sold. In addition, the developers believe that the sale of the Homestead resort's parent company, ClubCorp, in December 2006, may have had an impact on Homestead Preserve's sales.

Challenges and Lessons Learned

Many of the challenges the developers faced were related to the rural nature of the setting. Bath County—532 square miles (137,788 ha) in size—has no traffic lights and a population of roughly 4,800 people. "Coming back to a small community was an eye-opening experience," says Adams. "In some ways, it was refreshing, but in others it was challenging." The politics of a small community like Bath County "were even more intense," he says.

In addition, the developers were challenged in the early stages by the county's lack of a proactive approach to planning and its relative inexperience with large-scale development. "This is not a community that had a true comprehensive plan or up-to-date zoning ordinances," says Adams. "Whatever it had was just sitting on a shelf—designed to meet the requirements of the state."

The development team says the project's scale and complexity initially were overwhelming for the county's elected officials and small staff. For example, the county lacked clear rules for how its volunteer firefighters would sign off on plans or how decisions would be made about utilities. "We couldn't get a commitment that we would have enough water or sewer," says Adams. "The county had always offered these on a first-come, first-served basis, and they were reluctant to change." The development proved to be an education for the county and its officials regarding the benefits and use of impact fees, connection fees, and the like, and Adams and Killoren

The Celebration Associates Approach and Philosophy

We do not take words like integrity, perseverance, stewardship, loyalty, legacy, and excellence lightly. These core values infuse our every action and interaction. They inform not just the way we approach our projects, but also the partnerships we make, the relationships we build, and the way we view the world.

Our cornerstone philosophy—or in technological terms, our "community software"—is defined by access to and a balance of:

Place: a sense of place, a spirit and culture that immediately feel familiar and comfortable.
Health: a true sense of well being and health throughout the community.
Education: more than just schools and academies, education is a commitment to fostering lifelong learning for every resident.
Technology: state-of-the-art communications technology as an avenue to build and enhance local and global relationships.
Community: connected and engaged communities that create memories, are supportive, and nurture relationships through foundations, services, and more.

Source: Celebration Associates website, http://www.celebrationassociates.com/company/approach_philosophy.html.

Site plan.

say they have since become more proactive about involving elected officials and educating staff on the various aspects of development.

Adams and Killoren emphasize that they did not run into significant local opposition about developing the land, however. "There was less interference from neighbors and less not-in-my-backyard attitude than you typically find in such areas," says Adams. They credit the lack of opposition to the fact that they demonstrated a clear commitment to preserving the best the land had to offer through the bargain sale of most of the property to the Nature Conservancy and an easement on the vast majority of the rest. "We showed that we fully intended to be good stewards of the land," explains Killoren.

Other challenges relate to the land development costs. Because of the way the homesites were identified and because of the distance between homes—which is larger than in a typical clustered development—the infrastructure costs on a per-lot basis were higher than in many comparable developments. There are more linear feet of road per homesite, for instance. "The per-acre/per-lot development cost is not a useful tool," says Killoren. "We had to find other ways to assess value." Fortunately, the market has accepted higher costs at Homestead Preserve, as people are attracted to the community's high-end amenities and quality of life.

Adams and Killoren emphasize that the approach they have taken at Homestead Preserve is not appropriate for every site and every location. This approach to conservation-based development requires large landholdings that can be purchased at a reasonable price. The land needs to be at the right point on the urban-to-rural continuum—close enough to an urban center to make the land valuable and to attract enough qualified buyers while far enough out to make the land affordable for this type of development. Regardless of where the parcel is located, the market has to be able to support the higher costs that result from less-dense development. The developers say they benefited greatly from the fact that amenities already were in place to attract high-end buyers. Offering residents membership in the Homestead resort and its golf courses, tennis club, and other facilities meant that the developers did not have to add these amenities—or incur the associated costs of building and maintaining them.

Adams and Killoren see themselves on a continuum in which each of their developments enhances conservation aspects in different ways. At Celebration, Florida, they say, the conservation and green aspects of the development are "relatively passive." They call Homestead Preserve the "first generation of conservation-based development" and have continued to put conservation at the forefront of the process in subsequent developments.

Although conservation development may not be appropriate for every site, Adams and Killoren emphasize that it can be very profitable. "We hope our communities will set an example and show that when developers emphasize preservation, they actually enhance the value of their property," says Adams. "We're not only preserving natural landscapes for future generations, we're satisfying a desire that families have to be in a place where natural heritage still has meaning."

Notes

1. Bath County, Virginia, website, http://www.bathcountyva.org/.
2. Quoted in Meredith Guinness, "There's No Place Like Homestead Preserve," *PanachePRIVEE* (Fall 2006), www.panache-mag.com/Fall_06/Features/Homestead-Preserve/HomesteadPreserve.asp.

HOMESTEAD PRESERVE

LAND USE INFORMATION

Site area	11,561 ac/4,679 ha
Open space under easement	10,626 ac/4,300 ha
Developable site area:	2,311 ac
Number of residential units	450 planned, 20 completed
Number of lots sold	159
Percentage of residential infrastructure development complete:	56%
Gross residential density	1 unit per 26.69 acres (10.80 ha)
Average net density	1 unit per 2.08 acres (0.84 ha)

LAND USE PLAN

	Acres/Hectares	Percentage of Site
Residential (disturbed)	189/76	1.6
Roads	141/57	1.2
Developed open space (parks, common areas)	56/23	0.5
Land sold to the Nature Conservancy	9,250/3,743	80.0
Undeveloped open space (natural open space)	1,921/777	16.6
Sewer and power facilities	4/1.6	0.03

RESIDENTIAL INFORMATION

Lot Type	Lot Size (ac/ha)	Range of Initial Sales Prices
	0.5–13 (0.2–5)	$300,000 to $1,100,000

Unit Type	Unit Size (sq ft/m²)	Range of Initial Sales Prices
Spec home	1,800–8,200/167–762	$750,000 to $4,000,000
Custom home	3,000–12,000/279–1,115	$750,000 to $6,500,000

DEVELOPMENT COST INFORMATION

Site Acquisition Cost	**$14,814,206**

Site Improvement Costs

Excavation/grading	$1,898,279
Sewer/water/drainage	21,273,379
Paving/curbs/sidewalks	27,006,314
Landscaping/irrigation	3,955,042
Telecom/power	2,874,892
	$57,007,906

Construction Costs (Amenities)

Community center	$6,533,919
Equestrian center	491,667
Owners lodge	1,500,000
Cottages/pavilions/other	2,743,009
	$11,268,595

Soft Costs

Architecture/engineering	$7,171,238
Project management	32,187,424
Marketing and sales	37,675,889
Legal/accounting	788,985
Taxes/insurance	1,812,746
Construction interest and fees	3,988,386
Licenses, bonds, permits	1,602,112
POA fees	3,079,857
Homestead/foundation	8,507,274
	$96,813,911
Total Development Cost	**$179,904,618**

DEVELOPMENT SCHEDULE

Planning started	March 2002
Site purchased	January 2004
Sales started	January 2005
Construction started	March 2005
Phase 1 completed	April 2008
Phase 2 completed	Dec 2008
Project completion	2021 (projected)

DEVELOPMENT TEAM

Owner
Warm Springs Investment Company LLC
Hot Springs, Virginia

Developer
Warm Springs Management Company LLC, a wholly owned affiliate of Celebration Associates and Crosland
Hot Springs, Virginia

Site Planning
Design Workshop
Asheville, North Carolina
www.designworkshop.com

Urban Design Associates–The Highland Studio
Hot Springs, Virginia
www.urbandesignassociates.com

Architects
Urban Design Associates–The Highland Studio
Hot Springs, Virginia
www.urbandesignassociates.com

Frazier & Associates
Staunton, Virginia
www.frazierassociates.com

Robert Adam Architects
London, England
www.robertadamarchitects.com

John Reagan Architects
Columbus, Ohio
www.johnreaganarchitects.com

Versaci Neumann Partners
Middleburg, Virginia
www.versacineuman.com

Civil Engineers
The Timmons Group
Richmond, Virginia
www.timmons.com

Cole, Jenst & Stone
Charlotte, North Carolina
www.colejenststone.com

Open-Space Protection/Preservation/Management
The Nature Conservancy
Arlington, Virginia
www.nature.org

Virginia Outdoors Foundation
Richmond, Virginia
www.virginiaoutdoorsfoundation.org

Virginia Hot Springs Preservation Trust
Hot Springs, Virginia
www.homesteadpreserve.com

Conservation Advisers
Benchmark Advisors
Waynesville, North Carolina
www.benchmarkadvisors.com

Playground, a division of Intrawest
Vancouver, British Columbia, Canada
www.playground.com

Permar & Associates
Charleston, South Carolina
www.permar.cc/about.html

Envisioning & Storytelling
Blythe Development Company
Charlotte, North Carolina
www.blythedevelopment.com

Project Website
www.homesteadpreserve.com

Jackson Meadow

Marine on St. Croix, Minnesota

CASE STUDY

Special Features

- Sixty residential lots clustered on just 40 acres (16 ha) of the 145-acre (59-ha) site.
- Partnership agreements with adjacent landowners that expanded the development agreement to 320 acres (130 ha) and added to the conservation lands.
- A site design focused on preserving lands of high conservation values and incorporating natural features of the landscape into the design of the residential neighborhood.
- Strict design and building guidelines that preserve the architectural integrity of the community, in keeping with the Scandinavian vernacular of the surrounding area.
- Homes situated whenever possible to capture the sun, with south-facing roofs prefabricated to accommodate photovoltaic solar panels. (The homeowners association is studying whether solar panels are architecturally compatible with existing structures.)
- Innovative stormwater and wastewater treatment techniques, including an organic wetlands septic system, that reduce runoff and pollution.

Jackson Meadow is a conservation community set in the rolling hills overlooking the St. Croix River Valley, immediately west of the historic village center of Marine on St. Croix, Minnesota. Its developers used a clustered planned unit development (PUD) strategy to site 64 homes on 40 acres (16 ha) of a 145-acre (59-ha) residential community. (In early 2009, the parcel was replatted to 60 lots, combining several of the original homesites into larger lots.) This acreage is surrounded by protected land, including 53 acres (22 ha) that the developers bought and donated to the city in fee, and 120 acres (49 ha) to which they acquired the development rights and overlaid with a conservation easement.

Consistent with conservation development site planning principles, Jackson Meadow takes its cues from the Minnesota landscape. It is organized topographically, with a series of neighborhoods set around a central public green and connected by a looping road and pedestrian corridors. Footpaths connect various parts of the development and link to a six-mile (10-ha) trail system that surrounds the community. "The idea was to give people a place to live in the country but, by clustering the homes, to leave them with a lot of pristine open space," explains developer Harold Teasdale, who lives in Jackson Meadow with his wife, Carol, the community's director of marketing.

Cobbling together a parcel with so much open space was not easy. The county had no mechanism for transfer of development rights, so Teasdale enlisted the help of adjacent landowners, who essentially became co-developers of the project by allowing their land to be included in Jackson Meadow's acreage.

Origins

Marine on St. Croix is the oldest European settlement in Minnesota; it earned its name in 1839 with the opening of its first sawmill. Located alongside the St. Croix River, Marine grew into a lumber town; rich soil attracted farmers to the surrounding hilly land. Almost all of the buildings still standing in downtown Marine were constructed during the lumber-era boom, giving it an old-world feel. The Marine on St. Croix Historic District is on the National Register of Historic Places.

Today, quaint shops attract people to Marine on St. Croix's small downtown district. Walking paths line the river, allowing visitors and the city's approximately 700 residents to enjoy fishing and leisurely strolls. Marine on St. Croix is also close to a 700-acre (283-ha) state wildlife reserve, the Rose Warner Nature Center, which offers a diversity of wildlife, native plants, and grasses that are ecologically important to the area.

Jackson Meadow is a conservation community that combines award-winning architecture with abundant green space.

In the early 1980s, Ron Jackson, a longtime resident of Marine on St. Croix, decided to sell his 145-acre (59-ha) farm and retire to Arizona. A developer agreed to purchase Jackson's land, but the sale was contingent on his obtaining development approval from the city. His site plan proposed a conventional large-lot subdivision that would have sited 32 houses on oversized lots spread uniformly across the parcel. Residents believed that the plan—with its overly wide roads and large lots—signaled the beginning of the end of their rural way of life. They worried that other farms would follow suit, breaking up the landscape and undermining its rural character. When the development was derailed, the community looked to Harold Teasdale to craft an alternative solution. Teasdale already had experience as a developer in Marine on St. Croix. Even more important, Teasdale and fellow developer Bob Durfey showed that they were willing to work with the city to address the community's concerns.

The Vision

Most of the land in the agricultural region surrounding Marine on St. Croix was zoned for five- and ten-acre (2- and 4-ha) lots. "What are you going to do with five acres?" asks Teasdale. "You can't farm it. And there's no sense of community." So he and Durfey took a different approach.

As they planned and developed Jackson Meadow, Teasdale and Durfey followed two guiding principles: to preserve the landscape and to create a sense of neighborhood and community. Their goal was to develop a community in both a physical and a social sense, creating a new village surrounded by protected open space. "Our vision was to build a neighborhood that you could visit in 20 or 50 years and have it be every bit as inviting and vital as it is today," says Teasdale.

The developers believed the best way to preserve the site's rural character and open space would be to cluster housing on one part of the parcel. At the same time, shortly before Durfey and Teasdale evaluated the land and drafted the site plan, the city passed a new ordinance designed to address the community's concerns about the loss of farmland. The new ordinance required any developer building three or more houses to use a clustered development approach that would preserve 50 percent of the land as open space. The ordinance did not specify

Footpaths connect various parts of Jackson Meadow and link to a six-mile (10-ha) trail system and open space that surrounds the community.

which lands should be preserved, but Teasdale and Durfey recognized the natural resource values of their parcel and developed a site plan that would preserve the portion of the property with the highest conservation values.

Conservation development principles were at the center of the design process. Members of the design team first identified the resources and areas they hoped to preserve, and then laid out the clustered homesites in a way that was influenced by the development patterns of small Minnesota towns and the St. Croix River Valley.

With this context in mind, the project team had several goals for the development. They wanted it to:

- Respect the sense of place by integrating local historic architecture and forms into the project's housing styles and layout;
- Have minimal impacts on the bluffs and forest;
- Protect and restore native vegetation;
- Maintain an agricultural buffer around the development;
- Provide an interconnecting system of footpaths and trails; and
- Use innovative stormwater and wastewater treatment techniques to minimize water impacts.

The resulting site plan preserves more than 70 percent of the parcel.

The developers also worked with adjacent landowners to ensure that the project's open space would connect to that of surrounding properties. In order to preserve more land, two adjacent property owners agreed to combine all of their properties into one large parcel. Two other property owners still own their entire properties, but sold their development rights to the developers of Jackson Meadow. These lands are now under conservation easements, protecting them from development in perpetuity. Another adjacent property owner sold 53 acres (22 ha) to the developers of Jackson Meadow, who then contributed this land to the city. With the assistance of a grant from the Minnesota Department of Natural Resources, this property has been developed and preserved as a city park named the Hollow. The plan for Jackson Meadow thus began with a 145-acre (59-ha) site, but a total of 320 acres (130 ha) eventually were included in the final development agreement.

A careful analysis of the landscape to determine the best locations for the open space and for the dwellings was a key element of the planning process. The developers' priorities included protecting the viewshed, as well as ecological processes and natural resources. They walked the land, identifying the areas that should be protected as common resources, such as the viewing points from which one could look over the river valley. The resulting plan protects more than 70 acres (28 ha) of mature hardwood forest and 25 acres (10 ha) of restored prairie. Adjacent parcels include roughly 120 acres (49 ha) of preserved productive farmland. The 53 acres (22 ha) donated to the city is a steeply sloped parcel that contains virgin upland prairie grasses and mature woodlands. The community's homeowners association provides most of the money and labor for restoration activities, but the Minnesota Department of Natural Resources and the St. Croix Watershed Research Station have helped with some of the restoration efforts.

Planning and Design

The design team—consisting of the landscape architect, architect, and developers—collaboratively developed the project program and design guidelines. The landscape architecture firm of Coen + Stumpf took the lead in guiding the project through plat approval and infrastructure construction.

Marine on St. Croix's character was shaped by a grid of city streets that start near the river's edge and expand outward, up the steep bluffs that rise from the river. The development team wanted to complement the character of the existing community while translating the village template into a modern community design.

After examining the original Jackson family farmstead, the design team proposed a cluster of homes along the section lines laid out by the U.S. Public Land Survey in the 1830s. This gave central organization to the overall site plan. Building on the European "open-field" model—in which a cluster of houses surrounds a meadow—lots were organized around the surrounding land's topographical features, preserving the central open space for the enjoyment of all residents. To accomplish this, the design team arranged the houses to emulate the structure of a traditional midwestern village while also connecting the built environment to the landscape. About half of the houses are situated in an old-fashioned town grid, with lot sizes averaging about one-third of an acre (0.13 ha). The other lots range from one-half to two acres (0.2 to 0.8 ha). The configuration of the community is modeled after the city of Marine on St. Croix, explains Teasdale, with the looping road symbolizing the St. Croix River.

Rather than facing a street, houses face a public walkway that covers the utility right-of-way. Streets run behind the houses, and gravel driveways connect the streets with detached garages set along back lot lines. At the center of the community, a circular park acts as a wetland filtration site and commons that also serves as a skating rink and sledding hill in winter.

Homesites are pushed back from the edge of the bluff, which preserves the views from the town and river while also enabling residents of Jackson Meadow to enjoy sweeping views over the countryside. Setting the homes away from the bluff also helps minimize runoff and soil erosion.

Shane Coen, Jackson Meadow's landscape architect, emphasizes the flexibility of this approach: "Because each new house is responding to the land, to its neighbor's house, and the client's vision, ideal placement of a home is really an evolving and wonderfully complex puzzle to be solved," he says.

Sustainability

The developers incorporated sustainability principles and practices into multiple aspects of Jackson Meadow's development. A constructed wetland septic system was designed to service the clustered homes. Building a consolidated sewage treatment system rather than individual septic systems for each house allowed a portion of the property to be developed at a higher density, so that a greater amount of open space could be preserved. The constructed wetland system also naturally removes more pollutants and bacteria than a conventional system, resulting in much cleaner water seeping into the water table.

The innovative wetland septic system first delivers wastewater to a treatment cell, which is a shallow basin lined with an impermeable membrane and pea-sized gravel. The roots of wetland plants in the pool permeate the entire gravel layer. These plants and the bacteria that live among them purify the water that enters the treatment cell. This partially purified water then flows to a wetland infiltration cell, which is similar to the treatment cell but has no synthetic liner. Additional treatment in this cell's gravel bed removes even more pollutants before the purified water seeps back into the natural water table. Because the entire process occurs underground, residents do not even notice that their water is being purified beneath the community's open-space centerpiece.

Clustering the homes also minimized the roads and other impervious surfaces required, which helps reduce the amount of stormwater runoff. A natural conveyance system that carries stormwater to open-space areas also helps mitigate stormwater impacts throughout the site. Roadside swales and an inverse crown on the roadways—rather than an expensive network of curbs and gutters—are used to move stormwater. Wetland grasses are anchored in the swales to assist in the absorption process. This method of natural filtration is ecologically sound and more efficient than standard stormwater systems. The approach also supplies water to the native greenery in the community's open-space network.

Instead of installing the wide streets typically found in many suburban communities, the development team deliberately narrowed the roads that wind through the neighborhood, slowing traffic and reducing the project's infrastructure footprint. Zoning codes dictated a 24-foot (7.3-m) minimum roadway width, but the development team progressively reduced the width from 24 feet to 18 feet (5.5 m) through the PUD process. These narrower streets require 25 percent less pavement than traditional suburban streets. Some footpaths are constructed of gravel that is compatible with the natural surroundings.

The Minnesota Land Trust helped draft the conservation easements for Jackson Meadow to meet state open-space requirements. The Minnesota Office of Environmental Assistance partially funded the wetland waste management system, construction of an observation deck, creation of interpretive signs about the project's sus-

Houses at Jackson Meadow are clustered to emulate the structure of a traditional midwestern village. The dramatic white color scheme takes its cue from Nordic farmhouses.

tainability, and the printing of informational materials to educate the public about sustainable development.

The community's trail system—which is open to the public—extends for more than five miles (8 km) and connects to downtown Marine on St. Croix. Marine's elementary school is just a ten-minute walk from Jackson Meadow along the trail system. Plans are in place to link the trail system to the nearby 3,000-acre (1,214-ha) William O'Brien State Park, which is located on the northwest corner of the city.

Architecture and Design Standards

Jackson Meadow's houses are designed to blend in with the historical architecture of the surrounding area. The community's award-winning architecture builds on the language of the regional vernacular while adding modern design elements. Architect David Salmela designed all of the homes, which feature a dramatic white color scheme that takes its cue from traditional Nordic farmhouses and Marine on St. Croix's cultural history. The local vernacular also informs the architectural detailing and building materials, which include whitewashed cedar siding, front porches, and picket fences. All of the homes must adhere to strict design guidelines that maintain the architectural integrity of the community. For instance, all siding must be cedar (or an approved material of equal quality and appearance), roofs must be metal, and only picket fences are allowed.

The design team also carefully considered the spatial arrangement of auxiliary buildings. The houses (with one architectural exception) have detached garages, which create spaces between structures that give scale to the lots and model the village form. These garages feature high gable roofs, and many are topped with a home office, artist's studio, or sauna. Unlike most subdivisions, which prohibit doghouses, tool sheds, or other outbuildings, Jackson Meadow encourages additional structures. These extra buildings help create a village template, block winter winds, and replicate the feel of a Scandinavian farm.

Common design elements include energy-efficient galvanized steel roofs and modern interiors, but Salmela custom designs each home to accommodate the homeowner's lifestyle and specific needs—and to create diversity and character within the community. "Jackson Meadow is full of simple, beautiful structures, virtually the same, yet all different," he explains.

A Sense of Community

Jackson Meadow was designed to foster the sense of an old-fashioned rural hamlet. Front porches and walking trails encourage people to get to know their neighbors. "At the beginning, we worked the land, built the trails, and created the infrastructure of the natural wetlands septic system, but what kept us going was envisioning people and children playing on the land," says Carol Teasdale. "As humans, I think we need a strong sense of community to thrive."

Social events, some sponsored by the homeowners association, further encourage a sense of community. Homeowners also help maintain the community's hiking and biking trails and volunteer with ongoing prairie and woodland restoration efforts. "We're used as an example of how to get a community to take on restoration," Teasdale says. "You really have a sense of community when people are working together to restore the land."[1]

Marketing and Sales

Harold Teasdale says initial sales were slower than he would have liked, but he was prepared to wait it out. Sales began just before September 11, 2001, a moment in history when all things predictable vanished. Since then, all but a few of the Phase

I properties have sold. Phase II also lagged behind projections, but about half of the houses in Phase II have been sold. In spring 2009, prices for one-third- to one-and-a-half-acre (0.13- to 0.6-ha) lots in the neighborhood section of Jackson Meadow ranged from $79,900 to $110,000; the average price of lots outside of the village center was $150,000 to $160,000. (One larger lot was priced at $230,000.) As of January 2010, about 22 lots remained on the market.

Although marketing can be time consuming, Carol Teasdale favors the personal touch. She believes that there is no better way to understand the unique quality of Jackson Meadow than by visiting the entire site. Teasdale escorts potential buyers on walks around the neighborhood, introduces

Jackson Meadow is surrounded by 120 acres (49 ha) of open space that is protected by a conservation easement held by a local land trust.

them to owners, and provides tours of existing custom-built homes. As the sales process continues, she accompanies buyers to their first design meeting with David Salmela and builder Streeter & Associates. Teasdale explains that this intensive sales process both enables buyers to better understand the community and builds a strong sense of belonging from the outset.

Challenges and Lessons Learned

The city of Marine on St. Croix traditionally had resisted proposals for new subdivision development. Landscape architect Coen, who worked on Jackson Meadow for more than five years, describes the planning commission members as "extremely progressive but also very protective of their town." During early discussions, rumors spread that the city was trying to prevent Ron Jackson from developing his land. Some community members felt that individual property owners' rights should be more important than long-range community visions and plans.

The development plan went through several iterations. An early proposal included building homes around a village square with office space, a town hall for community gatherings, and affordable apartments, but residents resisted these ideas because they were worried that they would increase the density of the project. Others felt that they should keep downtown Marine as the area's central business district and feared splitting the small city in half.

Working with citizens, the local government, and the planning commission required patience. Throughout the planning process, Harold Teasdale and Bob Durfey sought advice from local citizens to ensure that the development met their concerns. They held numerous community meetings, at which residents voiced their concerns and hammered out their differences with the development team. It took two years of meetings, adjustments, legalities, and hard work before ground was broken in October 1998.

"One of the biggest challenges was working with a small city and the city council," says Teasdale, and this challenge was made even more difficult when the council membership turned over. Among the more contentious issues was how the houses should be placed on the lot. "We weren't supposed to have garages facing the roads," he says, "but with the alleys behind the homes serving as roads, could the garages face backward?" This issue was successfully resolved: the garages are set away from the houses and are accessed from the rear, leaving a wide expanse of aesthetically pleasing, neighborly feeling, and pedestrian-friendly front yards that contribute to the development's appeal.

In addition, Marine on St. Croix's planning code insisted on five acres (2 ha) of open space around every house. Teasdale argued that if the city offered a small density bonus for clustering, several lower-priced units could be included. Ironically, very little of the infrastructure called for by the current code exists in the historic part of the city. "If you were to rebuild the town according to its modern code, all of the charm that people value would be gone," says Coen.

Discussions of some of the community's sustainability features were particularly contentious. City engineers worried that the lack of a conventional stormwater management system would result in catastrophic flooding. "There were also a lot of discussions about narrowing the roads and how they drained," adds Coen. The city's codes also included a mandate for wide streets and engineered drainage. The design team's proposed narrow loop road with 20-foot-wide (6-m) lanes and sophisticated wetland filtration did not meet the existing code. To address these concerns, Coen says that it is essential for designers to go before the planning commission armed with a slideshow of historical precedents and current projects around the country that demonstrate the engineering integrity of ecologically sensitive and clustered neighborhoods.

Teasdale says that it was a challenge to swim against the conventions of real estate development. "Jackson Meadow is all about pushing upstream," he says. "You just have to be willing to get a whole series of no's, and keep asking the question, 'why not?' until you can finally bust through and get someone to say, 'well, maybe if this is done this way,' and then suddenly, 'yeah, I guess it would work if you did it that way.' And all you're looking for is that opening."[2] He adds that things would be easier for developers today. "We were plowing new ground when we started," he says. "I think we've paved the way for other developments."

The aesthetic of conservation-oriented developments like Jackson Meadow appeals to a unique portion of the marketplace. Some potential homeowners are turned off by the strict building requirements, such as the requirement for a detached garage or a whitewashed finish. "People have told me that we'd have sold all the homes if we didn't require them all to be painted white," says Teasdale.

In an area in which five- and ten-acre (2- and 4-ha) lots are the norm, it also can be challenging to sell people on smaller lot sizes at the same price point. It is important to market the community and the open space, not the individual lots. "You have to show people what this means," says Teasdale. "I bring people to my home and ask them where the lot line is. Of course, they can't tell."

Teasdale says that market perceptions are changing. "The world has moved in our direction," he says. "I don't need to own ten acres. If I have access to it, I don't have to own it all."

Notes
1. Quoted in "Jackson Meadow Special Advertising Section," *Midwest Home* (2009), http://www.midwesthomemag.com/media/Midwest-Home/Real-Estate-Relocation/Association-Maintained-Living/Jackson-Meadow/.

2. Quoted in Marisa Helms, "Jackson Meadow Aims to Be Model for Sustainable Growth," *All Things Considered*, Minnesota Public Radio (January 13, 2003), news.minnesota.publicradio.org/features/2003/01/13_helmsm_jacksonmeadow/.

JACKSON MEADOW

LAND USE INFORMATION

Site area[1]	305 ac/123 ha
Open space under easement	220 ac/89 ha; 72%
Number of residential units planned	60
Number of lots sold	38
Number of residential units completed	34
Percentage of residential development complete	57%
Gross residential density (units per ac/ha)	5/12
Average net density (per ac/ha)	5/12

LAND USE PLAN

	Acres/Hectares	Percentage of Site
Residential	40/16	13
Roads	6.25/2.53	2
Undeveloped open space (natural open space)	258.75/104.72	85
Total	**305/123**	**100**

RESIDENTIAL INFORMATION

Lot Size (ac/ha)	Range of Initial Sales Prices
Varied	$80,000–$125,000

Unit Size (sq ft/m²)	Range of Initial Sales Prices
1,800–2,900/167–269	$250,000–$800,000

DEVELOPMENT COST INFORMATION

Site Acquisition Cost	**$1,610,000**
Site Improvement Costs	
Excavation/grading/roads	$237,000
Sewer/water/drainage	$851,000
Paving/curbs/sidewalks	$32,000
Landscaping/irrigation	$165,000
	$1,285,000
Soft Costs (estimated)	
Marketing and sales	$125,000
Legal/accounting	$75,000
	$200,000
Total Acquisition and Development Costs	**$3,095,000**

DEVELOPMENT SCHEDULE

Planning started	June 1996
Sales started	October 1998
Site purchased	October 1998
Construction started	November 1998
Project completion	TBD (4 and 18 lots remain to be sold in Phases I and II, respectively, as of fall 2009)

DEVELOPMENT TEAM

Developers
Harold Teasdale and Bob Durfey
Minneapolis, Minnesota[2]

Owner
Jackson Meadow Company
Marine on St. Croix, Minnesota
www.jacksonmeadow.com

Land Planner
Coen + Partners
Minneapolis, Minnesota
www.coenpartners.com

Architect
Salmela Architect
Duluth, Minnesota
www.salmelaarchitect.com

Builder
Streeter & Associates
Wayzata, Minnesota
www.streeter-associates.com

Open-Space Protection/Preservation/Management
Harold Teasdale/Jackson Meadow Homeowners Association
Minneapolis/Marine on St. Croix, Minnesota

Project Website
www.jacksonmeadow.com

Notes
1. About 15 acres (6 ha) across the railroad tracks from the Hollow parkland were subsequently sold as open space to a non-Jackson Meadow homeowner, reducing the total project acreage from 320 to 305 (129 to 123 ha).
2. Harold Teasdale now lives in Jackson Meadow.

Santa Lucia Preserve

Monterey County, California

CASE STUDY

Special Features

- 18,000 acres (7,285 ha) of permanently preserved land.
- A land conservancy to manage the open space.
- More than 100 miles (161 km) of hiking, biking, and riding trails.
- Architectural design standards that build on traditional California architecture and complement existing historic structures.
- High-end amenities, including a state-of-the-art fitness center, pools, an equestrian center, and a world-renowned golf course.
- A 1920s-era hacienda offering lodging and dining services.
- Two hundred and ninety-eight homes carefully sited to ensure environmental and aesthetic integrity and to guarantee that almost none can be seen from other homesites or from any roadway.

In Monterey County, California, just three miles (5 km) from Carmel and Pebble Beach, the Santa Lucia Preserve uses limited development to preserve the scenic beauty and natural resource values of a large and unique piece of land. The 298 homesites and community amenities occupy only 10 percent of the 20,000-acre (8,094-ha) Rancho San Carlos. The homes at the Santa Lucia Preserve are carefully sited to ensure the environmental and aesthetic integrity of the landscape. The natural features of the land—hills, trees, and foliage—guarantee that almost none of the homes can be seen from one another or from any roadway. In addition, each approximately 2.5-acre (1-ha) homesite is positioned to ensure the owners' privacy within an average lot size of 22.5 acres (9 ha), although the actual lots range from 8 to 80 acres (3 to 32 ha), depending on vegetation and topography.

The developers, with the assistance of the Trust for Public Land, established the Santa Lucia Conservancy, a 501(c)3 nonprofit organization, as an integral component of the project design and governance. The conservancy protects and maintains the land's natural beauty and resources and ensures their enjoyment by future generations without further subdivision or development. It holds conservation easements on 30 percent of the property—approximately 6,000 acres (2,428 ha) purchased by property owners as part of the lots containing their homesites. The developer also transferred the fee interest in about 12,000 acres (4,856 ha) to the conservancy, which gives the conservancy oversight and management of 18,000 acres (7,285 ha) of oak woodlands, savannas, grasslands, and forests of redwood and pine that range in elevation from 100 to 3,000 feet (31 to 914 m).

Origins

The site has been home to families who valued the land, its climate, wildlife, and resources since the Rumsen Indians lived there as early as 500 B.C. In the 19th century, the ranch began as an assemblage of two Mexican land grants and 125 homestead parcels. Known as Rancho San Carlos, it was a prosperous working ranch with 1,000 head of cattle and several hundred horses. In the 1920s, George Gordon Moore bought the land, built a 37-room, Spanish-style home eight miles (13 km) from the nearest road, and converted the property into a gentleman's club with polo fields and an equestrian center. Moore hosted lavish parties and brought in Russian boars for hunting on the ranch.

The Santa Lucia Preserve in Monterey County, California, uses limited development to preserve the scenic beauty and natural resource values of the 20,000-acre (8,094-ha) Rancho San Carlos.

Ninety percent of the Santa Lucia Preserve is permanently protected from further development. The Trust for Public Land assisted the developers in establishing a land trust to manage the open space.

The descendants of these huge animals still roam the property today.

With the onset of the Great Depression, foreclosure of debts forced Moore to sell his 20,000-acre (8,094-ha) estate to the Oppenheimer family, which maintained the land as a cattle ranch until 1990, when the property began its metamorphosis from Rancho San Carlos into the Santa Lucia Preserve. Surprisingly, this 31-square-mile (8,029-ha) property survived the development that had split up all of the grand ranchos that had surrounded it.

When Tom Gray and his partner, Peter Stocker, came across the site in 1989, they were struck by the fact that an undeveloped parcel of this size remained intact in coastal California. They were even more surprised to find that the land had no entitlements for subdivision whatsoever. The former owners had won a lawsuit challenging the county's density requirement of one unit per 160 acres (65 ha) on the site, which left the property without clear zoning or land use requirements. Realizing that the land had been assembled over time, they initiated a title research process that resulted in the certification of 125 legal lots of record with Monterey County. These legal lots provided an exit strategy for subdividing the property, should no entitlements be secured from the county.

Gray, Stocker, and their partners closed on the property in March 1990 for a purchase price of $70 million. They knew that success would depend on their ability to create and sell 300 parcels for at least $1 million each. In addition to these homesites, their initial plan called for 50 units of employee housing and a 150-room hotel. Marketing studies, however, later proved that potential lot buyers would be turned off by transient accommodations, and the hotel plan was scrapped. Tragically, Stocker was killed two months later in a helicopter accident on the property, leaving Gray to go it alone.

The Vision

From the outset, the planning team envisioned something different from what had occurred in surrounding areas. "We didn't use the word

'development,'" says Gray. "We focused on lands that were suitable for settlement and those that were appropriate for conservation."

Preserving the integrity of the landscape was a driving principle from the outset. The team believed that the only politically acceptable proposal would be one that was consistent with the goals of the local environmental community. In addition, they believed that conservation would create certainty that views and vistas would remain the same for generations and that this legacy would increase land values, much like what happens on beachfront property—where the impossibility of building in front of homes on the beach creates value for owners.

To accomplish this, the development team committed to an extensive, ground-up environmental study. "This is a spectacular landscape. We needed to quantify it. What makes it so special? If we damaged the resources, we would diminish the value of the land," adds Gray.

Amenities at the Santa Lucia Preserve include a sports and aquatic center, a 37-room inn, an equestrian center, 100 miles (161 km) of hiking and riding trails, and a renowned golf course.

The vision for the Santa Lucia Preserve encompassed three core components: 1) long-term protection of the property's scenic vistas and habitat values; 2) construction of a residential community integrated into the landscape and compatible with the natural ecosystem; and 3) assured, permanent financial support for the preservation of the property's natural resources.

"This land had escaped development for 200 years," says Gray. "We wanted to preserve the landscape for at least another 200 years—longer, ideally, but 200 years was about as far as we could stretch our minds." The vision was to establish a community around preservation values, set amid preservation land.

The first step was to determine which parts of the land were most suitable for development and which were best for preservation. "By happenstance, this ended up being a 50/50 split," says Gray, "but from the beginning we said we'd protect 90 percent of the land." The environmental study identified the most ecologically valuable areas to be protected. The Santa Lucia Conservancy was formed to hold conservation deeds on this land, ensuring its ongoing preservation and maintenance. The protected land includes riparian areas, redwood groves, and habitat for endangered species, including the red-legged frog and Smith's blue butterfly.

The next step involved creating a land use plan for the remaining 8,000 acres (3,238 ha). The team paid careful attention to the siting of 298 homes, so that only 10 percent of the land would experience the impacts of development. Lots ranging from eight to 80 acres (3 to 32 ha) were designated, and an approximately 2.5-acre (1-ha) building envelope was specified for each lot. The remainder of each lot, exclusive of the building site, was subject to a conservation easement held by the conservancy.

The final step was the entitlement process. The ranch, which was the largest private landholding in Monterey County, was a prized piece of land, so the development team was not surprised to find that there was significant opposition to any sort of development. The environmental review and public hearings took six years. Then the land use plan was tied up in litigation before it was put on the ballot for referendum. The developers filed the plan in April 1994 and finally succeeded in gaining approval in August 1997. Although it was a long process, the victory was sweet. "When we started, nobody believed we'd succeed," says Gray.

Site Planning

The site planning process required what Gray calls a high-tech, high-touch process. Following Ian McHarg's approach to landscape design, the team mapped the resource values of the land. "We had 50 or more what I call 'ologists'—biologists, geologists, ecologists, and the like—studying the property," Gray explains.

The scientists' exhaustive studies resulted in maps, based on geographic information systems (GIS) data, that showed soils, fire and flood hazards, archaeological and historical resources, watershed and riparian-corridor resources, and a wide range of other natural resources. The data first were used to identify the 18,000 acres (7,285 ha) that would be preserved under the conservancy's guardianship. The maps then were used to site the homes, amenities, and infrastructure on the remaining 2,000 acres (809 ha) of the least environmentally significant land, where they would have minimal impact on the landscape and the plants and animals that live there. The development team's idea was to build homes on just 750 acres (304 ha) and use the remaining 1,250 acres (506 ha) for a golf course, other amenities, trails, and roads—essentially incorporating a 2,000-acre settlement in a 20,000-acre (8,094-ha) preserve.

The initial vision was to sell 2.5-acre (1-ha) lots surrounded by conservation land owned by a conservancy, but early market research showed that concept would meet with

The golf course at Santa Lucia Preserve is considered part of the 2,000 acres (809 ha) of development. To protect the groundwater supply, the greens and tees were lined, the course was sand-capped, and extensive drain fields were put under the fairways. The water captured by these conservation measures is returned to irrigate the course.

the landscape, while also providing owners with scenic views and privacy. "While the army of 'ologists' did their analyses, Dave Howerton of Hart|Howerton—the project's principal land planners and architects—and I spent the better part of three years looking for every great place for a family to build a house," says Gray, who describes this time-consuming process as "handcrafted."

Commitment to Conservation

One of the primary goals of the project was to ensure that 90 percent of the Santa Lucia Preserve is permanently protected from further development and will remain as open space forever. In addition to the 6,000 acres (2,428 ha) under conservation easements, 12,000 acres (4,856 ha) are owned by the Santa Lucia Conservancy, a 501(c)3 nonprofit. The developer endowed the conservancy with $25 million from a dedicated portion of lot sales. California law makes implementation of

resistance from the marketplace. To attract potential buyers and still meet their conservation goals, the development team instead divided the 6,000 acres (2,428 ha) that were not owned by the Santa Lucia Conservancy into parcels ranging in size from eight to 80 acres (3 to 32 ha), and then identified a 2.5-acre homeland or building envelope on which owners could build their home or other structures. The remaining part of each parcel was put under conservation easement. Gray points out that attitudes might have changed in the almost two decades since the team began its feasibility studies. In the early 1990s, conservation development was a truly novel idea. "People just wanted to know that they owned the land around their house," Gray says. "They would agree not to build or make other changes to this land as long as their neighbors agreed to do the same."

The development team carefully sited the buildable 2.5 acres (1.0 ha) on each parcel to ensure the environmental and aesthetic integrity of

Strict architectural design standards aim to make the community appear to have evolved over time. The guidelines build on the vernacular of California architecture but allow for modern interpretations.

mutually beneficial opportunities for scientific study.

The Santa Lucia Conservancy's mission is "to conserve and sustain the Santa Lucia Preserve, a unique California Central Coast landscape, by implementing a model of compatible development and sustainable conservation where natural landscapes are protected and restored for Santa Lucia Preserve residents and all future generations."

Architecture and Building Standards

The development team further sought to maintain the integrity of the Santa Lucia Preserve's landscape by connecting it to its past; the developers described what they were doing as "settlement" rather than "development." "If you come upon the land 50 years from now, we want it to look as though it had been settled over the past 200 years," explains Gray. "We asked ourselves, 'How would the land look if it had been settled over the last 200 years?'"

Strict architectural design standards aim to make the community

transfer fees almost impossible, so the endowment was critical to ensuring that there would be sufficient funds for the ongoing protection of the resource-rich open space. The conservancy safeguards and maintains a total of 18,000 acres (7,285 ha) for recreation, environmental research, and wildlife habitat. Its long-term mission is to establish a proven model of compatibility between human settlement and the conservation of natural resources and landscape.

The Santa Lucia Conservancy is governed by an independent board of directors and staffed by an executive director and two full-time resource managers. Its conservation programs include natural resource monitoring and management, habitat restoration, public education and outreach, and scientific research. Among the conservancy's plans is a pilot program to explore rotational cattle grazing as part of its natural resource management plan. In addition, the conservancy's interpretive programs provide opportunities for residents and local youth and adult groups to explore the natural landscape and to learn about its unique resources. Cooperative programs with other conservation and research organizations, as well as scholastic institutions, provide appear to have evolved over time. The California architecture takes its cue from the hacienda, stables, and outbuildings that have been on the land since the early 1900s. "These structures set the tone for the design of the community buildings and influenced the architectural standards for residential homes," explains Lisa Guthrie, the Santa Lucia Preserve's director of clubs and services.

Before building commenced, Gray asked six world-class architects to test the draft architectural guidelines by designing houses for six parcels. Howerton and Gray wanted to make sure that the guidelines would allow for ample creativity and diversity. Gray reflects on the experience: "It was a fascinating experience to sit in a room with these world-class egos and have them push against our design guidelines and push against each other and engage in this intellectual debate over how restrictive the design guidelines should be."

The design guidelines build on the vernacular of California architecture but allow for modern interpretation. They encourage three basic styles: hacienda, California Arts and Crafts or cottage, and board-and-batten ranch house and barn. To avoid a "cookie-cutter" look, residents are encouraged to explore various options within the design guidelines. An outside professional review board, consisting of two licensed architects and a representative from the Santa Lucia Conservancy, enforces the architectural guidelines.

The Market

The development team, recognizing that the Santa Lucia Preserve was not a typical development project, realized that success would depend on capturing the target market—by necessity, an affluent segment of the population. The developers needed to sell 300 parcels at a price of at least $1 million each and believed that the beauty of the land would attract prospective buyers.

To test its assumptions, the team conducted extensive market research. It used profiling and focus groups to identify prospective buyers' needs and desires. Results suggested that the target market was family oriented, held conservation as a value, and had high net worth. The legacy of passing land on to future generations would appeal to the target market; security and privacy were also priorities. Because the community's houses cannot be seen from the road, those who wanted to express their wealth or architectural creativity through their home would be unlikely to buy there.

Market research also showed that a golf course and other high-end amenities would be good investments and might be critical to the project's financial success. Focus groups indicated that more than one-third of prospective buyers would not purchase at the Santa Lucia Preserve unless it had a golf course. (Ironically, the same focus groups that showed support for a course also indicated that 10 percent of potential buyers would *not* purchase a site if there *was* a golf course.)

The golf course was controversial. To blunt the opposition, the golf course was considered part of the 2,000 acres of development. "From the beginning, we said that the 350 acres on which the golf course sits was included in the developable acreage," says Gray. "We weren't claiming the golf course as part of the preserved land. Still, it was the most controversial aspect of the project. The environmental community has strong negative opinions about golf courses. Mostly, they complain about the 'excessive' use of water, but they also object to the use of chemical fertilizers and pesticides." To protect the groundwater supply, the greens and tees were lined, the course was sand-capped, and extensive drain fields were put under the fairways. The water captured by these conservation measures is run though the project's treatment plant and returned to irrigate the course. About a third of the course's irrigation water comes from this recycling system. Another third is derived

The homes at the Santa Lucia Preserve are carefully sited to ensure the environmental and aesthetic integrity of the landscape and to guarantee that almost none of the 298 homesites can be seen from one another or from any roadway.

from tertiary treated effluent, and the last third from nonpotable well water.

Marketing and Sales

Homesites at the Santa Lucia Preserve initially ranged in price from $1 million to $4 million. Lots went on sale in 1999, and sales were brisk from the outset. As of January 2010, all but 15 of the 298 residential lots have been sold. To date, 93 homes have been completed or are under construction; another 23 are in the design review process.

Like many innovative development projects, the Santa Lucia Preserve has benefited from positive publicity. Articles showcasing the community have appeared in golf and high-end shelter magazines. "You don't have to push this on anybody," says Mark Baxter, the project's director of marketing. "*Travel and Leisure Golf* voted us the number-one golf community [in 2007]." But Gray emphasizes that the Santa Lucia Preserve is really not a golf community. "It's a community that happens to have a golf course. Most of the houses are miles away from the course. Only a few sit alongside the fairways."

Challenges and Lessons Learned

Working with a large, relatively pristine piece of land in an area already known as a world-class destination is inherently challenging, particularly when it is the largest privately held parcel in the region. In the case of the Santa Lucia Preserve, environmentalists opposed any development on the 31-square-mile (8,029-ha) tract of land. When their opposition failed, they called for a maximum density of one home per 160 acres (65 ha)—a density that Gray believed would cause more environmental damage, through the re-subdivision and fragmentation over time by owners of the large parcels into four 40-acre (16-ha) sites without conservation guarantees, than the more balanced conservation approach proposed by the developers. The team spent years studying the land and its values to ensure the best design for both nature and homeowners.

Although it took seven years to gain approval for the site plan, Gray credits the success of the project to the detailed planning that the team put into the project. "We knew we were going to have to over-prepare our environmental information to blunt the opposition from environmentalists," he says. "We needed scientific evidence to support our proposal, to answer questions from naysayers, and to convince the regulators and political decision makers that we had the best plan for the land." The team sought to make the process as transparent and straightforward as possible.

The detailed planning process also ended up driving the design and development of the community to its intended end. "The community that

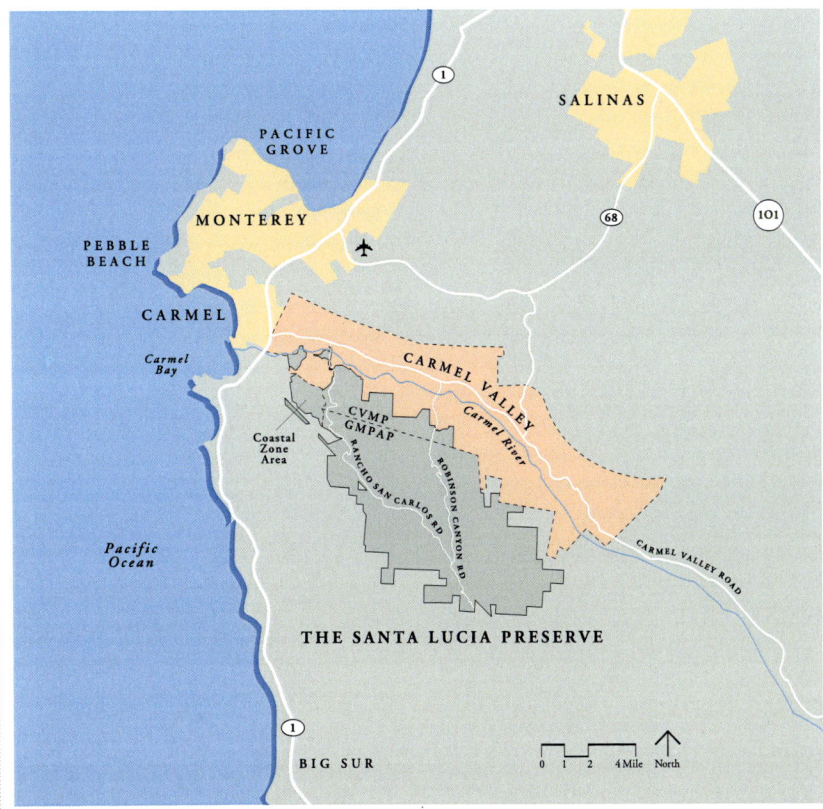

Location map.

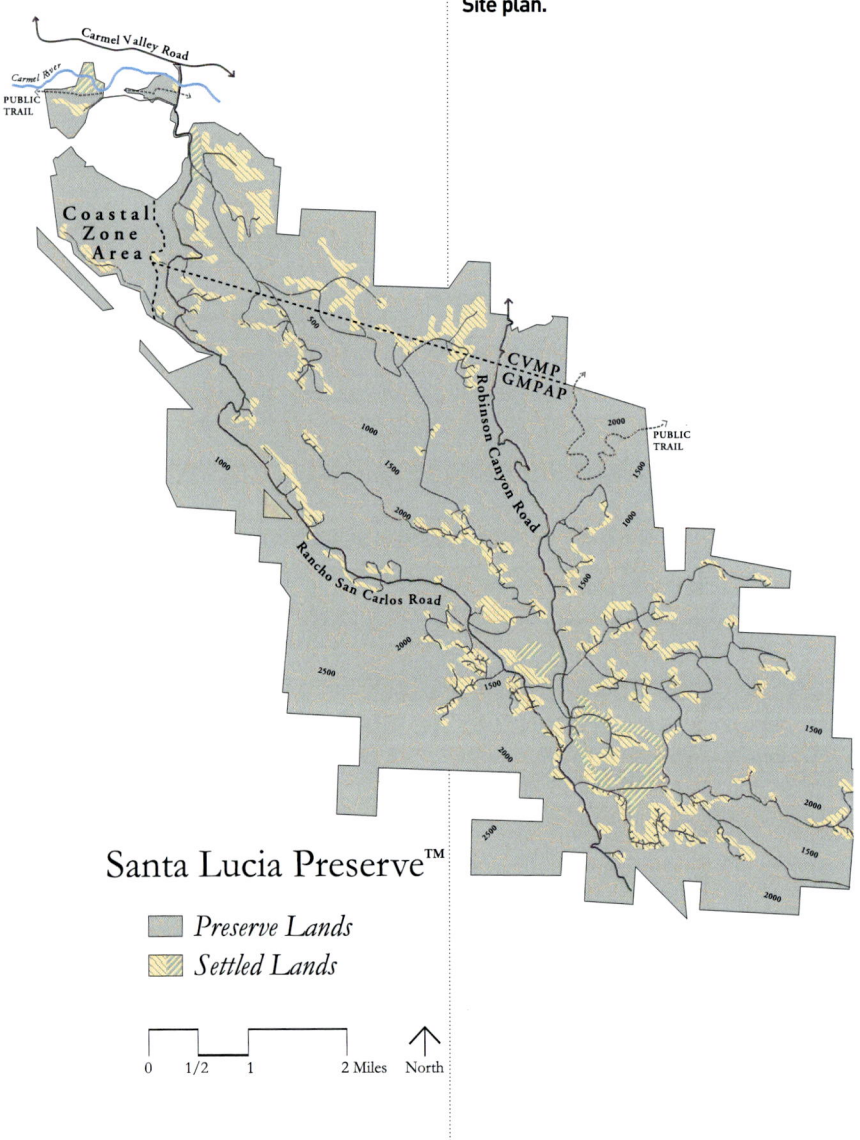

Site plan.

exists today is almost exactly the project for which we applied to create in 1994," says Gray.

Does the development team wish it had done anything differently? Gray laments some of his public relations decisions. "I learned a lot about the dirty nature of politics," he says. "We all know it happens, but it's different when it happens to you." He describes the referendum process that would decide the fate of the Santa Lucia Preserve: "We naively thought the referendum process was a two-way street. We thought we had a democratic right to a voice, so we went to where the opposition was passing out leaflets and passed out our own information. We wanted to provide a counterbalance and to correct misrepresentation of what we were doing. It ended up in the headlines as the big, bad developer beating up on the environmental community. I made a very bad PR decision. I gave the environmentalists credibility."

Although the Santa Lucia Preserve was far ahead of its time in terms of adhering to environmental principles, Gray says if he were to design a community today, he would focus attention not just on land conservation but on other issues of sustainability as well. "I wish we'd thought more about other sustainability issues, such as energy conservation—using passive energy sources—and water," he says.

We did a lot with water, but you can always do more."

Today, the Santa Lucia Preserve is a community in which residents can enjoy thousands of acres of unspoiled nature with friends and family. In addition to the natural beauty of the landscape, residents have access to a wide range of amenities, including 100 miles (161 km) of private hiking and riding trails; a sports and aquatic center; an equestrian center; a 1920s-era, 37-room hacienda offering lodging and dining; and a renowned golf course. The community also holds organized events that encourage residents to enjoy the open space, including hikes and mushroom-gathering expeditions. Other events, such as a yearly cattle round-up and horsemanship exhibition, hark back to the land's earlier days as a working ranch. One of the most popular events is a black-tie performance of the opera *A Midsummer Night's Dream*, held under a canopy of redwoods.

Gray says that this sense of community is the real reward. "The most exciting part of the process is the community that has developed. The owners share common values about family, legacy, and conservation, which lead to lasting friendships among the residents."

SANTA LUCIA PRESERVE

LAND USE INFORMATION

Site area	20,000 ac/8,094 ha
Open space under easement	18,000 ac/7,285 ha; 90%
Number of lots	298
Number of lots sold	279
Number of houses completed or under construction	93
Percentage of residential infrastructure complete	98%
Gross residential density (units per acre/hectare)	0.015/0.037
Average net density (acres/hectares per unit)	67/166

LAND USE PLAN

	Acres/ Hectares	Percentage of Site
Residential	750/304	3.75
Roads	120/49	0.6
Developed open space (parks, golf course, common areas)	420/170	2.1
Undeveloped open space (natural open space)	18,000/7,285	90
Town center/mixed-use/school	620/251	3.1
Sewer and power facilities	90/36	0.45
Total	**20,000/8,094**	**100**

RESIDENTIAL INFORMATION

Lot Type	Gross Average Lot Size (ac/ha)	Range of Initial Sales Prices
Single-family detached	67/27	$1,000,000 to $4,000,000

DEVELOPMENT COST INFORMATION

Site Acquisition Cost	**$70,000,000**
Site Improvement Costs	
Excavation/grading	$25,000,000
Sewer/water/drainage	45,000,000
Paving/curbs/sidewalks	30,000,000
Telecom/power	45,000,000
Total	**$145,000,000**
Amenity Construction Costs	**$80,000,000**
Soft Costs	
Architecture/engineering	$6,000,000
Project management	5,000,000
Marketing and sales	7,000,000
Legal/accounting	5,000,000
Taxes/insurance	5,000,000
Construction interest and fees	10,000,000
Licenses, bonds, permits	3,000,000
Total	**$41,000,000**
Total Development Cost	**$336,000,000**

DEVELOPMENT SCHEDULE

Planning started	February 1989
Site purchased	March 1990
Sales started	March 1999
Developer buildout	December 2008

DEVELOPMENT TEAM

Owner
Rancho San Carlos Partnership, LP
Carmel, California

Developer
Tom Gray
Carmel, California

Marketing and Sales
The Preserve Land Company
Carmel, California
www.santaluciapreserve.com

Land Planner and Architect
Hart|Howerton
San Francisco
www.harthowerton.com

Open-Space Protection/Preservation/Management
Santa Lucia Conservancy
Carmel, California
www.slconservancy.com

Other Key Team Members
Don Wilcoxon
COO/CFO, Santa Lucia Preserve

Lisa Guthrie
Director of clubs and marketing, Santa Lucia Preserve

Legal
Brian Finegan
Land use and entitlements attorney
Salinas, California

Environmental Planning
Denise Duffy & Associates
Monterey, California
www.ddaplanning.com

Project Website
www.santaluciapreserve.com

Serenbe

Fulton County, Georgia

CASE STUDY

Special Features

- As a result of zoning changes, a county master plan that calls for 80 percent of the 40,000-acre (16,188-ha) Chattahoochee Hill Country region to be preserved as green space.
- Zoning overlays that allow increased density on developed parcels, enabling more than 70 percent of the land to be preserved in perpetuity.
- Residential and small commercial facilities that are clustered in three hamlets, each of which takes its form and character from the surrounding landscape.
- An omega-shaped form that allows the built environment to follow the undulations of the land.
- A 25-acre (10-ha) organic farm that provides produce for Serenbe's three restaurants, as well as for residents of the community and the surrounding Chattahoochee Hill Country.
- A system of interconnecting pathways and trails that reaches all parts of the community.
- An innovative, chemical-free private wastewater treatment system that cleans wastewater, which then is used to irrigate yards and the community's cow pasture.

Serenbe is a 1,000-acre (405-ha) mixed-use conservation community located in the Chattahoochee Hills of Fulton County, Georgia, just 32 miles (52 km) from downtown Atlanta. It is the first development to be approved since the Fulton County Board of Commissioners adopted the Chattahoochee Land Use Plan, which calls for rural green space to be preserved by focusing development in historic villages and hamlets. This comprehensive land use plan covers 40,000 acres (16,188 ha) in Fulton County and calls for 80 percent of it to remain as green space.

The plan for Serenbe—which has been designed to be fully integrated into its natural surroundings—encourages architectural diversity amid untamed stretches of nature. In addition to residences, the community includes a country inn, shops and restaurants, a 25-acre (10-ha) working organic farm, and riding stables and an equestrian center. Building sites are limited to 220 homes, including live/work spaces, and commercial buildings. The developers preserved 70 percent of the property by clustering the residences in small hamlets, which are connected by looping country roads and footpaths designed to make Serenbe a walkable community. In addition to preserving rolling hills, woodlands, streams, and meadows that provide habitat for wildlife, the plan protects the ruins of an early farm settlement and some Native American archaeological sites.

Origins

Marie and Steve Nygren discovered the property now known as Serenbe on an outing to introduce their children to the Georgia countryside. In 1991, they fell in love with a 60-acre (24-ha) farm and purchased the property, with its 1905 farmhouse amid rolling terrain, as a weekend home. A few years later, the Nygrens sold their home in Atlanta and their stake in the Peasant Restaurant Group and relocated to Serenbe.

Within a few years, the Nygrens had converted the farm buildings into a country inn and a guesthouse, and added a pool, fishing pond, croquet lawn, and hiking trails. They believed that people would be attracted by the opportunity to spend a relaxing weekend in the country. "We invited people to come and relax," says Nygren. "Just being in nature was enough of a draw."

The Nygrens were attracted by the area's rural character, but worried that it would not last. When they saw bulldozers clearing forests nearby, their first impulse was to buy more land. Steve Nygren purchased 1,000 acres (405 ha) adjacent to the farm, but knew that his pockets were not deep enough to stop

Serenbe is a rural, mixed-use hamlet with 220 homes, live/work units, a country inn, and shops and restaurants surrounded by abundant green space.

development from spreading outward from Atlanta. "I quickly realized we could never buy enough land to protect ourselves," he says.

Nygren then set about learning how other communities were protecting rural landscapes. After visiting Prairie Crossing, "I realized we weren't thinking big enough," says Nygren. "What they did at Prairie Crossing was great, but people developed traditional housing right next to that development."

Nygren began talking to neighbors and developers about the need for balanced growth. He learned that those who wanted to develop in a different way—those who espoused new urbanism—often found it difficult because communities did not understand what these developers were doing. His research into the issues led him to conclude that the only way to protect the Chattahoochee Hill Country would be to bring together landowners, conservationists, and developers to come up with a mutually agreeable land use plan. "I realized right away this wouldn't be easy," he says. "I listened in on their conversations. On one side of the room, I overheard the developers murmuring about the tree-huggers. On the other, people kept talking about greedy developers. As I listened in, I couldn't help but think, 'We'll never get these people to talk to each other.'"

Fortunately, Nygren was able to convince these different interest groups to work together. He began to forge a coalition of people in the community who wanted development to occur in a different way. At first, many residents were skeptical that high-density villages could be developed on the urban edge without destroying the area's rural character, but the coalition of believers grew. Nygren and his colleagues held coffees, dinners, desserts, and public meetings to discuss the need for balanced growth—growth that would provide homes for people to live in and at the same time protect the rural character they cherished.

After two years, the group succeeded in changing the county zoning laws, with a zoning overlay that affects the owners of 36 large land parcels and more than 20,000 acres (8,094 ha) in and around Serenbe. The zoning overlay ensures that 80 percent of the region's open space will be permanently protected by conservation easements and that in three designated areas 20 percent *more* housing per square mile will be allowed than the zoning code previously stipulated. The Serenbe Institute Land Trust, which is a separate entity from the homeowners association, holds the easement, but it plans to transfer the easement to the Chattahoochee Hill Country Trust when that entity is established.

Site Plan

The vision for Serenbe is to protect both the site and the region from typical suburban sprawl and to integrate ecologically sound planning principles with the design philosophies of walkable neighborhoods that include a mix of homes, shops, restaurants, and other facilities. In short, the team wanted to replicate the neighborhoods of 100 years ago, in which people knew their neighbors and walked to shops and community activities. Sidewalks and pathways connect all the homes and commercial areas. The hiking, equestrian, and bicycle trails within Serenbe also connect with a 98-mile (158-km) regional greenway system that is being created by the PATH Foundation, a nonprofit organization dedicated to developing multipurpose, off-road trails throughout Georgia.

The master plan for the settlement calls for three hamlets with a range of housing options for single people, families, and empty nesters, as well as a wide range of economic and cultural diversity. The land design allows the homes and buildings to flow with the terrain, disturbing the natural landscape as little as possible and eliminating the need for mass grading. Buildings are clustered along a serpentine omega form fitted to the undulations of the land. The development team designed the built

Serenbe has a 25-acre (10-ha) organic farm, plus riding stables and an equestrian center. The farm provides produce for Serenbe's three restaurants, as well as for residents and the surrounding community.

The Blue Eyed Daisy Bakeshop is a LEED-certified building. Serenbe's town center also includes a barbecue restaurant, a tack store, a gourmet grocer, art galleries, and several boutiques.

environment to fit the natural fall of the land, and carefully considered the scale and angle of each building during the design phase. Every house backs up to a forest, farmland, or other open space.

Serenbe includes a 25-acre (10-ha) certified organic farm that grows vegetables, herbs, flowers, and fruit. A farmers market held each Saturday during the growing season attracts residents from many parts of the Chattahoochee Hill Country. Stables were built using local wood, a natural solution that helps the building to blend in with its surroundings. The community also includes a country inn, several restaurants, an art gallery, shops, and a cooking school.

Each of the three hamlets has its own personality, taking its cues from the surrounding environment and characteristics.

Selborne, the first hamlet to be developed, was 80 percent built out as of fall 2009. It is home to about 150 residents and serves as the community's artistic center, with restaurants, a gourmet grocer, art galleries, and several boutiques. Winding lanes snake between cottages built in the Arts and Crafts style and loft-style townhouses. The community is marked by attention to detail, such as streetlamps specifically created by a local artist for the hamlet.

Grange, which is currently under construction, is home to the stables and organic farms, which host an organic produce market weekly during the growing season. Grange builds on the community's agricultural past with an agrarian aesthetic. A barbecue restaurant, a tack store, a feed and seed shop, and arts and crafts studios are planned for this hamlet. A carefully designed site plan protects the hilly terrain to provide sweeping views of the surrounding area and give homeowners the feel of living in a mountain retreat.

Mado, yet to be built, takes its name from a Creek Indian word meaning "things in balance." In addition to homesites, the development team plans to build a destination spa, an upscale boutique hotel, and a vegetarian restaurant here.

Architecture and Design

One of Serenbe's most pleasing aspects is its architectural diversity. The developers anticipated attracting prospective buyers looking for a weekend retreat, as well as those who were looking for a permanent, year-round home. To meet the needs of people at various stages of their lives, the developers incorporated a range of home sizes and types, including live/work units, townhouses, cottages, and larger estate homes. Each is offered in a variety of architectural styles that draw from and sometimes update the local architectural vocabulary.

Live/work units, for instance, provide compact spaces for living and working. The ground floor of each of the two- or three-story units is a storefront that can be used as an artist's studio, a workshop, or retail space; living quarters are located above. The architectural style of these buildings draws on local examples from historic downtowns, as well from Federal, Greek Revival, and Italianate styles.

All of the homes at Serenbe are built to the standards of the EarthCraft House program, a local green-building program that sets standards for energy efficiency, air quality, water conservation, and resource-efficient building materials and systems. Building according to high environmental standards results in lower utility bills and increases resale values. Commercial buildings also were built in accordance with environmental principles. The Blue Eyed Daisy Bakeshop, for instance, is the smallest Silver LEED–certified building in the nation. To ensure the quality of workmanship, the development team provides initial purchasers with a list of approved builders; buyers

---

Vision and Values

We share a vision for Serenbe as a place where people authentically live, work, learn, and play in celebration of life's beauty, and where connections between people, nature, and the arts are nourished. This vision can only be achieved for future generations if we commit ourselves now to building a community that is a living part of its natural surroundings, not something built at nature's expense.

From the ground up, we have taken a new look at development; every facet of Serenbe's design is grounded on traditional values and the principles of environmental sustainability.

At Serenbe we value:
- **Nature** . . . because people can live more fully when connected to nature's wonders.
- **Passion** . . . because living passionately is the most rewarding of lives.
- **Art** . . . because artists live lives of great passion, and can help the rest of us do the same.
- **Community** . . . where people are accepted for who they are, not what they are.

Source: Serenbe community website, www.serenbe.com.

Cottage Living magazine named Serenbe one of its top-ten neighborhoods in 2008. The community offers many different types of houses, at varying price points to meet the needs of people at all stages of life.

who want to use another builder can submit their request for review by the development team.

Building materials also were selected to blend with the surroundings. Native plants and organic landscaping techniques are used exclusively throughout the community.

Sustainability

The development team designed Serenbe's infrastructure to be low impact and environmentally friendly. Rather than creating concrete spillways that concentrate stormwater runoff, the community's runoff is directed into a natural system of vegetated filter strips and shallow channels of dense vegetation. These natural filters remove pollutants while dispersing water flow.

Serenbe also features an innovative, state-of-the-art wastewater treatment system, which is separate from the county's sewer system. The natural system uses constructed wetlands, filtration basins, and circulating pumps to treat the community's wastewater without any chemicals. Once treated, the plant's effluent is pumped to an application field in the community cow pasture and released into the ground via piped subsurface drip lines. Treated, clean water also is pumped to each individual homeowner's yard to be used for subsurface drip irrigation.

Art, Culture, and the Environment

The development team created the Serenbe Institute for Art, Culture, and the Environment to ensure that the developers' conservation vision would become reality. The nonprofit institute sponsors programs that bring residents together to learn about low-impact lifestyles and living in harmony with the environment, sustainable development, and new ways of thinking and planning for the future. It also sponsors art exhibits and classes, with a special emphasis on "earth-centered" arts that celebrate the cultural and ethnic heritage of the Chattahoochee Hill Country.

The institute is funded by fees from the sale of homesites and houses. All buyers pay a transfer fee—either 1 percent of the total purchase price of a home or 3 percent of the total purchase price of an unimproved lot—to the institute at closing. One-half of the money

Site plan.

received is placed in an endowment fund that will be a perpetual source of revenue for the institute from interest and dividends; the other half is used for programs and to manage the institute's day-to-day activities, including community events and programs as well as other community initiatives. Additional revenues come from annual memberships, corporate sponsorships, and other sources.

Marketing and Sales

Positive publicity and word of mouth are the best marketing available, and Serenbe has received significant local and national recognition for setting a new standard in responsible development. In August 2008, *Cottage Living* named Serenbe one of its top-ten neighborhoods, a list that "celebrates the best places to enjoy life just right—communities where neighborly houses, pedestrian-scaled streets, and a healthy environment aren't a thing of the past." In 2008, the ULI Atlanta District Council awarded Serenbe its first-ever Award for Excellence in Sustainability.

Serenbe offers many different types of homes at many different price points, to meet the needs of a diverse group of people at various stages of life. When the community's estate lots—which range in size from one-eighth to one-half of an acre (0.05 to

0.20 ha)—first went on the market, they sold for $235,000 to $499,000. Although the pace of sales slowed with the market downturn, Serenbe's lots held their value in subsequent phases of the development. In 2009, the cottage homes in Selborne ranged in price from $500,000 to $600,000; luxury homes and townhouses in the Selborne and Grange hamlets are selling for more than $1 million, up to as much as $1.5 million.

Annual homeowners association (HOA) fees, ranging from roughly $600 for live/work units to almost $900 for estate lots, are assessed on all properties to support the maintenance of common areas, the irrigation system, the recycling center, private streets, signage, and other expenses. Trash removal service is also provided by the HOA and is billed separately at $25 per month in the annual statement.

Serenbe's shops and restaurants have proven to be a major draw, bringing outside money into the community and enhancing the value of the homes and businesses. In just a few years, Serenbe has become a destination for Atlantans in search of a day trip to the country or a farm-to-table dining experience. Its restaurants have built a reputation for excellence, in part due to the freshness of their vegetables, which often are served within hours of being picked from Serenbe's organic farm. The community also sponsors frequent weekend festivals, farmers markets, and other events that attract people from nearby Atlanta and beyond.

"There are many reasons to move to Serenbe, but the one heard most often is the quality of life," says Serenbe's website. "Where else can you live like this?"

SERENBE

LAND USE INFORMATION

Site area	1,000 ac/405 ha
Open space under easement	700 ac/283 ha (projected)
Number of residential units at buildout	1,000 (projected)
Number of lots sold	100
Percentage of residential development complete	10%
Gross residential density (units per ac/ha)	1/3
Average net density (per ac/ha)	3/7

LAND USE PLAN FOR PHASE I

	Acres/ Hectares	Percentage of Site
Residential	43.9/17.5	19.5
Roads (inside access)	14.7/5.9	6.6
Roads (outside access)	5.3/2.1	2.4
Developed open space (parks, common areas)	8.9/3.5	4.0
Undeveloped open space (natural open space)	147.6/59.0	65.7
Town center/mixed-use/school	3.5/1.4	1.6
Sewer and power facilities	0.7/0.3	0.3
Total acreage	**224.0/89.6**	**100.0**

RESIDENTIAL INFORMATION

Lot Type	Lot Size (ac/ha)	Range of Initial Sales Prices
Estate	0.25–0.5/0.10–0.2	$250,000–$500,000

Unit Type	Unit Size (sq ft/m²)	Range of Initial Sales Prices
Live/work	1,100–3,500/102–325	$280,000–$550,000
Townhome	1,700–4,000/158–372	$350,000–$1,000,000
Cottage	900–6,000/84–557	$265,000–$900,000

DEVELOPMENT SCHEDULE

Planning started	2000
Site purchased	1991–2000
Construction started	2004
Sales started	2004
Phase I completed	2005

DEVELOPMENT TEAM

Owners
The Nygren Family
Palmetto, Georgia

Rawson Haverty, Jr.
Atlanta, Georgia

Developer
Serenbe Development Corporation
Palmetto, Georgia
www.serenbe.com

Site Planner
Phillip Tabb
College Station, Texas

Architect
Lew Oliver Inc.
Atlanta, Georgia
www.wholetownsolutions.com

Open-Space Protection/Preservation/Management
Serenbe Institute
Palmetto, Georgia
www.serenbeinstitute.com

Other Key Team Members
Southeastern Engineering, Inc.
Marietta, Georgia
www.seengineering.com

Morgan Constructors
Atlanta, Georgia
www.morganbartos.com

Project Website
www.serenbe.com

Spring Island

Beaufort County, South Carolina

CASE STUDY

Special Features

- 1,200-acre (486-ha) nature preserve.
- Mobley Nature Center, staffed by three full-time naturalists who manage Spring Island Trust's wildlife conservation program.
- Two clubhouses with private dining facilities; club members have a choice of golf or social membership plans.
- Extensive tree preservation and natural buffers on and around homesites.
- Wide range of recreational amenities, including a golf course, a community swimming pool, four clay tennis courts, a 30-acre (12-ha) equestrian center, 35 miles (56 km) of trails, a fitness center, and private boat docks.
- Site plan with 285 estate homesites that range from two to ten acres (0.8 to 4 ha) and 125 small cottage homesites that range from 0.25 to 0.75 acres (0.1 to 0.3 ha).

Spring Island is a master-planned conservation community on the South Carolina coast between Hilton Head and Beaufort, near Savannah, Georgia. In addition to a golf course, tennis courts, a fitness center, a swimming pool, and a host of other amenities common to many high-end planned communities, Spring Island boasts a nature center, a 1,200-acre (486-ha) nature preserve, and 30 miles (48 km) of walking, biking, and equestrian trails. James J. Chaffin, Jr., and James W. Light, principals of the development firm Chaffin/Light Associates, designed the community to ensure the preservation of its natural beauty and established the Spring Island Trust to maintain the preserved green space. The result is a community in which coastal living and an active lifestyle coexist with stringent environmental protection regulations.

Origins

During the early 19th century, the 3,000-acre (1,214-ha) Spring Island was a major cotton plantation, enabling owner George Edwards to become the wealthiest man in South Carolina—a distinction he enjoyed for more than 50 years. After the Civil War, cotton farming became less lucrative, and the cotton fields of Spring Island reverted to their natural state. The island then was used as a hunting preserve, and visitors also enjoyed fishing, horseback riding, and walking through nature. Unlike the other sea islands in the Carolinas, Spring Island remained in private ownership; it has had just four owners since its initial purchase in 1706. The Walker family, which bought it in the 1960s, lived there for six months of the year. Like its previous owners, the family took care of the island and preserved its resources, including the historic ruins of the Edwards mansion, which was built of tabby, a native material made of crushed oyster shells.

In the late 1980s, a group of investors that had an option on Spring Island planned to build 5,500 housing units and sought to build a bridge from the mainland. Coincidentally, developers Chaffin and Light were involved in developing another community on nearby Callawassee Island. Recognizing that it would be easier to build a bridge from Callawassee Island than from the mainland, the investors contacted Chaffin to discuss the possibility of an easement for this purpose. Chaffin responded that they would entertain the idea only if the developers would lower the density at the proposed Spring Island project. "I don't think density is a four-letter word," says Chaffin. "In fact, density is a necessity for responsible land use, especially with transit-oriented development. But

Spring Island is a 3,000-acre (1,124-ha) conservation community on the South Carolina coast. Originally proposed for 5,500 housing units, the island now has 407 residential units and a 1,200-acre (486-ha) nature preserve.

A majority of the land on Spring Island is undeveloped. It is protected by a conservation easement held by the Spring Island Trust.

density should take its cue from the land. The appropriate density depends on what you are trying to accomplish and what the land tells you to do." In Chaffin's opinion, the land on Spring Island clearly was not well suited for the 5,500 homes and two golf courses that the original developers proposed. "It was one of the most beautiful and fragile ecosystems that I'd ever seen," he says.

The owners' request for a permit to build a bridge from the mainland was denied because the bridge would have crossed over Class A fishing waters. Chaffin refused to provide the easement they needed to build a bridge from Callawassee Island. Instead, Chaffin purchased a one-year option on Spring Island to explore the feasibility of a different kind of community. What he envisioned was a conservation-based community that subordinated development to the island's existing natural character and beauty.

Commitment to Nature

Chaffin and Light had worked together for many years. After going to college together in the 1960s, they worked for Charles Fraser—the developer of Hilton Head Island, Sea Pines Plantation, and other well-known planned communities—from 1968 to 1978, developing master-planned communities, primarily in the southeast and Puerto Rico. By the late 1980s, their firm, Chaffin/Light Associates, was becoming known for its environmentally sensitive treatment of the land at communities it had developed in Colorado and the Pacific Northwest. But Spring Island presented a new challenge and a new opportunity. Chaffin and Light wondered: "Could the main amenity of this community be the environment? Our philosophy was to create a community within a park, not a park within a community."

Chaffin believed that the time was right for this new approach. Studies of the baby boomer generation showed that an increasing number of people indicated that they were concerned about environmental issues and were willing to pay to protect the environment. "People were more interested in their well-being than in being well-off," he says.

Chaffin/Light set about exploring the feasibility of a low-density development on Spring Island with nature as its main amenity. Extensive market research suggested that people would respond to the idea of a community within a park. It appeared that the natural setting of Spring Island would help Chaffin and Light differentiate their product. But research also showed that the people who could afford to buy in a low-density development like the one Chaffin and Light proposed would demand high-quality amenities. "The golf course was our insurance," says Chaffin.

With the initial research showing that their idea would be financially viable, Chaffin and Light set about evaluating the land. They used McHargian overlays to better understand the island and its resources, and engaged naturalists and planners to determine which land should be protected and which was appropriate for development. The resulting site plan set aside 1,200 acres (486 ha) of the most sensitive land as a nature preserve, and Chaffin and Light established the Spring Island Trust to ensure its preservation and maintenance. In addition to preserving areas for keystone wildlife habitat, the Spring Island Trust's three full-time naturalists focus on educating members of the community to assume stewardship responsibilities for the land.

"We felt that for the community to be successful—for the idea to last—we needed to establish an ethos," says Chaffin. "The naturalists at the trust have Thursday morning bird watching, Saturday morning kayaking, and other environmentally based activities to help people to get over their biophobia and understand the environment in which they live. Our homeowners are people from urban areas—from Charleston, Chicago, Philadelphia—who may not have experience with nature. Our mission was to get them to enjoy walking in the woods and to appreciate the nature that surrounds them."

One of the on-site naturalists also works with individual architects and builders, reviewing the plans for each of the proposed homes and helping them understand the constraints of the land and how to design and build a home that will have minimal environmental impact. "The demarcation between nature and development is blurred," says Chaffin. "The third person we hired at Spring Island was a naturalist."

The protected wetlands and woodlands in the nature preserve provide a rich habitat for many plant and animal species. Naturalists have identified more than 90 tree species on the island—more than three times the number found on neighboring barrier islands. There are also more than 400 species of plants and bushes. This provides fertile habitat for a wide variety of animals, including wild turkeys, deer, quail, woodpeckers, fox squirrels, egrets, herons, and other marsh birds. Spring Island is also home to great horned owls, barred owls, red tail and

Spring Island's Mission Statement

The mission of Spring Island residents is to preserve the natural surroundings that we have inherited so that we might take pleasure in the peaceful enjoyment of its marshes, forests, and fields. This restorative sense of solitude is furthered by the studied decision to set aside more than one-third of our maritime forest as a nature preserve, and permit only 400 families to share the experience of Spring Island. Everything that is natural and beautiful about the island will be maintained, and human presence will always be subtle and unassuming.

As stewards of Spring Island, we recognize our obligation to plan for the preservation of this natural asset into the future. The programs in place have been designed to ensure that future generations will carry on this philosophy, thus enabling them to enjoy the same unique attributes that first drew us here.

Source: Spring Island website, www.springisland.com/club/scripts/public/public.asp?NS=PUBLIC.

Cooper's hawks, eagles, mink, otters, foxes, and bobcats. During the design and development process, the Spring Island team also took care to preserve the shell mounds and camps of the indigenous people who once called Spring Island home, as well as the ruins of the plantation houses and outbuildings of early European settlers.

Spring Island's policies and guidelines emphasize coexistence with its sensitive environment. The golf course, for instance, is what Chaffin calls a "model of restraint." The designs for several holes—including one that features a rookery, where golfers can pause to view wood storks, ibis, egrets, and herons—use natural management practices. During the buildout phase, the developers took care to preserve as many trees and other natural features as possible. Where trees needed to give way to development, they were transplanted to other parts of the island. Because of the emphasis on tree preservation, it is very difficult to tell how many houses are on the island. Land management principles continue to be reviewed and enhanced. Scientists from several fields routinely meet to review how their practices are affecting keystone species.

Siting and Design

The site plan includes 285 "estate" homesites that are two to ten acres (0.8 to 4 ha) in size and 125 smaller "cottage" homesites that range from one-quarter to three-quarters of an acre (0.1 to 0.3 ha). Regardless of their size, the homes are situated to blend with their natural surroundings and sited for minimal specimen tree disturbance. The development plan also called for unpaved roads and setbacks for homes that are twice the county minimums. The homesites are designed to blend seamlessly with their surroundings. "The homes at Spring Island don't intrude into nature," boasts Spring Island's website. "Rather, they fit within it."

Homeowners are allowed a small envelope of residential landscaping around their houses, but are required to maintain natural vegetation at the periphery of their lots to screen the houses from view. One result of the landscaping policy is that very few homes can be seen from the island's major roads. The natural vegetation also provides habitat for indigenous wildlife.

Life at Spring Island

Creating a sense of community was another guiding principle for development. The development team elected to have a centrally located post office rather than mailboxes in front of each house. Chaffin explains that this takes mail delivery vehicles off the road and "gets people to come to

Spring Island has two clubhouses with private dining facilities, as well as many other amenities. Mobley Nature Center is staffed by full-time naturalists who manage the Spring Island Trust's wildlife conservation program, maintain trails and open space, and conduct educational programs for residents and schoolchildren.

a central place every day and bump into each other." Other community-building events include regular talks by naturalists and visiting artists, art workshops, concerts, kids' camps, and cultural events.

Spring Island also offers many of the amenities that homeowners typically expect to find in a high-end community, including a private, Arnold Palmer–designed golf course. The golf course, which is widely viewed as one of the finest residential courses in the country, also has the distinction of being a Certified Audubon Cooperative Sanctuary. A 30-acre (12-ha) equestrian facility with 35 miles (56 km) of riding trails, private tennis and fitness facilities, community boat docks, and 30 freshwater and four saltwater fishing ponds provide additional recreational opportunities for residents. Like the homes, all of these facilities are designed to blend into the natural environment.

Still, nature remains Spring Island's most important amenity. "When you live on Spring Island, nature becomes an amenity just as golf is," says Chris Marsh, one of Spring Island's naturalists. "Of the 3,000 acres that are on Spring Island, over 1,200 are protected permanently as nature preserve. In addition, the Spring Island Trust works very closely with all the Spring Island members to ensure that they understand how their stewardship of their individual properties also contributes to Spring Island as one 3,000-acre nature preserve." Steve Roper, the club manager, adds: "Spring Island is probably the most unusual club or residential community that I have ever been a part of or witnessed. Forget about the golf, the tennis, and the sports facilities that most other clubs have, it's all the other stuff that makes Spring Island the special place that it is."

The Spring Island Trust, which holds the conservation easement on the 1,200 acres (486 ha) of protected land, designates a member to serve on the homeowners association's board of directors. In addition, a stewardship committee, consisting of three Spring Island Trust members and two homeowners association members, helps provide guidance and advice on issues of mutual interest, such as the maintenance of trails. "The hottest issue is the maintenance of the roadside," says Chaffin. "Some people believe it should have a manicured look with mowed grass, while others think it should be allowed to revert to its natural state."

Marketing and Sales

Marketing Spring Island was initially a challenge because there was no other nature-based, private club community to use as a model. Chaffin and Light capitalized on their reputation, focusing on people who knew them from prior experience. They added to this list people who had visited Spring Island or the surrounding area.

To generate interest and cash, Chaffin and Light created a "founders program" through which they offered the initial 35 investors first pick of a homesite and a discounted membership. As they brought people to the island, the developers got their investment back. The infusion of $10 million in "founder" sales helped Chaffin/Light obtain debt financing. "The $10 million in sales on an island with no bridge, no beach, and no roads gave the local banks confidence that we were on to something," explains Chaffin.

The developers believed that traditional marketing techniques would be ineffective. "It is a story that is very hard to tell in an ad," says Chaffin. Ad placement was also an issue. "We didn't want to sell ads in golf magazines, because we didn't want to become known as primarily a golf community."

The developers did place a few black-and-white teaser ads in more generic publications they believed would reach their target audience, such as the *New York Times* and *National Geographic*, but this was a very small portion of their effort and amounted to less than 10 percent of the money spent on marketing. Rather, the development team focused on owner referrals. Chaffin and Light believed that the best way to sell the island was to bring others to see and experience its natural beauty and to explain what they were trying to do there. They allowed the founders to use the island for shrimp and oyster roasts, and also sponsored dinners in the off-island homes of the founders for friends who might be interested.

The marketing team crafted a logo and tagline that capitalize on the development's unique relationship with nature. Focusing attention on the community's ties to nature, the logo features birds, a crab, and a tree. The tagline—"Spring Island. It was the first of its kind. It is the last of its kind."—seeks to prompt curiosity and a sense of urgency.

Still, initial sales were slow. Chaffin/Light closed on the property in April 1990; the next year or two brought little additional interest—a fact that Chaffin believes may have been attributable to the U.S. invasion of Kuwait. Over time, however, Spring

Island's environmental bent and recreational amenities attracted national attention. In mid-1991, an editorial in the New York Times discussed the community's innovative approach. Articles also appeared in golf, equestrian, and sporting magazines, as well as in several shelter and lifestyle magazines, such as Southern Living, Luxury Living, Architectural Digest, and Southern Accents. Once the community had what Chaffin calls "visible viability," sales picked up considerably: 1993 to 1995 were "fabulous years." When the developers turned over management of the community to the homeowners association in 2000, all but ten sites had been sold.

Spring Island has an award-winning golf course and many other recreational amenities, including a community swimming pool, tennis courts, an equestrian center, a fitness center, and miles of trails.

There are many historic structures on Spring Island, as well as more than 400 species of plants and animals, including eagles, wild turkeys, deer, fox, quail, egrets, herons, and great horned owls.

Spring Island received a ULI Award for Excellence in 2000.

As of the end of 2009, there were 237 homes finished and six under construction. Many of the members are original owners. In most years, roughly 10 percent of the homes are on the market; during the economic downturn of early 2010, there were 38 homes—or 16 percent—on the market. Project staff say that this is not bad, given the current economic conditions.

This is within market norms, although sales sometimes take longer because there tend to be fewer qualified buyers for these high-end properties. Homeowners are loyal to Chaffin/Light's concept, however. "People looking to downsize ask me, 'What have you got for me now?'" says Chaffin. "In fact, we're looking into the possibility of a "downsized" home neighborhood.

Challenges and Lessons Learned

Spring Island was unique in many ways, which made its future uncertain. It was the first high-end development along the Carolina coast that did not have a beachfront and among the first developments based on the philosophy of offering nature as a primary amenity. Initial sales were slow, and resulted mainly from word of mouth and owner referrals. "Spring Island attracted people with a certain value system," says Chaffin. "It is not for everyone."

Chaffin asserts that this sense of community enhances quality of life and thus real estate values. "Quality of life has less to do with the architecture, land planning, or interior design than it does with the friends people make and the quality of service they get every day." He emphasizes that authenticity is key. Spring Island builds on indigenous architecture and preserves the integrity of the land's history, as well as nature. Chaffin also says it was critical to attract top-quality food and beverage service to the island.

Marketing was a challenge early on. Traditional marketing approaches were ill-suited for this nontraditional community, and sales were initially slow. In addition, Chaffin emphasizes that conservation development requires, first and foremost, the right piece of property. According to Chaffin, "the success of Spring Island was due in large part to its uniqueness, to the fact that centuries after the first person set his claim to the island, nature there still governed supreme."

Site plan.

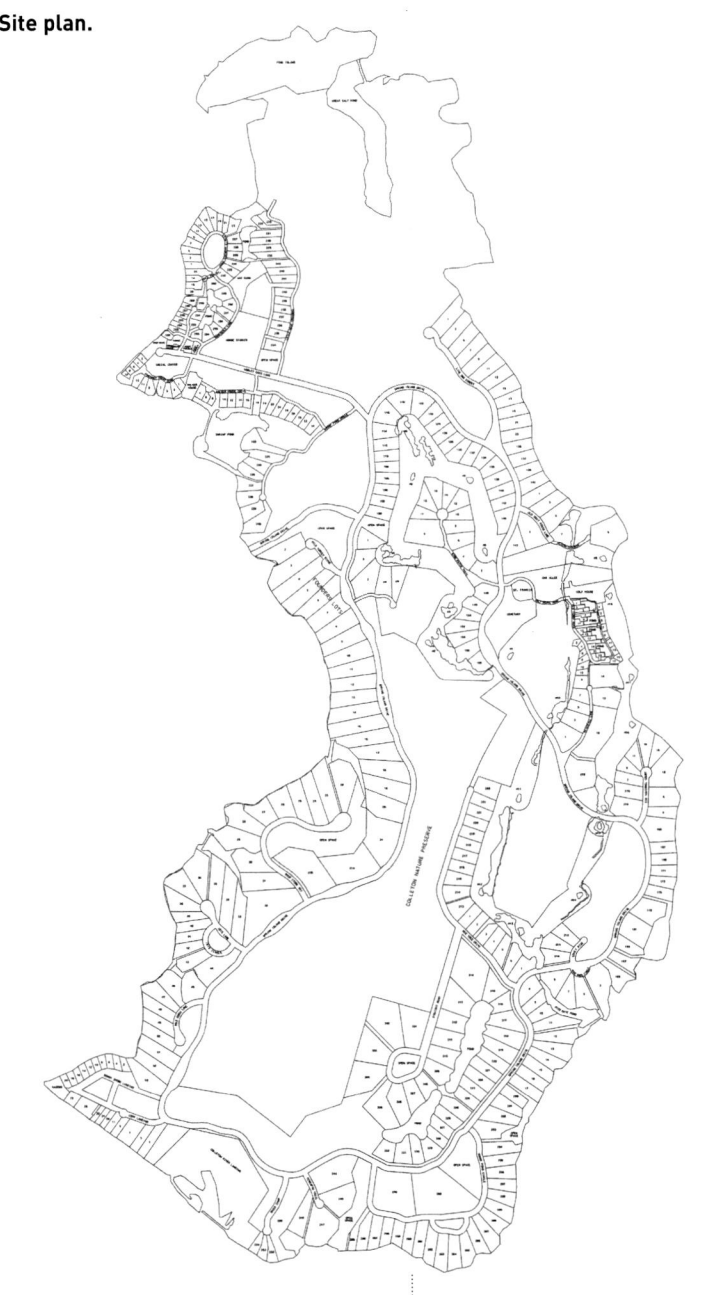

SPRING ISLAND

LAND USE INFORMATION

Site area	3,000 acres/1,214 ha
Number of residential units planned	407
Number of residential units completed (2009)	237
Gross residential density (units per ac/ha)	0.14/0.35

LAND USE PLAN

	Acres/ Hectares	Percentage of Site
Residential	1,600/648	53
Roads/surface parking	30/12	1
Natural open space	1,200/486	40
Developed open space (golf course)	120/49	4
Other	50/20	2
Total	**3,000/1,214**	**100**

DEVELOPMENT COST INFORMATION

Site Acquisition Cost	**$15,000,000**

General Costs

Master planning/engineering/landscaping	$4,324,582
Bridge construction	1,873,823
On-island main roads	1,196,201
Paving	624,904
Wastewater facility (bulk plant)	1,802,349
Water facilities	636,503
Bulkhead/promenade	1,490,679
Causeway	623,859
	$12,572,900

Lot Development Cost	**$8,262,777**

Amenity Construction Costs

Golf club facilities	
Golf course	$5,857,769
Maintenance facility/pump house	589,997
Golf clubhouse	3,577,994
Walker Landing facilities	7,231,545
	$17,257,305

Soft Costs

Project management	$11,769,000
Marketing and sales	17,417,000
Construction interest and fees	8,760,000
Operating losses during sellout	10,638,000
	$ 48,584,000
Total Development Cost	**$101,676,982**

DEVELOPMENT SCHEDULE

Site purchased	1990
Lot sales began	1990
Construction started	1991
First residences built	1991
Developer buildout	2000

DEVELOPMENT TEAM

Developer
Chaffin/Light Associates
Okatie, South Carolina
www.chaffinlight.com

Planners
Robert Marvin/Howell Beach & Associates
(master planning/site planning)
Walterboro, South Carolina
www.marvinbeach.com

Edward Pinckney/Associates Ltd. (master planning)
Bluffton, South Carolina
www.pinckneyassociates.com

Community Building Architects
Thomas & Denzinger Architects
Beaufort, South Carolina
www.thomasanddenzinger.com

Historical Concepts
Peachtree City, Georgia
www.historicalconcepts.com

Golf Course Architect
Palmer Course Design Company
Ponte Vedra Beach, Florida
www.palmerdesign.com

Project Website
www.springisland.com

Storm Mountain Ranch

Steamboat Springs, Colorado

CASE STUDY

Special Features

- Almost 800 acres (324 ha) under conservation easement, including 200 acres (81 ha) preserved for agricultural use (hay production).
- Working cattle ranch with red Angus cattle.
- Equestrian facilities with 12 paint horses.
- Restored trout streams and ten acres (4 ha) of ponds offering world-class fly fishing.
- Extensive multiuse trail system for hiking, horseback riding, cross-country skiing, and mountain biking.
- Architectural guidelines and attention to detail that enhance the Western design motif.
- Awapa Lodge, an owners' lodge that provides a place for homeowners to gather, relax, and get to know one another.
- Five owner cabins that provide a place for owners to stay when building their homes and for guests to stay after the owner's homes are built.
- Sold out in only 12 months, generating $44 million in sales.

Storm Mountain Ranch is a gated luxury ranch community located in Colorado's Yampa Valley, less than five miles (8 km) south of Steamboat Springs. This high-end conservation development is situated on 1,063 acres (430 ha), almost 800 acres (324 ha) of which are under conservation easement. The remaining acreage is divided into just 14 lots, providing a density of roughly one house per 76 acres (31 ha). Homes are strategically situated to maximize privacy and access to nature while minimizing the impact of development on the land. The working ranch is surrounded by Routt National Forest and features numerous amenities, including four luxurious fishing cabins—also known as owners' cabins—as well as a 7,400-square-foot (688-m^2) owners' lodge built in the style of historic national park lodges, and a 3,000-square-foot (279-m^2) hand-crafted log "hideout cabin" with modern conveniences and authentic Western decor. Storm Mountain Ranch—which also features world-class trout fishing in ten acres (4 ha) of ponds and three miles (5 ha) of freestone Walton Creek, equestrian facilities, nine miles (14 km) of trails, and a herd of red Angus cattle—was developed as an exclusive sanctuary for people who love the Western outdoors.

Through its limited development approach, Storm Mountain Ranch balances the preservation of the land's natural resources with the desire of people to enjoy old-fashioned ranch living. "Storm Mountain Ranch is a model for protective development in a Colorado valley facing unprecedented growth pressure," says Lee Dusa, former president of Colorado Open Lands, a statewide land conservation organization. "Storm Mountain Ranch demonstrates there is a way to successfully marry environmental and agricultural protection with limited habitation by man. Homeowners on Storm Mountain Ranch are participants in creating a new model for land development in the West, one based on stewardship, agricultural production, and environmental preservation."

Origins

Ranching has been a central part of life in the Yampa Valley for decades. While tourism has become Steamboat Springs's primary economic driver, cow and sheep ranching, hay and wheat farming, and coal mining remain key industries in the area. In the 1980s, a large parcel adjacent to what is now Storm Mountain Ranch was sold and developed into a housing project known as the Fox Estates. Sunwest Corporation then bought the remaining land and operated the property as a large cattle ranch and corporate retreat for trophy elk and bear hunting.

Storm Mountain Ranch is a high-end, low-density conservation community located in the Yampa Valley, near Steamboat Springs, Colorado.

In the early 1990s, Jamie Temple, a developer, came across the property when he was looking for a ranch on which to build a home. He purchased the Storm Mountain property from Sunwest Corporation in 1994. In his quest to name the ranch, Jamie was inspired by his father, Jim Temple, the founder and developer of the Storm Mountain Ski Area, which later became the Steamboat Ski Resort. During an early meeting with a marketing group, Jamie looked out the window and saw Storm Mountain and Walton Creek Canyon engulfed by a storm. (Later, Olympic skier A.J. Kitt created the ranch's logo and brand, which he originally drew on the back of a napkin.) In 1998, Jamie Temple and his brother Jeff formed Storm Mountain Development, Ltd., and began to plan a small, high-end residential community at Storm Mountain Ranch.

Commitment to Conservation

Colorado law allows anyone who owns at least 35 acres (14 ha) of rural property to build a home on that parcel without going through the local county planning or subdivision process. Routt County's land preservation subdivision ordinance was designed to avoid the patchwork development that results from this law by rewarding developers who agree to cluster homesites with an expedited planning process and a density bonus. The county's ordinance would have allowed one homesite per 28 acres (11 ha) at Storm Mountain Ranch, or 37 homesites total. The developers, however, felt that a lower density—just one home per 76 acres (31 ha)—would be more in keeping with their vision of land conservation, continued food production on the land, and marketing strategy—so only 14 homesites were created.

At the core of their development strategy is an emphasis on preserving the pristine environment of Walton Creek Canyon—which surrounds a blue-ribbon trout stream that flows through the property—and protecting the ranching heritage of the Yampa Valley. The overall design of the property was dictated by a preservation ethic and recognition of the great value of preserved open space and wildlife habitat. The development team spent a full year undertaking a comprehensive inventory of the ranch to identify areas to protect from development—including riparian zones, wildlife habitat, and productive ranchlands. House lots and roads then were sited to ensure that these resources would not be affected by the development.

Each ranch lot, called a homestead, is roughly 70 acres (28 ha), fee simple. A building envelope, ranging in size from one to three acres (0.5 to 1.5 ha), is placed on each lot to

Vision and Values Statement

The Storm Mountain Ranch (SMR) homeowners are committed to sustaining an uncrowded, peaceful, spiritual, and pristine environment. In an effort to preserve these qualities at the ranch for future generations of owners, the use of the ranch facilities and land is solely dedicated for the enjoyment of the owners' family and friends.

This vision of SMR is accomplished through the following values:

- Homeowners taking pride in using the common facilities and guest cabins as extensions of their own homes.
- Pursuing a casual lifestyle through family retreats and interactions with neighbors in the ranch community.
- Enjoying safe adventures such as fishing, hiking, horseback riding, cross-country skiing, snowshoeing, and observing wildlife on the property, and the many recreational opportunities in the adjacent national forest.
- Honoring nature as a learning environment while maintaining a high-quality agricultural program.
- Acting as good stewards of the ranch and the greater Steamboat Springs community.
- Observing, in both spirit and word, all ranch rules and regulations.

Source: Storm Mountain Ranch website, www.stormmountainranch.com/storm_mountain_ranch/index.php.

limit the developable portion. One home and one guest home—limited to 2,000 square feet (186 m²)—may be built on a homesite. Most of the land outside the building envelope is under conservation easement. This protects the portion of each lot with the highest conservation value. Hay meadows were preserved by siting homes along the tree line at the edges of the meadows. The site plan protects hundreds of acres of meadows, timbered hillsides, nine acres (4 ha) of ponds, and two miles (3 km) of Walton Creek. Many miles of recreation trails loop through the conservation lands, allowing glimpses of the mountains, the valley floor, and a wide variety of wildlife.

In 1997, Jamie Temple donated the development rights on 793 acres (321 ha) of conservation land to the Yampa Valley Land Trust, a nonprofit

Storm Mountain Ranch, situated on 1,063 acres (430 ha), includes hay meadows, forest land, nine acres (3.6 ha) of ponds, and two miles (3 km) of Walton Creek.

In addition to 14 homes, Storm Mountain Ranch includes Awapa Lodge, which provides a gathering place for homeowners' families and friends. Other amenities are guest cabins and equestrian facilities.

organization dedicated to preserving the agricultural, scenic, wildlife, and open-space values of northern Colorado. Included in this easement is the Meadows Conservation Area which guarantees that more than 200 acres (81 ha) of open hay meadows will stay in agricultural production. This area, which is farmed by ranch employees, produces more than 100 tons of hay per year. Some of the hay is kept to feed the horses at Storm Mountain Ranch; the revenue from the sale of the remaining hay goes to the Storm Mountain Ranch Homeowners Association.

Two additional conservation areas provide critical habitat for wildlife, including moose, elk, mule deer, black bear, golden and bald eagles, porcupine, and ermine, as well as for brown, rainbow, brook, and cutthroat trout. The old-growth forests of the Hill Side Conservation Area abut Routt National Forest. Hiking trails throughout the conservation areas provide opportunities for Storm Mountain Ranch residents to enjoy the lush scenery and view abundant wildlife.

State-of-the-art forestry and wildlife management practices ensure the ongoing management and protection of the natural resources at Storm Mountain Ranch. The homeowners association (HOA) oversees land management and restoration activities. In addition, the working ranch includes a ranch manager's house, a horse barn, a shop, outbuildings, and other facilities for maintenance and haying operations. The HOA employs a full-time ranch manager and two wranglers. The ranch manager oversees the agricultural operations and shares his love of horses and ranching lore with residents. "In a world of dwindling resources, it's imperative to keep agricultural land in production," says Jeff Temple, a fifth-generation Routt County resident. "The farmer and rancher exercise a special kind of stewardship of the land. I love riding horses but, for me, the working ranch is as much about the meadows' protected hay operation as it is about the opportunity to ride, rope, and wrangle."

The development team capitalized on the land's unique natural features to provide additional amenities. Irrigation ditches were widened and drop structures installed to turn the ditches into prime habitat for several varieties of trout.

Storm Mountain Ranch has several miles of blue-ribbon trout streams as well as an extensive multipurpose trail system.

Design Guidelines and Amenities

The developers' commitment to preserving and enhancing Storm Mountain Ranch's natural features and aesthetic was furthered by careful attention to detail in design and construction. The community's stone and timber entryway, wooden bridges, rugged stacked log-rail drift fences, and custom lighting were designed to integrate with the natural surroundings and to emulate the architectural character of the region and its national parks. While homeowners were given considerable latitude in the design of their homes, they were required to follow a comprehensive set of design guidelines to ensure that the community would have a comprehensive feel and that the homes would blend harmoniously with their natural surroundings.

In addition to its 14 homes, Storm Mountain Ranch includes the Awapa Lodge (from a Ute word meaning "the land of many waters"), which sits at the edge of a nine-acre (4-ha) lake teeming with trout. With a commercial kitchen, bar, TV, and pool table, this owners' lodge provides a gathering place for homeowners and their families and friends. Other amenities are five guest cabins, and equestrian facilities that include 12 horses, a barn, and an arena. All of these amenities are housed in buildings reminiscent of the Old West. The Western-style wood-and-stone horse barn, for example, has a double-pitched gambrel roof that is intended to shed snow while maintaining large hayloft capacity.

Storm Mountain Ranch also contains many miles of carefully planned and maintained trails for hiking, horseback riding, mountain biking, cross-country skiing, and snowshoeing. The trails connect Storm Mountain Ranch to the Routt National Forest. Footpaths also meander along Walton Creek and along the spring creek streams in the front meadows of the ranch, providing excellent access for fishing and wildlife viewing.

Storm Mountain Ranch received the Colorado Smart Growth Award in 1998 from the governor of Colorado.

Fishing at Storm Mountain Ranch

Water runs like a thread through the canyon, lakes, and ponds at Storm Mountain. It cascades from lake to lake. Creeks and ditches flow all year round. Walton Creek, the North Fork, the Middle Fork, and the South Fork connect the homesteads to the canyon and meadows like a strand of pearls, and the meadows' smaller spring creek fisheries make the landscape come alive.

Storm Mountain Ranch is committed to creating and maintaining high-quality fish habitat. You can fish the creek, the ponds, the lakes, and the meadow meanders. You can fish in waders, from the shore, or from one of the lake's flat-bottomed wooden Adirondack guide boats elegantly handcrafted of cedar. There are big fish, fighters, and plenty of them.

Walton Creek, teeming with brook, cutthroat, and rainbow trout, had great private fly-fishing to begin with. First a trout ecologist, Dr. William Walsh, studied the creek and irrigation system. Then Steve Herter, a world-famous fly-fisher and master planner of the fishing empire, enhanced and added to the original habitat to provide ideal conditions for raising big fish. Consulting with land planners, Herter designed fishing lakes with bottoms contoured to provide superior trout habitat, allowing the fish to grow big and strong. He also transformed the irrigation ditches to create a fly-fisher's dream in the meadows—an amazing array of flowing spring creek fishery. Storm Mountain's commitment to fishing is so strong that the ranch's registered brand is "Hook, Line, and Sinker."

Source: Adapted from Storm Mountain Ranch, "An Empire of Fishing," http://dreampursuits.com/fishing.html.

Marketing and Sales

In the early 1990s, the concept of building a luxury, low-density community with a working ranch was quite innovative. As a result, the developers met with initial resistance from banks for financing. "This was a foreign concept," says Jeff Temple. "Since then, many people have tried to emulate these types of communities, so it is easier to get an audience with the banking community."

Construction began in 1998, and sales of the 14 lots—priced at more than $2.5 million each—began in 2000. Storm Mountain Ranch was marketed as a luxury ranch community on its website, as well as in national publications and in periodicals targeting the West, including the *Wall Street Journal* and *Cowboys and Indians*.

The project sold out in just 12 months, exceeding expectations. By fall 2009, 12 homes had been completed on the 14 homesites. Home value appreciation has exceeded the area market; one home resold for $7.4 million in 2007. While only about 35 percent of the owners are full-time residents, some owners spend half the year there, taking advantage of the excellent year-round amenities such as skiing and fishing.

Temple credits the success of Storm Mountain Ranch to the development team's single-minded attention to detail and quality. "The high-end amenities and superb architecture struck a chord with the market," he says. Temple also notes that the conservation aspect of the project helped build goodwill in the community. "Routt County supported us from the beginning because we did what we said we would do—preserved open space and continued food production on the land. We are also very involved in the local community." In addition, he cites the proximity of Storm Mountain Ranch to Steamboat Springs as a huge plus. "People see this as a healthy, beautiful place to live—a legacy property where families can get together, a place where memories are created."

The Next Step

Jeff Temple and a group of six other partners are building on Temple's success and the lessons learned at Storm Mountain Ranch to create a larger conservation community at

Marabou, a land preservation subdivision that comprises 62 homesteads on 1,717 acres (695 ha) of ranchland five miles (8 km) west of Steamboat Springs. "I'm excited about Marabou," Jeff Temple says. "After Storm Mountain Ranch, I didn't think I'd have an opportunity to create another ranch preservation community. I saw things we missed and things that could be done better. It's not often you are able to learn from your mistakes and create another community of this scale."

Temple says he is taking what he learned at Storm Mountain to provide more of the high-end amenities typically found at luxury resorts. He said he was surprised by how many of the owners at Storm Mountain Ranch asked for a swimming pool, fitness

Each ranch lot is roughly 70 acres (28 ha), but the building envelope is limited to one to three acres (0.5 to 1.5 ha).

Sustainability at Marabou

Jeff Temple and six new partners took the lessons he learned at Storm Mountain Ranch to create a conservation community at Marabou, a 1,717-acre (695-ha) ranch conservation community with 62 homesteads located five miles (8 km) from downtown Steamboat Springs, Colorado. The development sets aside 77 percent of the land as common open space, with trails connecting the homesites to the preserved land.

Marabou's core philosophies are land stewardship, energy efficiency, water conservation, waste reduction, and environmental education. This all-encompassing commitment to the environment will ensure that the natural beauty of Marabou's mountain setting is preserved, the natural wildlife habitats are enhanced, and wildlife carrying capacity is increased. By incorporating green building technologies, adopting a "light-on-the-land" master plan that clusters homesites and maximizes open space with green agricultural and ranching operations, and using 100 percent renewable energy certificates, Marabou has achieved a better-than-carbon-neutral footprint. All of Marabou's amenity buildings have incorporated recycled building materials, energy efficiency, and electricity from clean, renewable wind power. They also use materials that promote improved indoor environmental quality and environmentally conscious landscaping practices. The team developed design guidelines for green building; a $10,000 incentive is available for homeowners who incorporate green building techniques into the design of their home.

Marabou also serves as a model for green agricultural ranch operations, incorporating rotational grazing, which is better for the land, animals, and people. Grass-fed cattle are fattened on natural forage, not in feedlots and not on grain. No hormones or antibiotics are used, yielding healthier cattle that are healthier to consume. Perhaps Marabou's biggest legacy will be to create a new sustainability model for other developments through leading by example.

facilities, and a spa, so Marabou includes those elements. It also has a 26-seat theater, 22 miles (35 km) of trails, and over 1,300 acres (526 ha) of preserved open space, as well as fly-fishing on ten acres (4 ha) of ponds and along 2.5 miles (4 km) of Elk River.

The other main difference is Marabou's increased focus on sustainability. The new community, like Storm Mountain Ranch, has been built around land preservation principles; more than three-quarters of the site will be permanently protected. "When designing this project, preserving the land and protecting the wildlife were our first priorities and will continue to be the most critical part of this community," says Jeff Temple. But the development team has also incorporated best practices in sustainable development into the planning, design, and construction of the community. "When we developed Storm Mountain Ranch, we were focused on saving the land," he explains. "I wish we'd done more with sustainability, but we just didn't know that much about it at the time. At Marabou, everything we're doing is focused on sustainable solutions to saving energy and resources."

The Marabou community has achieved better-than-carbon-neutral status, as verified by a third party. It also has received a U.S. Environmental Protection Agency award for exemplary green procurement, the Gold Nugget Award from the National Association of Homebuilders for best public/private recreation use facility, and the Sustainable Business of the Year 2007 award from Steamboat Springs.

Sales at Marabou have been brisk, exceeding expectations. As of January 2010, just two and a half years after the homesites went on the market, 40 of the 62 offered had been sold.

Site plan.

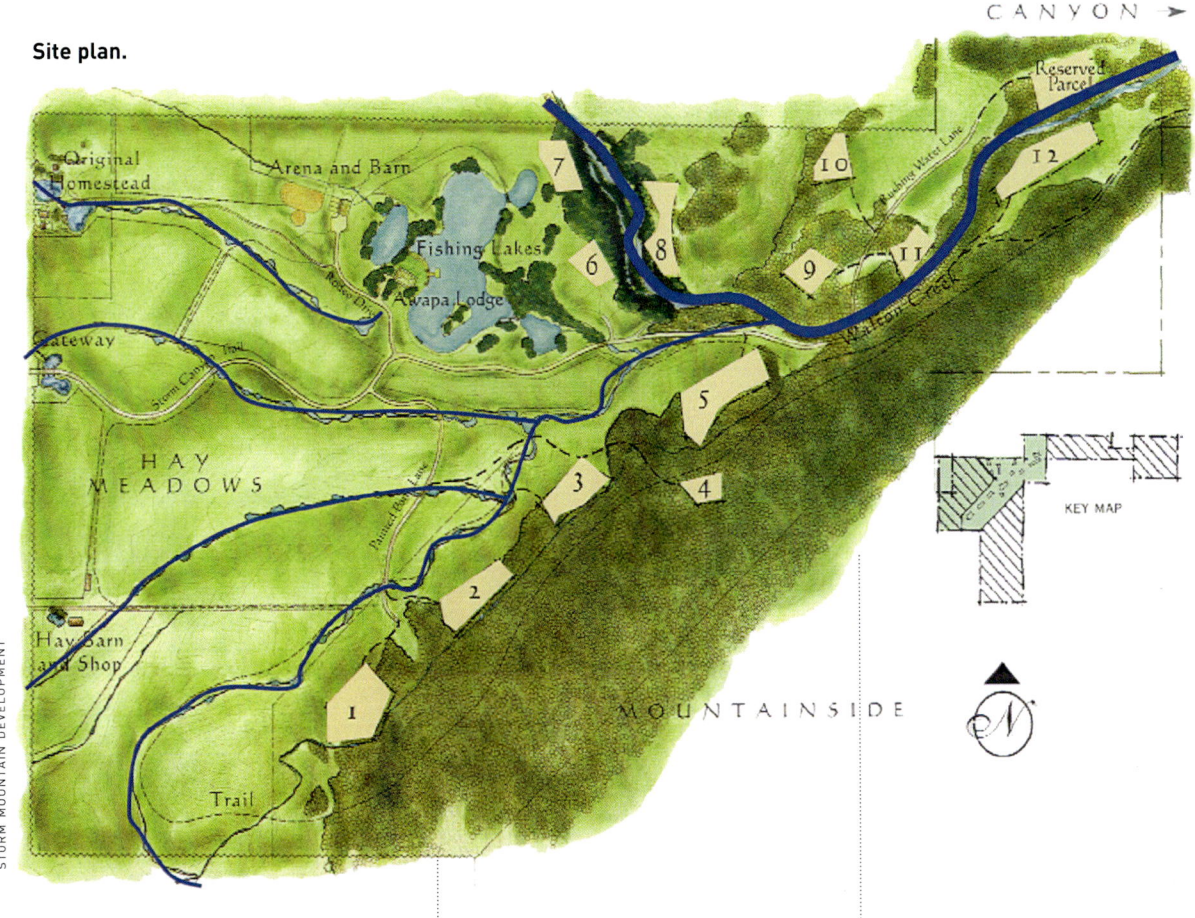

STORM MOUNTAIN RANCH

LAND USE INFORMATION

Site area	1,063 ac/430 ha
Open space under easement	793 ac/321 ha
Number of residential lots	14
Number of lots sold	14
Percentage of residential development complete	86%
Gross residential density	1 unit per 76 ac/31 ha

LAND USE PLAN

	Acres/ Hectares	Percentage of Site
Residential	42/17	4
Developed open space (parks, common areas, ponds)	121/49	11
Undeveloped open space (natural open space)	900/324	85

RESIDENTIAL INFORMATION

Lot Type	Lot Size (ac/ha)	Range of Initial Sales Prices
Residential	70/28	$2,500,000–$3,800,000

DEVELOPMENT COST INFORMATION

Site Acquisition Cost	**$7.5 million**
Site Improvement Costs	
Roads	$4,500,000
Ponds and fishery work	2,200,000
Buildings	7,500,000
Electric/phone	400,000
Front gate and fencing	500,000
Bridges	1,200,000
Total	**$16,300,000**
Acquisition and Development Costs	**$23,800,000**

Soft Costs

Architecture/engineering	$3,500,000
Project management	2,000,000
Marketing and sales	500,000
Commissions	1,800,000
Legal/accounting	400,000
Taxes/insurance	500,000
Construction interest and fees	2,600,000
	$11,300,000
Total Development Cost	**$35,100,000**

DEVELOPMENT SCHEDULE

Site purchased	1994
Planning started	1997
Construction started	1998
Sales started	1999
Developer sellout	2000

DEVELOPMENT TEAM

Owners
Jamie and Jeff Temple
Steamboat Springs, Colorado
www.duewestland.com

Developer
Storm Mountain Development
Steamboat Springs, Colorado
www.duewestland.com

Land Planning/Site Development
Braun Associates Inc. (BAI)
Edwards, Colorado
www.braunassociates.com

Architects
Bob Fitzgerald
Naka Designs
www.nakadesigns.com

Open-Space Protection/Preservation/Management
Yampa Valley Land Trust
Steamboat Springs, Colorado
www.yvlt.org

Project Websites
www.stormmountainranch.com
www.marabouranch.com

Tryon Farm

Michigan City, Indiana

CASE STUDY

Special Features

- Clustered housing in seven settlements; the design and architecture of each settlement reflect its surroundings.
- Natural wetlands sewage system.
- Beautifully restored 1896 Queen Anne farmhouse converted into a bed-and-breakfast.
- Self-governance through a homeowners association.
- A one-150th interest in Tryon Farm's communal land owned by each homeowner. Homeowners do not own the land on which their home is built, but they have access to all of the common areas.
- Besides fishing, boating, hiking, and other outdoor activities, the opportunity for residents to help with farm activities such as planting vegetables or feeding goats and chickens.

Tryon Farm is a 170-acre (69-ha) conservation development in Michigan City, Indiana, just over an hour east of Chicago. The project's homes are clustered in seven settlements, allowing almost 75 percent of the site to be preserved as rolling pasture, meadows, woodlands, and ponds. The site's rural character is reinforced by a restored prairie and 150-year-old beech trees, but it is located just five minutes from the South Shore commuter rail line, providing residents with ready access to Chicago and other cities.

Origins

Michigan City emerged in the late 19th century as a thriving Lake Michigan port town that connected Indianapolis and the rest of the state with commerce from the East Coast. The Tryon family homesteaded Tryon Farm in the 1860s, and in 1896 built the brick Queen Anne home that remains on the property and that is now used as a bed-and-breakfast guesthouse. After World War II, the Tryon family sold the farm to the Werner family, which continued to use it as a dairy farm. By 1990, when architect and developers Ed and Eve Noonan purchased the farm, it was being used to grow corn, beans, and other crops.

The Noonans envisioned a sustainable residential community that would fit into its rural surroundings. Architect Ed Noonan's emphasis was on site planning and high-quality house design. "We're on a farm that for five generations had never been able to make enough money to just live on it," he says. "We wanted to do something in which you have the advantages of the big farm, without the burden of taking care of it."

The Noonans saw a way to preserve the best of the land and the rural character of the area. Their long-time dream was to show that there was an alternative to the "McMansions" and sprawling subdivisions that are spreading out from cities all across the United States. They also believed that a market for this type of community existed among people who wanted to live in a simpler, more sustainable manner and still be connected with nearby urban centers.

The Noonans looked to Prairie Crossing and other early conservation development projects for ideas on how to achieve their mission. As they began the site planning process, they sought to protect the best features of the land by clustering Tryon Farm's homesites in seven settlements.

Tryon Farm is a 170-acre (69-ha) conservation development in Michigan City, Indiana, about an hour east of Chicago.

Planning

One of the Noonans's goals in building Tryon Farm was to create a density-neutral project. "We wanted to show that this could be done without having to change zoning laws or get a variance," says Eve Noonan. Local zoning called for a minimum lot size of one acre (0.4 ha) for each house, but planned unit development (PUD) zoning allowed density transfers within the site. The Noonans used the PUD to create a plan that clustered 150 homes in several settlements and put 120 of the 170 acres (49 of the 69 ha) into a land conservancy.

A natural features analysis helped to determine which land should be protected and where housing should be placed. The roads have been built on the farm paths that the dairy cows once used to travel to the fields where they grazed. Walking and studying the site enabled the development team to nestle the houses into the landscape, disturbing it as little as possible while providing protected long views of the wetlands, prairie, and farmland. The preserved land wraps in and among the settlements, so that all residents have access to open space right outside their doors.

An early resident bought the original brick farmhouse and converted it to a bed-and-breakfast. The Noonans believe that the B&B has helped reduce the footprint of the development: Guests can stay at the B&B, so homeowners can purchase a smaller house because they do not need an extra bedroom for the occasional guest.

Tryon Farm is being built gradually, with each settlement relating to the landscape. The houses come in a variety of models, depending on the settlement in which they are located. Local vernacular architecture is used to enhance the sense that Tryon Farm belongs among the family farms that surround it. Homes that can be seen from the road, for instance, have pitched roofs that mirror the style of century-old Indiana farmhouses.

The Farmstead settlement, the first to be built, consists of 17 houses of different sizes, price points, and types. The scale and materials of the houses respect the farmhouse, barn, and sheds that have been built on the farm over the past 100 years. Cars are contained in European-style red-gravel courtyards ringed by enclosed garages. The settlement also has cultivated gardens in a walled enclosure, enhancing the feel of community in a natural, rural setting.

The Woods settlement is secluded within a forested area. The homes in this settlement include tall, narrow "treehouses" that are elevated above the ground, providing views to the canopy of woods around them. These homes are smaller than those in the Farmstead settlement; some are only 760 square feet (71 m^2). Some of the houses are covered with Cor-Ten steel which, as it rusts, blends in with the surrounding woods. Others are built with cedar siding. The forested setting provides privacy.

Berms were built so that the one-story houses in the Pond settlement recede into the dunes around a wetland pond. The houses are organized in private courtyards with views of the pond. Grass roofs help control cooling and heating, and enable the houses to blend seamlessly into the surrounding dunes.

The Noonans also have defined the features of the remaining settlements, each of which will be situated to fit within and respond to its surroundings. Design features of the homes in these settlements will reflect unique characteristics of the landscape. In the Grove, for instance, dwellings will be built on either side of a creek, tucked behind the existing hedgerow. The developers plan to use the pattern of existing white pines to give form and space to the settlement. Each of the subsequent neighborhoods or settlements will be similarly named and situated to respond to the landscape.

Governance

Tryon Farm is a "land condominium." Residents do not own the land on which their homes are located;

Tryon Farm homes are clustered in seven small settlements, allowing almost 75 percent of the site to be preserved as rolling pasture, meadows, woodlands, and ponds.

instead, each family owns an equal share—a one-150th interest—in the entire settlement. Homeowners care for and pay taxes only on their houses, but they are assessed a monthly fee for the maintenance of communal land and facilities. The monthly assessment pays for insurance, snow removal, road maintenance, garbage pickup, and the biological sewage treatment system. The property manager, First American Management Company, provides financial management and bookkeeping, and maintains road access and common areas. In 2009, each home was assessed $200 per month, but the developers anticipate the cost will go down as more families move to Tryon Farm and share the expenses.

The community is self-governed by the Tryon Farm Homeowners Association, which has an elected board responsible for community decision making. Each settlement also has a committee responsible for the unique issues of that settlement. All homeowners have an equal vote, regardless of the size of their homes or whether they are part-time or full-time residents.

The Tryon Farm Institute, a nonprofit land conservancy, was created to assume ownership of the 120 acres (49 ha) under conservation easement. Creating a conservancy not only guarantees that the acreage will be preserved,

©JOHN HINES

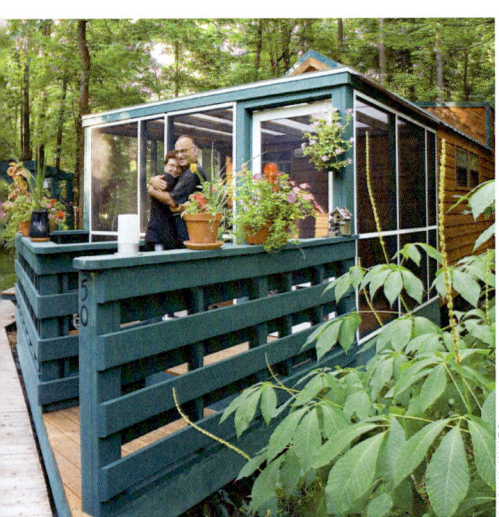

Houses at Tryon Farm range in size from small cottages used as weekend getaways to large year-round homes. As a result, the project attracts buyers of varying demographics and incomes.

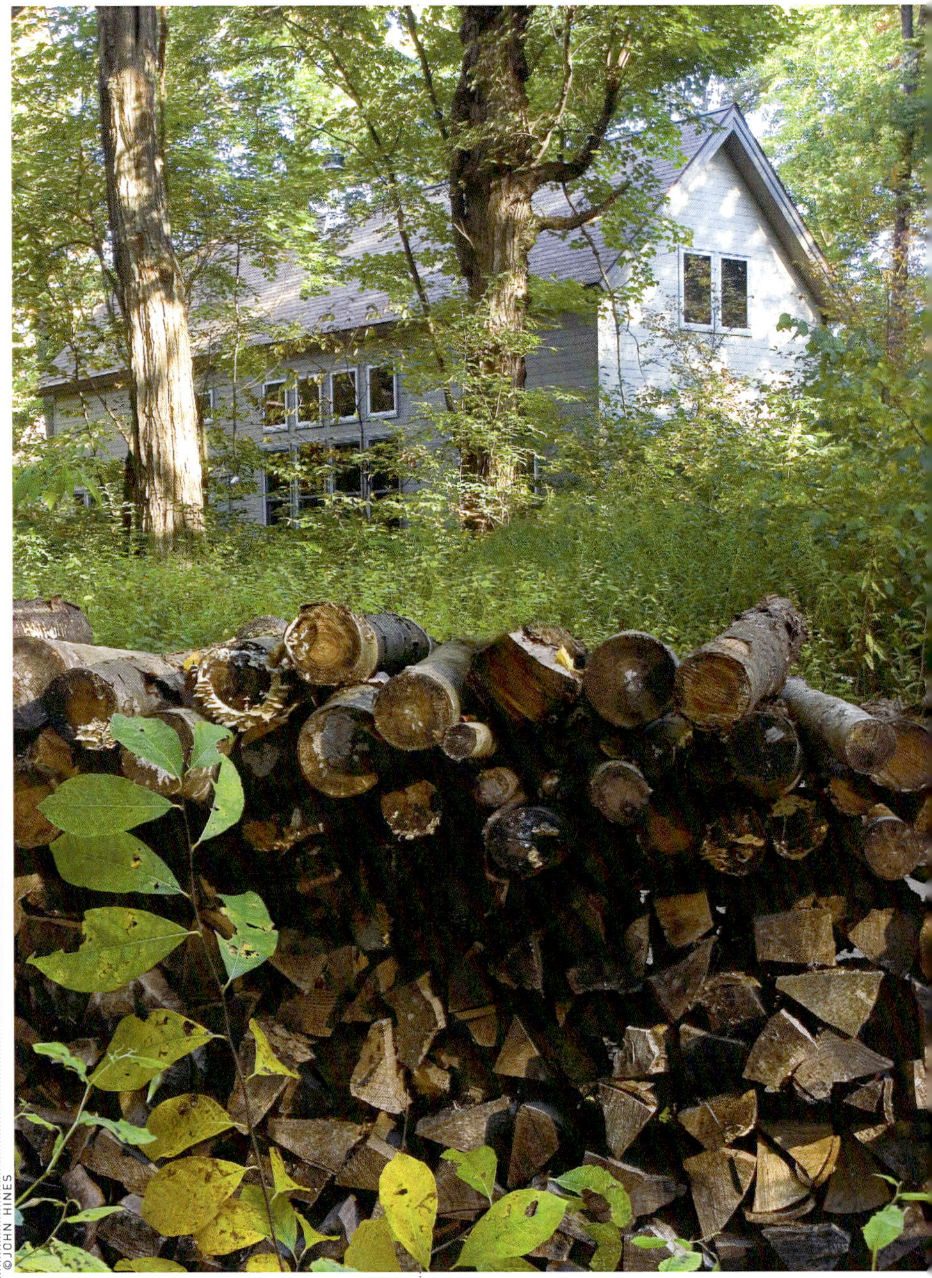

©JOHN HINES

it also saves homeowners from having to pay taxes on what would have been valued as a 120-acre common area. The conservancy manages special projects for wildlife habitats, wetland protection, and educational programs, funded by the monthly assessments.

Green Building and Sustainability

Tryon Farm's homes incorporate a variety of green building practices. The houses are well insulated and have high-efficiency heating systems. Many have bamboo floors and recycled-denim insulation. Although these green features make the homes more expensive to build than production or tract houses, they are far less costly than custom homes. The Noonans say that their commitment to "building well" has translated into a higher per-square-foot price for Tryon Farm homes than those in comparable subdivisions.

Tryon Farm has a natural wetlands sewage treatment system that operates independently of a municipal system. The sewage water goes into an 18-inch-deep (46-cm) pool with a gravel bed covered by tuberous plants. The oxygen from the plant roots cleans the water, and the nutrients in the waste feed the plants. The purified water is pumped into the fields of hay and alfalfa that are grown for livestock feed.

With the help of the Indiana Department of Natural Resources (DNR), the development team also built four ponds in places that had been drained by the farmer. When planning the ponds, the team looked at how water entered the site and how it flowed across the land. "We were the first people the DNR had come across who wanted to build ponds even though government regulations didn't require it," says Ed Noonan. The ponds, natural wetlands, and protected forests provide habitat for an abundance of wildlife, including more than 200 varieties of birds.

Life on the Farm

Tryon Farm provides many opportunities for residents who wish to participate in the life of the farm. In addition to fishing, bird watching, boating, cycling, hiking, and other outdoor activities, residents are encouraged to help with farm activities such as planting vegetables, feeding goats and chickens, and splitting firewood. The developed portion of Tryon Farm also features shared garden plots with picnic tables and grills, as well as a mowed area for outdoor recreational pursuits such as playing ball, flying kites, and other activities.

Tryon Farm also sponsors workshops on crafts, bicycle repair, organic gardening, landscaping, and other topics throughout the year. Movies are shown in the Tryon Farm dairy barn.

Owners also use the barn for potluck suppers, meetings, and other activities. An electronic newsletter keeps residents posted on events at Tryon Farm, as well as what is happening in the surrounding area.

Tryon Farm is not just a farm in name. The community has a bartering arrangement with a neighboring farmer to grow alfalfa for livestock feed at Tryon Farm. In exchange for caring for the farm, the farmer leaves some of the feed for the animals at Tryon Farm and sells the rest. Tryon Farm also has set aside land for community-supported agriculture, in case residents are interested in starting such a project sometime in the future.

Marketing and Sales

Houses at Tryon Farm range in price from approximately $150,000 to $460,000. In the first couple of years, home values increased steadily, but sales slowed in 2006 with the decline in the real estate market. As of early 2010, more than 60 families live at Tryon Farm.

Most resales have involved people selling smaller cottages to build larger houses at Tryon Farm. Several years ago, for instance, the Dennis family bought a 600-square-foot (560-m^2) cabin at Tryon Farm as a weekend getaway. They fell in love with the community, citing the benefits of the conserved

> ### Guidelines for a Healthy Environment, an Energetic Community, and a Nurturing Home
>
> Tryon Farm is based on a set of goals for creating a healthy environment, an energetic community, and a nurturing home. Specific goals include the following:
>
> Goals for land development:
> - Save the farmland and the woodlands;
> - Establish wetland habitats;
> - Reestablish prairies;
> - Clean sewer water for irrigation;
> - Control stormwater;
> - Reduce road width;
> - Manage waste;
> - Establish gardens;
> - Protect open space; and
> - Use government help.
>
> Goals for the homes and settlements:
> - Cluster the houses;
> - Protect privacy;
> - Make simple designs;
> - Use good materials;
> - Build well;
> - Design private courtyards;
> - Place windows for sunlight, privacy, and long views; and
> - Keep night lighting low.

land, the fabulous architecture, and the attention to detail. Within a few years, the Dennises sold the cabin and bought a 2,000-square-foot (186-m²) home as a new permanent residence.

Marketing has been a challenge. In addition to their website, the Noonans rely almost exclusively on word of mouth and news articles. The most effective paid ads were in *Conscious Choice*, a lifestyle magazine focused on sustainable living. "We found that that magazine targeted the right demographic," says Eve Noonan. "We ran a half-page ad every month for the last five or six years. We'd probably still be doing that if *Conscious Choice* hadn't gone out of business." Tryon Farm also has benefited from articles in the *New York Times*, the *Wall Street Journal*, *Dwell*, and *Country Living*, as well as local publications such as the *Chicago Tribune* and the *Chicago Sun-Times*.

The developers also stress the importance of getting out the word beyond prospective buyers. They attend meetings and seminars to describe their project and its benefits, and say they have met many people who are interested in their ideas, including planning officials, architects, developers, and builders. "People are excited to see tangible examples that show there are alternatives to sprawl," says Eve Noonan. "Increasing awareness among developers and architects and builders is really important to do."

Tryon Farm features the following amenities and benefits for residents:

- A plan that put houses within the preserve rather than separate from it;
- Emphasis on land conservation and preservation of natural beauty and resources;
- 120 acres of the 170-acre (49 of the 69-ha) parcel left open for farming, recreation, scenic views, and wildlife habitat;
- Several wetland ponds, prairies, meadows, and woods to roam;
- Horses, pasture, and stables located next door;
- Goats and chickens living in the original farm buildings;
- A bonfire circle in the Middle Meadow;
- A large area with shared garden plots and picnic tables, and a mowed area for kite flying, baseball, and other activities;
- Free firewood, chopped and split from trees that fall on the land;
- Events such as movies, bike hikes, potluck suppers, bird walks, discussions, and seminars at the old barn, restored prairie, and farmed fields; and
- Architects working with purchasers to fit their needs.

Lessons Learned

Like many other developers, the Noonans say the biggest hurdle for conservation development is the outdated regulations that stipulate minimum lot sizes and minimum road widths, and utility requirements that interfere with the goal of land preservation through clustered housing. The developers wanted to build narrow roads to reduce impervious surfaces, slow traffic, and encourage walking, but local codes required wide roads that would allow easy access for fire trucks. The Noonans argued that the trucks could easily turn around, using part of the farmland off the paved surface. After considerable discussion and debate, the developers were allowed to reduce the road widths. They also had to convince the city to let them use a constructed wetlands for on-site sewage treatment, instead of running miles of city sanitary lines.

There was some initial apprehension on the part of the local community. "We are amid farms," says Eve Noonan. "We are often seen as the big, bad developer. Many of the people here are wary of anyone who has not lived here for four generations." The Noonans have been successful in overcoming much of the initial distrust. In fact, two of the owners of the farms that abut Tryon Farm are in the process of putting part of their land in conservancy.

The Noonans explain that their approach to developing the property in phases has been critical to their success. "Building settlement by settlement means we can change things as we go—revise as we learn," says Eve Noonan. "We are building the infrastructure as we go, so we don't have a big outlay for the roads or other infrastructure. This helps with financing. We can develop at the same rate that we're selling, whether that is quickly or at the slow pace of a down market."

The financial risk also has paid off. By protecting sand dunes, forested areas, and other natural features, the developers saved thousands of dollars in site grading and infrastructure costs. "I think, in lots of ways, we have found out financially that this kind of development can be very successful," says Ed Noonan. "That is not just good news for everybody's pocketbooks, but also good news for Mother Nature."[1]

Most of Tryon Farm's residents come from the surrounding area. About one-third of the families at Tryon Farm are full-time residents; most of the others live in Chicago or other nearby cities and use Tryon Farm as a weekend retreat. Tryon Farm is particularly attractive to professionals whose jobs allow them to extend their weekends from Thursday to Tuesday.

Tryon Farm attracts buyers of varied demographics and a wide range of interests. "Some of my friends warned me that we were going to attract tree huggers or former hippies," says Eve

Goats and chickens still live in the original farm buildings at Tryon Farm. In addition, there are shared garden plots for the residents.

Site plan.

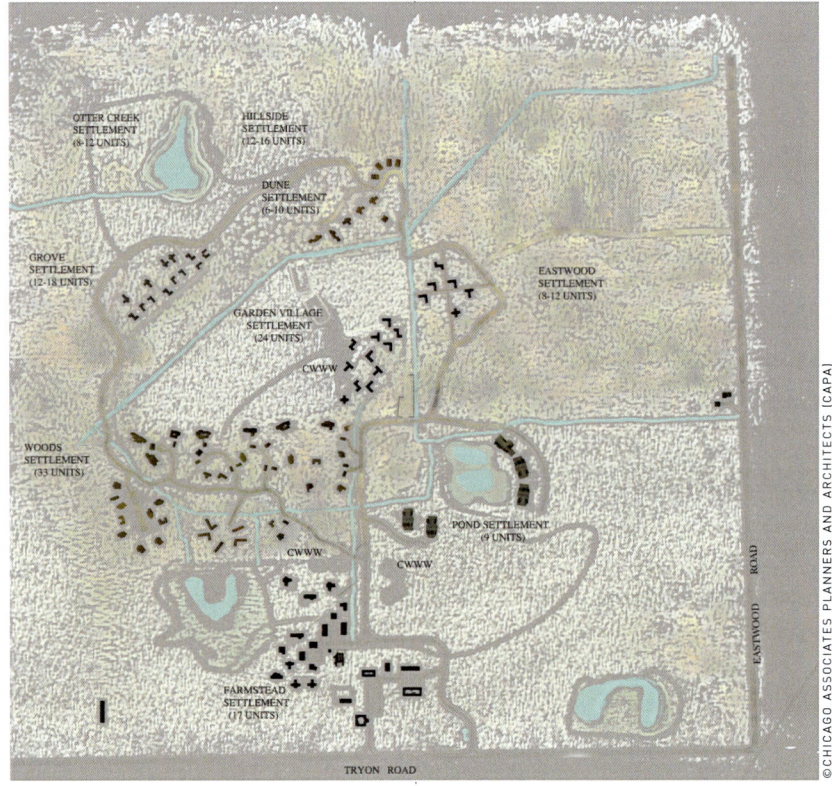

Noonan, "but we have bankers, doctors, and lawyers, as well as teachers, therapists, and writers who are in need of more affordable housing options." Still, she says, there is a shared ethos. "The project attracts people who are pretty sure of themselves and their place in the world and who have a love of the land—people who are not worried about not having lot lines. Most early buyers see themselves as pioneers on a wonderful adventure."

These shared values translate to a strong sense of community. Eve Noonan says that most buyers plan to stay for a long time and are committed to making it work: "People feel as though their good ideas will be heard." Tryon Farm's residents take an active part in the community. They have fixed up the barn and maintain the communal gardens. Homeowners admit that governance can be difficult in a community in which land and labor are a shared expense. "It's more interdependent than a regular subdivision, but it is still a subdivision," says Ed Noonan.[2] "We had to break that territorial imperative of the lot." One of the liveliest discussions has involved the idea of an ecologically friendly swimming pond that would be maintained without chlorine or other chemicals. Some residents argue that this could be a great community amenity—serving as a wildlife sanctuary for most of the year but providing a place for kids to swim in the summer—but others argue that a swimming pond would be too reminiscent of a country club.

Eve Noonan says Tryon Farm is everything she and Ed hoped it would be—and more. "The residents here are excited about saving Mother Nature," she says. "There is a sense of a commitment to a cause—that helping the environment is important. That makes you feel good."

Notes

1. Quoted in Steve Wright, "Conservation Subdivisions: Good for the Land, Good for the Pocketbook," *On Common Ground* (Winter 2006): 17.
2. Quoted in Amber Bravo, "Farm Team," *Dwell* (November 2007): 110, http://www.amberbravo.com/article-pdfs/farmteam.pdf.

TRYON FARM

LAND USE INFORMATION

Site area	170 ac/69 ha
Open space under easement	132 ac/53 ha; 75%
Number of residential units planned	150
Number of lots sold/residential units completed	64
Percentage of residential development complete	45%
Gross residential density (units per ac/ha)	1/2.5
Average net density (units per ac/ha)	3.3/8.2

LAND USE PLAN

	Acres/ Hectares	Percentage of Site[1]
Residential	40/16	24
Developed open space (parks, common areas)	10/4	6
Undeveloped open space (natural open space)	85/34	50
Roads	12/48	7
Constructed wastewater wetland (CWWW) and sewer	23/9	14

RESIDENTIAL INFORMATION

Lot Type	Lot Size (ac/ha)	Range of Initial Sales Prices
Condominium deeded with limited common use	0.33–1/0.13–0.41	$45,000–$100,000

Unit Type	Unit Size (sq ft/m²)	Range of Initial Sales Prices
Single family and attached	400–2,500/37–232	$125,000–$465,000

DEVELOPMENT COST INFORMATION

Site Improvement Costs

Excavation/grading	$100,000
Sewer/water/drainage	300,000
Walkway paths	50,000
Landscaping	80,000
Telecom/power	30,000
Total	**$560,000**

DEVELOPMENT SCHEDULE

Multi-phases planning started	1996
First homes occupied	1998
Project completion	2020 (projected)

DEVELOPMENT TEAM

Owner/Developer
Edward Noonan & Associates
Chicago, Illinois
www.chicagoassociates.net

Planners/Architects
Chicago Associates Planners and Architects (CAPA)
Chicago, Illinois
www.chicagoassociates.net

Open-Space Protection/Preservation/Management
Tryon Farm Institute
Michigan City, Indiana
www.tryonfarm.com

Project website
www.tryonfarm.com

Note
1. Percentage may not total 100 percent, due to rounding.

Daniel Island, in Charleston, South Carolina.

NOAA Coastal Services Center. *Alternatives for Coastal Development: One Site, Three Scenarios.* www.csc.noaa.gov/alternatives.

Northeastern Illinois Planning Commission (NIPC) and Chicago Wilderness. *Conservation Design Resource Manual: Language and Guidelines for Updating Local Ordinances* (2003).

O'Neill, David J. *Environment and Development: Myth and Fact.* Washington, D.C.: ULI-the Urban Land Institute, 2002. www.nonprofitcenters.org/uploads/tx_ncndb/1f8538e36a.pdf.

Stein, Susan M., et al. *Forests on the Edge: Housing Development on America's Private Forests.* USDA Forest Service, Pacific Northwest Research Station, General Technical Report PNW-STR-636 (2005).

Trust for Public Land. *Local Greenprinting for Growth.* Washington, D.C.: Trust for Public Land, 2004. www.tpl.org.

Tuttle, Craig Q., Jill C. Enz, and Steven I. Apfelbaum. *Cost Savings in Ecologically Designed Conservation Developments.* Brodhead, Wisconsin: Applied Ecological Services Inc., 2007.

Websites

American Farmland Trust
www.farmland.org

American Planning Association
www.planning.org

Center for Watershed Protection
"Better Site Design"
www.cwp.org/Resource_Library/Better_Site_Design/index.htm

Chicago Wilderness Coalition
www.chiwild.org

The Congress for the New Urbanism
"The Smart Code"
www.cnu.org/node/2645

The Conservation Fund
www.conservationfund.org

Greener Prospects (Randall Arendt)
www.greenerprospects.com

LandChoices
www.landchoices.org

Low Impact Development Center Inc.
www.lowimpactdevelopment.org

The Nature Conservancy
www.nature.org

Smart Communities Network
www.smartcommunities.ncat.org

Smart Growth Network
www.smartgrowth.org

Trust for Public Land
www.tpl.org

Appendix A

Examples of Conservation Development by Region

New England
Connecticut
Long Hill Farm, Guilford
Strathmore Farms, Madison
Old Farm, Middletown

Maine
Agamenticus Estates, South Berwick

Massachusetts
Battle Road Farm, Lincoln
Dunovan's Farm, Norwell
Jarvis Farm, Westford
Myers Farm, Greenfield
Partridgeberry Place, Ipswich

Rhode Island
Brown's Farm, Kingston
Fieldstone Estates, North Kingston
Trim's Ridge, Block Island
Wickford Point, North Kingston

Vermont
South Village, Burlington

Mid-Atlantic
Maryland
Cooke's Hope, Easton
Paternal Gift Farm, Highland
Terra Maria, Howard County

New Jersey
Fern Valley, Tewksbury Township

New York
Mendon Green, Mendon
Stone Ridge, Marbletown

Pennsylvania
Canterbury, Doylestown, Bucks County
Farmview, Bucks County
Garnet Oaks, Delaware County
Indian Walk, Doylestown, Bucks County
Lamborne, London Grove,
    Chester County
Ponds at Woodward, Kennett Township
Ringfield, Chadds Ford Township
Weatherstone, West Vincent,
    Chester County

Southeast
Alabama
The Preserve, Hoover

Florida
Centerville, Leon County
The Park at Wolf Branch Oaks,
    Mount Dora

Georgia
Fieldstone, Walker County
Serenbe, Fulton County

Louisiana
River Ranch, Lafayette

North Carolina
Balsam Mountain Preserve, Sylva
Stratford Hall, Weddington

South Carolina
Dewees Island, Charleston County
Spring Island, Beaufort County

Virginia
Birch Hollow Hamlet, Loudoun County
Bundoran Farm, Albemarle County
Farm Colony, Stanardsville
Fields at Cold Harbor, Hanover County
Homestead Preserve, Bath County

Midwest
Illinois
Fields of Long Grove, Lake County
Prairie Crossing, Grayslake

Indiana
Tryon Farm, Michigan City

Michigan
50 Conservation Subdivisions in
    Hamburg Township

Minnesota
Fields of St. Croix, Lake Elmo
Inspiration, Bayport
Jackson Meadow, Marine on St. Croix
Wild Meadows, Medina

Ohio
Hidden Creek at Darby, Galloway

Wisconsin
Hawksnest, Delafield
The Preserves at Hunter's Lake, Ottawa
Sugar Creek Preserve, Walworth County

Southwest
Arizona
DC Ranch, Scottsdale
Fairfield, Pima County
Rocking K Ranch, Pima County

New Mexico
Galisteo Basin Preserve, Santa Fe

Texas
Chimney Rock, Flower Mound
Creek Road Ranch, Blanco County
Montgomery Farm, Allen
The Woodson Place, Rains County

West
California
Angwin Eco-Village, Napa County
Santa Lucia Preserve, Monterey County
Tejon Ranch, Lebec

Colorado
Catamount Ranch, Steamboat Springs
Heartwood Cohousing, LaPlata County
Marabou Ranch, Steamboat Springs
Ranch at Roaring Fork, Carbondale
Storm Mountain Ranch, Steamboat
    Springs
Wildcat Ranch, Snowmass

Idaho
Hidden Springs, Ada County

Montana
Ameya Preserve, Livingston
Moonlight Basin, Bozeman

Wyoming
Sand Creek Ranch, Buffalo

Appendix B

How to Evaluate a Conservation Development Ordinance

LandChoices, a nonprofit organization based in Milford, Michigan, has developed the following checklist for public officials, planners, and developers to evaluate whether their local land use ordinance encourages the development of conservation subdivisions.

- Does your ordinance designate preserving a minimum of 50 percent of the buildable land, in addition to the unbuildable wetlands, steep slopes, and floodplains in new subdivisions?
- Does your ordinance encourage developers to preserve land by offering incentives, such as 1) allowing narrower streets and eliminating curbs and gutters (using swales instead, along with rain gardens, to absorb excess water) in order to lower costs, recharge groundwater, and reduce stormwater runoff and pollution; and 2) providing a smooth review process to eliminate risk and uncertainty?
- Does your ordinance designate conservation subdivision design as a "by-right permitted use" option?
- Does your ordinance require all involved in the process—the developer, planning commission members, abutting landowners, officials, staff, etc.—to conduct a site walk on the property before any engineering plans are put into place in order to identify the conservation areas to be preserved?
- Does your ordinance require a qualified landscape architect or physical planner experienced with conservation subdivisions to be involved from the beginning of the project?
- Does your ordinance require an inventory and site analysis map of existing features?
- Does your ordinance require an inexpensive conceptual sketch plan showing areas of proposed development and areas of proposed conservation before expensive and highly detailed design drawings are created for the preliminary plan stage?
- Does your ordinance plan ahead to create interconnected open-space networks by linking together the conserved land in conservation subdivisions?

Appendix C

Conservation Subdivision Fact Sheet

The fact sheet on the facing page was created by LandChoices, a national nonprofit organization helping landowners preserve land. It can be duplicated and distributed.

LandChoices is a national 501c3 non-profit organization helping landowners preserve land

Thank you to the University of Connecticut Cooperative Extension NEMO Project and The Natural Lands Trust for parts of the information below.
Images courtesy Randall Arendt, "Conservation Design for Subdivisions", Island Press, 1996

Copyright 2007 LandChoices. You are welcome to share this document as long as you provide attribution to LandChoices.

Conservation Subdivisions

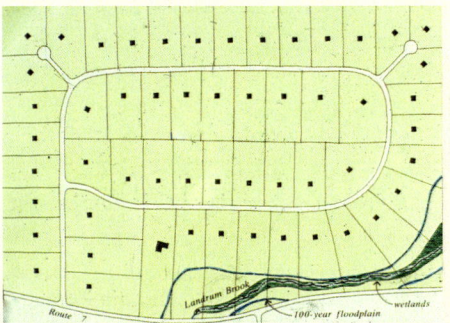 

Conventional Subdivision (above left with 2 acre house lots) vs. **Conservation Subdivision** (above right with just under 3/4 of an acre, 30,000 sq. ft., house lots) with the SAME number of home sites (55) on a 130 acre site

Preserving your community's water quality, rural character, natural lands, working family farms, wildlife and home values…
Which would you rather have in your community?

Advantages to communities

- This is NOT "clustering". **Conservation subdivisions preserve *50% to 70% or more** of the *buildable* land in unsewered rural areas in place of conventional "all lawn" lot sizes of two to five acres. This is a much higher quality and percentage of land than **"clustering".
- **Protects clean water** in lakes, rivers and streams and reduces stormwater run-off and treatment costs
- **Conserves groundwater** as natural areas infiltrate water and reduce flooding
- **Clean air:** Most trees and vegetation are left intact, helping combat climate change
- **Preserves your town's rural character**, forests and fields, wildlife, and tourism/agricultural economies
- **Saves money:** Preserves land at no cost to your community; reduces demand for public land acquisition
- **Same number of home sites** as conventional subdivision development
- **Fair to developers and landowners:** Proven more profitable and faster selling while reducing costs
- **Fair to homeowners:** Higher home appreciation rates
- **Reduces costs:** Municipal service costs are cheaper when homes are not widely scattered
- **Trails through natural lands:** Children and adults exercise and improve health while enjoying nature

*Conservation subdivision design can be used in areas served by public utilities (sewer, water) where the underlying density is higher, but the open space percentages would be correspondingly lower, for obvious reasons. In urban, sewered, high density areas zoned at 2-3-4 units per acre, preserving 40% open space, in addition to the unbuildable wetlands, floodplains, and steep slopes, is the norm. In rural, suburban edge areas at densities of 5 to 10 acres per dwelling, easily 70% (or more) of the land can be preserved.
**Community officials and planners often mistakenly confuse conservation subdivisions with an outdated technique called "clustering".

 LandChoices, P.O. Box 181, Milford, MI 48381 **www.landchoices.org**

Appendix D

Resources

Organizations That Can Help with Conservation Development

Audubon International
46 Rarick Road
Selkirk, NY 12158
518-767-9051
www.auduboninternational.org
Known primarily for its certification of green golf courses, Audubon International offers several other programs designed to encourage environmental planning and design. The Audubon Signature Program, for instance, provides comprehensive environmental planning assistance to new developments. The program helps landowners and developers design for the environment so that both economic and environmental objectives are achieved. Once construction is complete, involvement in an Audubon Signature Program ensures that managers apply sustainable resource management practices in the long-term stewardship of the property.

The Conservation Fund
1655 North Fort Myer Drive
Suite 1300
Arlington, VA 22209-3199
703-525-6300
www.conservationfund.org
The Conservation Fund is a national land conservation organization that works to balance environmental and economic goals. The fund buys land for conservation and works with landowners, businesses, and government to find solutions to conservation and economic development problems.

Lady Bird Johnson Wildflower Center, Sustainable Sites Initiative
4801 La Crosse Avenue
Austin, TX 78739
512-232-0100
www.wildflower.org/sites
The Sustainable Sites Initiative is an interdisciplinary effort of the American Society of Landscape Architects, the Lady Bird Johnson Wildflower Center, and the U.S. Botanic Garden to create voluntary national guidelines and performance standards for sustainable land design, construction, and maintenance practices.

LandChoices
P.O. Box 181
Milford, MI 48381
248-685-0483
www.landchoices.com
This national nonprofit organization offers landowners and communities methods for preserving land and ideas for creating conservation subdivisions. It provides sample ordinances and case studies of conservation developments.

Land Trust Alliance
1660 L Street, NW
Suite 1100
Washington, DC 20036
202-638-4725
www.landtrustalliance.org
This national conservation organization represents 1,700 local land trusts across the United States. It provides training, technical assistance, and information on tax policy and best practices in land conservation and in the use of conservation easements.

National Association of Home Builders
1201 15th Street, NW
Washington, DC 20005
202-266-8200; 800-368-5242
www.nahb.org
NAHB is a national nonprofit organization representing homebuilders and residential remodelers with 800 affiliated state and local homebuilder associations. It offers information on green building and creative land design.

Natural Lands Trust
Hildacy Farm Preserve
1031 Palmers Mill Road
Media, PA 19063
610-353-5587
www.natlands.org
Programs of this Pennsylvania-based land trust include "Growing Greener: Conservation by Design," which offers model conservation development ordinances, keys to conservation subdivision design, case studies, and publications.

North American Land Trust
100 Hickory Hill Road
P.O. Box 67
Chadds Ford, PA 19317
610-388-3670
www.nalt.org
The North American Land Trust provides major landowners with planning services integrating conservation incentives, such as conservation easements, limited development options, bargain sales, reserve life estates, transfer of development rights, and land stewardship and management assistance balanced with the landowner's financial goals.

Urban Land Institute
1025 Thomas Jefferson Street, NW
Suite 500 West
Washington, DC 20007
202-624-7000
www.uli.org
The mission of this international nonprofit organization is "to provide leadership in the responsible use of land and in creating and sustaining thriving communities worldwide." ULI offers courses, workshops, and publications on best practices in real estate development.

Books

Arendt, Randall. *Conservation Design for Subdivisions: A Practical Guide to Creating Open Space Networks*. Washington, D.C.: Island Press, 1996.

_____. *Envisioning Better Communities: Seeing More Options, Making Wiser Choices*. Chicago: Planners Press, 2010.

_____. *Growing Greener: Putting Conservation into Local Plans and Ordinances*. Washington, D.C.: Island Press, 1999.

_____. *Rural by Design*. Chicago: American Planning Association, 1994.

Benedict, Mark A., and Edward T. McMahon. *Green Infrastructure: Linking Landscapes and Communities*. Washington, D.C.: Island Press, 2006.

Burchell, Robert, et al. *Sprawl Costs: Economic Impacts of Unchecked Development*. Washington, D.C.: Island Press, 2005.

Forman, Richard T.T. *Land Mosaics: The Ecology of Landscapes and Regions*. Cambridge: Cambridge University Press, 1995.

Lerner, Steve, and William Poole. *The Economic Benefits of Parks and Open Space: How Land Conservation Helps Communities Grow Smart and Protect the Bottom Line*. Washington, D.C.: Trust for Public Land, 1999.

McElfish, James, and Rebecca Kihslinger. *Nature-Friendly Land Use Practices at Multiple Scales*. Washington, D.C.: Island Press, 2009.

McHarg, Ian L. *Design with Nature: 25th Anniversary Edition*. New York: John Wiley & Sons, 1995.

McQueen, Mike, and Ed McMahon. *Land Conservation Financing*. Washington, D.C.: Island Press, 2003.

Perlman, Dan L., and Jeffrey C. Milder. *Practical Ecology for Planners, Developers, and Citizens*. Washington, D.C.: Island Press, 2005.

Rocky Mountain Institute. *Green Development: Integrating Ecology and Real Estate*. New York: John Wiley & Sons, 1998.

Periodicals

Amundsen, Jason. "EcoSystem: Subverting the Subdivision: Conservation Development in the United States." *Ecosystem Marketplace* (June 13, 2006).

Arendt, Randall. "Enhancing Subdivision Value through Conservation Design," *On Common Ground* (Summer 2001).

Burney, Teresa. "Intentional Grounding." *Big Builder* (May 2006).

Fleckenstein, Neil. "Conservation Subdivisions Coming to the Panhandle," *Florida Planning* (June 2006). www.talltimbers.org/images/ttlc/conservationsubdivision.pdf.

Haines, Anna. "An Innovative Tool for Managing Rural Residential Development: A Look at Conservation Subdivisions." *The Land Use Tracker* (Summer 2002). www.uwsp.edu/cnr/landcenter/tracker/Summer2002/conssubdiv.html.

Hobbs, Richard J., and David A. Norton. "Towards a Conceptual Framework for Restoration Ecology." *Restoration Ecology* (June 1996): 93–110.

Johnston, Douglas M., John B. Braden, and Thomas H. Price. "Downstream Economic Benefits of Conservation Development." *Journal of Water Resources Planning and Management* (January/February, 2006): 35–43.

Mamosar, Alan P. "Sustainable Suburbia: The Beauty and Promise of Conservation Design." *Conscious Choice* (April 2001). http://consciouschoice.com/2001/cc1404/sustainablesuburbia1404.html.

Martin, Frank Edgerton. "New Ruralism." *Landscape Architecture* (June 2001): 50–54.

Milder, Jeffrey C. "Using Limited Development to Conserve Land and Natural Resources." *Land Trust Alliance Exchange* (Spring 2006): 14–19.

Mohamed, Rayman. "The Economics of Conservation Subdivisions: Price Premiums, Improvement Costs, and Absorption Rates." *Urban Affairs Review* (January 2006): 376–399.

Versaci, Russell. "New Ruralism: Developers Are Looking to our Agrarian Past to Create Communities." *Old-House Journal's New Old House* (Spring 2008): 10–12.

Wright, Steve. "Conservation Subdivisions: Good for the Land, Good for the Pocketbook." *On Common Ground* (Winter 2006): 12–16.

Reports

Alliance for the Chesapeake Bay. *Forest Friendly Development: Chesapeake Bay Watershed Case Studies* (2005).

American Institute of Architects. *Livability 101 for Communities* (2005). www.ala.org/liv_liv101.

Center for Watershed Protection. *Better Site Design: A Handbook for Changing Development Rules in Your Community*. Ellicott City, Maryland: Site Planning Roundtable, 1998.

Centers for Disease Control and Prevention. *Designing and Building Healthy Places*. www.cdc.gov/healthyplaces.

Conservation Research Institute. *Changing Cost Perceptions: An Analysis of Conservation Development* (February 2005). www.nipc.org/environment/sustainable/conservationdesign/cost%5Fanalysis/Cost%20Analysis%20Report.pdf.

Fowler, Laurie, and Seth Wenger. *Conservation Subdivision Ordinances*. Athens, Georgia: Institute of Ecology, University of Georgia, 2001.

Heid, Jim. *Greenfield Development without Sprawl: The Role of Planned Communities*. Washington, D.C.: ULI–the Urban Land Institute, 2004.

Lacy, Jeff. *An Examination of the Market Appreciation for Clustered Housing with Permanent Open Space*. Amherst, Massachusetts: Center for Rural Massachusetts, University of Massachusetts, 1990.

McCann, Barbara, and Reid Ewing. *Measuring the Health Effects of Sprawl*. Smart Growth America and Surface Transportation Project (2003). www.smartgrowthamerica.org.

McMahon, Edward T., and Michael Pawlukiewicz. *The Practice of Conservation Development: Lessons in Success, ULI Land Use Policy Forum Report*. Washington, D.C.: ULI–the Urban Land Institute, 2002.

The Nature Conservancy and Chicago Wilderness, *Conservation Development in Practice* (2005).

Nelson, Nanette. *Evaluating the Economic Impact of Community Open Space and Urban Forests: A Literature Review*. Athens, Georgia: The Institute of Ecology at the University of Georgia, 2004.